The Geography of Defence

The Geography of Defence

Edited by Michael Bateman and
Raymond Riley

Published on the occasion of the Annual Conference of the
Institute of British Geographers, Portsmouth Polytechnic,
January 1987

IBG PORTSMOUTH 87
PORTSMOUTH 87
PORTSMOUTH 87
PORTSMOUTH 87
PORTSMOUTH 87
PORTSMOUTH 87

CROOM HELM
London & Sydney

Croom Helm Ltd, Provident House, Burrell Row,
Beckenham, Kent BR3 1AT

Croom Helm Australia Pty Ltd, Suite 4, 6th Floor,
64–76 Kippax Street, Surry Hills, NSW 2010, Australia

British Library Cataloguing in Publication Data

The Geography of defence.
1. Military geography — Great Britain
2. Great Britain — Military policy
I. Bateman, M. II. Riley, Raymond
III. Institute of British Geographers.
Conference (1987: Portsmouth Polytechnic)
355'.0335'41 UA647

ISBN 0-7099-3933-7

Printed and bound in Great Britain by Mackays of Chatham Ltd, Kent

Contents

Acknowledgements

Figure 2.2 is reproduced by kind permission of Gerald Duckworth and Co. Figure 2.6 is based on information from the York Archaeological Trust. Whilst not copyright, we would like to acknowledge that Figure 2.10 was taken from the reproduction in H. Carter's *An Introduction to Urban Historical Geography*, published by Edward Arnold (Publishers) Ltd. Figures 2.9 and 2.11 are based on line drawings Figures 10 and 18 respectively, in M. Aston and J. Bond, *The Landscape of Towns*, published by J.M. Dent & Sons Ltd., and are reproduced with their permission. Figure 6.6 is Crown Copyright and is reproduced by permission of the Ordnance Survey. Finally, we would like to thank Vickers Shipbuilding and Engineering Ltd., for their permission for us to reproduce Plate 6.1.

Preface

The decision to hold the 1987 Annual Conference of the Institute of British Geographers in Portsmouth presented a unique opportunity. Frequently the hosts of previous IBG conferences have published a series of regional essays, concentrating on documenting the region and its development in some detail. It was felt that Portsmouth was both already well documented, with the publication of two regional atlases in 1975 and 1985, and that the processes leading to what may be termed the new geography of the region, relating to the emergence of high technology industry, were well explained in the existing literature. On the other hand, we were convinced that Portsmouth's very *raison d'être*, that of a city devoted in the past to the needs of the nation's defence, with a considerable residue of that function still present, should provide the focus for a broader geographical appraisal. At the same time, a book devoted solely to Portsmouth might at best be reasonably comprehensive, but at worst and more likely, be excessively parochial. This book therefore represents a wider canvas on which the geographical impact of defence has been painted. It is firmly rooted in Portsmouth as the reader will quickly realise, but it is presented as an attempted synthesis of many of the geographical effects of national government defence policies, many of which have received little attention in the past.

Michael Bateman and Raymond Riley
Department of Geography, Portsmouth Polytechnic

List of Contributors

Gregory Ashworth, Senior Lecturer, Geografisch Instituut, Rijksuniversiteit, Groningen, Netherlands

Michael Asteris, Principal Lecturer, Department of Economics and Economic History, Portsmouth Polytechnic

Michael Bateman, Dean of the Faculty of Environmental Studies, Portsmouth Polytechnic

Mark Blacksell, Senior Lecturer, Department of Geography, University of Exeter

John Bradbeer, Senior Lecturer, Department of Geography, Portsmouth Polytechnic

Keith Grime, Lecturer, Department of Geography, University of Salford

Trevor Harris, Faculty Research Fellow, Faculty of Social and Cultural Studies, Brighton Polytechnic

Graham Moon, Lecturer and Research Officer, Social Services Research and Intelligence Unit, School of Social and Historical Studies, Portsmouth Polytechnic

Kelvyn Jones, Senior Lecturer, Department of Geography, Portsmouth Polytechnic

Fiona Reynolds, Secretary of the Council for National Parks

Raymond Riley, Principal Lecturer, Department of Geography, Portsmouth Polytechnic

1

The Geography of Defence — An Overview

Michael Bateman

It is an unfortunate fact that man has found it impossible to live in a state of peace. Instead, throughout their history, most nations have had to make elaborate preparations for their defence. Of course, it may be argued that equal efforts have been put into offensive preparations, but whatever the real purpose, expenditure on military hardware, facilities and personnel is immense. Certainly, when measured on a world scale, it is difficult to comprehend the scale of the sums involved. Some estimates suggest that the equivalent of the total Gross National Product of Africa (including South Africa) is spent annually for this purpose (Kennedy, 1974). Yet it is only recently that geographers have begun to examine the effects of this preoccupation in terms of its wider effects with particular attention being paid to the spatial economic effects of defence spending, for instance, Short (1981) and Lovering (1985).

It would of course be misleading to suggest that geography has ignored the military. The contribution of geography to warfare, as opposed to defence *per se*, was recognised very early and spawned texts devoted to so-called 'military geography' (e.g. Maguire, 1900). Such writings were usually devoted to the contribution which a specialist knowledge of the terrain and local conditions could make to successful battle strategies. We are told that General Sherman in the American Civil War, wrote in 1844, 'Every day, I feel more and more in need of an atlas, as the knowledge of geography in its minutest details, is essential to a true military education' (Maguire, 1900, p. 7). Much more recently, O'Sullivan and Miller have written in an introduction to a book entitled *Geography of Warfare* that, 'the justification for writing this book is that the fundamental strategic and tactical problems are geographical in nature' (O'Sullivan and Miller, 1983, p. 7). At least in wartime, therefore, a geographical perspective is seen to be essential to both participant and observer.

Yet it seems fair to suggest that many of the combative actions of the military in wartime are essentially short-lived, perhaps even ephemeral, although the consequences may be more long-lasting. A knowledge of basic geography, or more properly topography, may be extremely useful to an understanding of the actions taken during the 1967 Arab–Israeli War, or of the British Task Force's approach of the re-taking of the Falklands in 1982. In the longer term, however, the geographer probably has much more to contribute to an understanding not of the military action itself, but to the economic and social effects consequent upon that action. What, for instance, was the geographical impact of the Israeli settlement of the West Bank, and how has the economy of the Falklands altered as a result of the maintenance of a large British garrison there? Certainly the social and economic impact of such military actions has been considerable and deserves close analysis. Equally, the physical alterations to the landscape in the form of new buildings, airfields and military installations can be quite far-reaching.

Much of the effect of the military, however, stems not from military action itself, since thankfully the waging of war is not its full-time occupation, but from its other activities. Plainly, much time, effort and finance is expended on preparing for the event of war, or, in other words, defence. The theme of this book, therefore, is related very much to the military, but concerns itself not with military action, rather with military defence and particularly its social, economic and physical consequences. It has to be said that in practice it is not always easy to separate out these consequences as three distinct effects of military defence, since they are obviously interrelated. However, the approach taken by this book is to document each in turn, examining the physical impact of defence functions both historically and in the present day, the economic consequences of decisions to spend government finance on defence, as well as the economic constraints which have determined both temporally and spatially the patterns of defence spending, and finally, some of the social consequences which have arisen from the decisions to locate defence facilities and installations in particular locations. The papers clearly reflect the importance of a detailed consideration of the role of externalities, many of which are aspatial, which control spatial patterning. Since all major allocative decisions are taken by central government and since all outcomes are at a finer spatial scale, defence-related decisions are an excellent example of the aspatial influencing the spatial. As the papers in this book will emphasise, this process is by no means new and it is often necessary to adopt an historical perspective to the analysis of defence policies in order fully to explain current spatial outcomes. As an introduction to the papers which follow, it is worthwhile outlining some of the major themes which emerge in a little more detail.

DEFENCE AND THE ENVIRONMENT

The morphological impact of defence on cities has always been considerable and remained so until the era of so-called nuclear defence. Many Roman towns were military garrisons (*castra*), although this was not necessarily their sole function. For such towns, however, the need to defend the settlement against attack was an important consideration in determining its form, and as such the *castrum* frequently left its mark on subsequent urban settlements. In the Middle Ages, there were few urban settlements in Europe which were immune from the need to fortify against an enemy, at least to some degree. Some towns were elaborately fortified, with a wall encompassing a tightly packed mosaic of houses, workshops and public buildings; still others were designed solely as garrison settlements (e.g. Aigues Mortes, in Southern France, was designed as a base for the Crusades).

Many major cities have had to defend themselves against successive threats of attack, both through considerable changes in military technology and as the cities themselves have grown in size. The effects of these changes have been to render some fortifications obsolete, calling for their replacement by others. Their successors were usually further out from the centre of the city and often called for a more elaborate arrangement of physical defences in order to cope with the greater sophistication of the weapons which might be used against them in an enemy attack. The successive fortifications of cities such as Paris are excellent examples of this, where the previous defensive features have been well preserved in the present day street pattern. It matters nothing that many of these cities, however elaborate their defences, were never subject to an enemy attack. The morphological impact is still not only very discernible, but also an important constraint on many aspects of the cities' current growth and development.

Some towns and cities have been influenced not only by the need to defend themselves from attack, but also by the necessity for housing defence personnel and their equipment. Some of these settlements may be termed garrison towns, whilst others merely accommodate extensive training facilities. In Britain, towns and cities such as Aldershot in the present and Portsmouth in the past, come readily to mind, although in terms of the scale of the presence of the military, many smaller settlements are virtual company towns owned by the Ministry of Defence. Examples are Catterick in North Yorkshire, with its army facilities, Middle Wallop in Hampshire, where the Army Air Corps is situated. Cranwell, in Lincolnshire, where the RAF training school is located, and numerous settlements on and around the Salisbury Plain, where the army predominates, both in the settlements themselves and the surrounding rural areas, which are frequently given over to training facilities.

It is in many of these smaller settlements that one becomes aware of a conflict between military use and the needs and wishes of the local community. Of course the argument can be advanced that national defence accords with the needs and wishes of the community and society at large and that a major presence of the services in one settlement is a small price to pay for the nation's safety. In terms of the geographical effect of such presence, however, the argument is largely irrelevant since much of the defence-related activity, both in the United Kingdom and elsewhere is highly localised.

It is this local impact, when a local community and environment has to bear the community cost of maintaining a defence force, which deserves closer attention from geographers than has often been the case hitherto. In some countries, major conflicts have come to light in the recent past, such as that which occurred on the Larzac plateau in southern Aveyron, near Millau in the extreme south of the Massif Central in France. There in 1971, the French military attempted a sixfold increase of its tank-firing-range to a total area of almost 17,000 ha. It involved a total take-over of land which to the outsider would not have appeared to be particularly productive in agricultural terms, which was geographically remote, and which was situated in an area which had a prolonged history of population loss. Yet it was bitterly opposed, with the opposition stretching far beyond the local *communes* involved, since it represented a total disruption of the traditional sheep-rearing economy of the region and perhaps more importantly became a symbol of a local community pitted against the power of the state. Eventually after ten years, and immediately following the election of the socialist President, François Mitterand, the government drew back from the proposed appropriation. (See Ardagh, 1982, for a fuller discussion of this particular issue.)

In the United Kingdom, the conflicts are commonplace and come in a variety of guises. The disfigurement of landscape through its use for military exercises is particularly unfortunate, but perhaps no less so than the restrictions which have to be placed in certain marine zones where artillery practice may take place. Not all such conflicts are to be found in the remoter parts of the country, since even in the relatively crowded South East of England, major areas are devoted exclusively to military use, such as the ranges at Bordon in North Hampshire and at Bisley in Surrey. In the air, the military are able to declare exclusion zones, similar to those which occur around major civil airports. This has led in the recent past to a major conflict between those who wish to use the airspace for recreational flying, especially gliding, and the military authorities who see in such dual use dangers to both civilian and military aircraft. Some such exclusions can be somewhat controversial, such as the 200 sq. km. exclusion zone which was declared around the USAF base at Upper Heyford, Oxfordshire, in January 1986. Since there was already a similar zone in force around the RAF base at Brize Norton, also in Oxfordshire, this second and neighbouring zone left only a four mile corridor free for civilian flying between the two, unless special permission had been sought and given by the traffic controllers concerned.

The dual use of many of the highland zones of Britain both for recreation and by the RAF to train pilots in low level flying techniques has frequently led to bitter complaints. Certainly the sight and sound of a pair of Jaguar jets following the contours of a Lake District valley, well below the summits of the surrounding fells is both intrusive and incongruous, particularly within a National Park. Yet the RAF, it has to be pointed out, must train their pilots in such flying techniques and it is unfortunate that all of the suitable terrain also happens to be prized for its landscape and recreational value. Such conflicts are difficult to resolve, but deserve a wider debate than is usually permitted by the central government departments concerned.

DEFENCE AND THE ECONOMY

Modern defence spending of course comprises a major part of the budgets of many industrialised countries. Even if we accept that governments of different political persuasions may place a varying emphasis on such expenditure, the fact remains that it has always proved to be one of the most thirsty of any government budget headings. From 1978 to 1985, the spending on defence equipment alone in Britain amounted to more than £34 billion. Ninety-five per cent of this figure has been spent on equipment supplied by British firms, comprising a major stimulant to the British economy (*Financial Times*, 19 February 1985). It is not surprising that we can now talk of defence industries and include within that category companies which are both large and almost totally dependent for their existence on contracts from the Ministry of Defence. Indeed, many British companies depend on the military spending of central government for well over 80 per cent of their business — perhaps best illustrated by the shipbuilding yards whose only way of avoiding extinction was to specialise in naval craft.

A detailed analysis of the experience of the British shipbuilding industry has been provided by Peck and Townsend, in which they describe the way in which the division of British Shipbuilders Corporation (formed in 1977) into separate divisions in 1980, included a warshipbuilding division. The division not only was the only profitable one in the period 1980–2, but it also suffered least from job loss in the period 1977–83, with a decline of only 6.9 per cent, compared with an average for all the five divisions of British Shipbuilders of 27.7 per cent (Peck and Townsend, 1984, p. 323). Essentially, government orders for naval craft have acted as a safeguard for those shipyards specialising in the construction of warships whilst other yards have proved to be very vulnerable in the face of a worldwide decline both of orders for new ships and for ship-repair facilities.

Whilst orders for military equipment can be invaluable for many companies, and indeed may form the basis of a company's manufacturing output, the relationship between defence and research and development in general is perhaps an even more intimate one. In the UK, this intimacy has been increasing considerably during the 1980s. Of the advanced industrialised countries, the UK is amongst the highest spenders in terms of the proportion of its spending on research and development which is devoted to the defence sector. Of the total amount spent on research in the US, 28 per cent is devoted to military research, whilst in the UK and France, the figures are respectively 27 per cent and 22 per cent. A contrast is provided by the Federal Republic of Germany, with a level of only 4 per cent of its research budget being related to the military and, even more strikingly, Japan, where the level is a mere 0.35 per cent (*Financial*

Times, 3 December 1985). Even more notable is the level of increase in spending on defence-related research. Between 1972 and 1983, Britain's total budget for research rose slightly, from £7.01 billion to £7.33 billion (at 1983 prices), but whilst spending on fundamental science declined by approximately 20 per cent, and civilian applied research went up by only 2 per cent, that on defence-related research and development claimed an additional 22 per cent expenditure. Of the expenditure on defence research, just over 75 per cent is spent in industry, with the rest being spent by government research establishments.

It is difficult to determine how much of such expenditure is of benefit to either the community or industry in general, other than that derived directly from the defence function. The stimulus to the private sector of this expenditure is obviously quite considerable, although in fairness it should be pointed out that a proportion of the spending does go towards the development of products which have a more general use, at least in the longer term. Indeed, there is no doubt that certain developments, such as early work on micro-computers and the use of the silicon chip was pioneered in government research establishments (Breheny and McQuaid, 1985). Yet it is equally true that all too often, the development of a product for military use may not be compatible with the requirements for an apparently equivalent civil use, even if the restrictions of secrecy were to allow the ready transfer from one sector to the other. A particularly poignant example is provided by the problems of the Westland Helicopter company, which had hoped to develop both a military and a civilian version of a new helicopter to replace its Sea King craft. The fact that it failed to do this, largely because of the lack of firm orders from the British government for a military version, led to the need to seek a refinancing deal for the company and the political embarrassments for the British government which were set in train in late 1985 and early 1986.

The effects of spending on research and development for military purposes both on the individual firm and on the region is well illustrated by Breheny and McQuaid in their study of the origins and development of the M4 corridor in southern England (Breheny and McQuaid, 1985). At the level of the firm, they indicate that certain contractors to the Ministry of Defence are highly dependent on such contracts. One example cited is that of British Aerospace, which in 1983 had a turnover of £2.3bn, of which £1bn was accounted for by military aircraft, £692m by guided missiles and £143m on space projects. Indeed, only 19 per cent of the company's turnover was related to the production of civil aircraft (Breheny and McQuaid, 1985, p. 30).

Of course, this high dependence on contracts from central government brings with it a vulnerability to the vicissitudes of government policies. Not only is the success of the firm dependent on the size of the government order, but it is also dependent on political decisions which may determine where a particular order is placed, or even whether it is placed at all. The precarious nature of companies which have a high dependence on defence contracts has become particularly obvious during the current recession. In some cases, firms which have received government orders have thereby gained a guarantee of work for their employees into the next decade. On the other hand, those which have not received orders are put in considerable jeopardy. Nowhere is this more vividly illustrated than in the case of the UK shipbuilding industry. In January 1986, the Ministry of Defence announced the placing of orders worth £300 million with the Cammel Laird yard at Birkenhead on Merseyside to produce three Upholder class conventional submarines. At the same time, the Vickers yard at Barrow-in-Furness, a part of the same group, received an order worth £200 million for the Royal Navy's seventh Trafalgar class submarine (*Financial Times*, 4 January 1986). In the case of the former, it was anticipated that the order would not only ensure the continued existence of the 1,300 jobs at the yard, but create a further 800 jobs over the next decade. The importance of defence contracts for the Birkenhead Cammel Laird yard had already been demonstrated in 1984, when with only two other orders remaining on its books, the British government placed an order for a Type 22 destroyer, thus ensuring its viability for a further four years.

The broader effects of the placing of these orders were twofold. On the one hand, it established the Vickers–Cammel Laird group as the only viable submarine-building (as opposed to re-fitting) facility in the UK. On the other, it meant that the future of the Scott–Lithgow yard on Clydeside was thrown into some jeopardy, since it was hoped that at least some of the contracts awarded would have gone to the Scottish yard. The other submarine-building facility which failed to receive an order was the Yarrow yard, also on Clydeside. Given that it is unlikely that the government will order any further conventional submarines in the immediate future and that the first Trident nuclear submarine will almost certainly be built at Vickers' Barrow-in-Furness yard, one can see the predicament in which the other yards find themselves. A company like Scott–

Table 1.1: Average expenditure (£m) on defence by regions in the UK, 1974/5–1977/8 (1978 survey prices), and percentage distribution

Region	Average expenditure 1974/5–1977/8	Per cent UK total
North	240.8	3.8
Yorkshire/Humberside	277.8	4.4
East Midlands	423.9	6.7
East Anglia	219.2	3.5
South East	2562.5	40.6
South West	986.8	15.6
West Midlands	360.5	5.7
North West	430.1	6.8
Wales	157.8	2.5
Scotland	477.0	7.6
Northern Ireland	175.1	2.8

Source: Adapted from Short (1981).

Lithgow, for instance, has become increasingly dependent on defence contracts, as the demand for first its ships and later its semi-submersible oil rigs, into which it had diversified, has declined. The financial value of defence contracts was also underlined at the same time as these naval contracts were announced, since Marconi Underwater Systems, a Portsmouth based company, were awarded a contract to supply 2,000 Sting Ray advanced lightweight torpedoes for the RAF and the Royal Navy, with the condition that if the company's profits exceed a certain level, then they must be shared with the Ministry (*Guardian*, 4 January 1986).

At the regional level, the effect of such contracts is also very marked, a fact which has caused a close analysis of the regional impact of defence spending both in the UK and abroad (see for instance Todd, 1980, Kunzmann, 1985 and Markusen, 1985). Once again Breheny and McQuaid's evidence shows that there was a remarkable concentration of companies which obtained defence contracts in the south, south-west and south-east. This is particularly noticeable in contracts related to advanced electronics and communication systems. Companies such as Racal and Ferranti operate within the M4 corridor and it is no surprise to find a high representation of companies such as Plessey, Marconi and GEC in the Portsmouth area.

Short's pioneering work quantified this regional bias of defence spending in the UK during the mid to late 1970s, as indicated in Table 1.1. When the analysis is undertaken on a *per capita* basis, the bias towards the southern growth regions of the country becomes even more pronounced, with the South West (£231.9 expended *per capita* in the region), the South East (£151.7), East Anglia (£121.6) and the East Midlands (£113.5), coming well ahead of regions which have traditionally been in receipt of government assistance through regional development programmes. The region with the least expenditure *per capita* was Yorkshire and Humberside (£56.8), with Wales (£57.0) only slightly above, and the North West (£65.6) and the West Midlands benefiting more by only a small degree.

DEFENCE AND SOCIAL STRUCTURE AND RELATIONS

Whilst some attention has been paid to the economic effects of defence-related activities at both the urban and regional levels, the parallel social relationships have not been accorded the same attention by geographers or indeed by other disciplines. This is unfortunate when one considers the impact of a large presence of military personnel and their families in particular localities. The location of the military is very significant in determining many of the social and demographic characteristics of the area and there is no doubt that this was equally true in the past as it is today. Schneider and Patton's recent detailed study of Solano County, containing the small community of Vallejo which houses the naval yard and base of Mare Island, illustrates well the demographic and social imprint of the military (Schneider and Patton, 1985). They note a larger than average presence of people over the age of fifty years, which is explained by the tendency for service personnel to retire in the area. In addition, there is a large number of children and teenagers, and there are high birth rates, low marriage rates and high divorce rates. The racial composition of the community varied significantly from that of the state, with Blacks accounting for 16 per cent of the population and a growing number of Philippinos, dating back to the Second World War, when many Philippine men joined the US Navy.

The social transformation of a community such as that described by Schneider and Patton is by no means a characteristic unique to the recent past. Naval bases such as Portsmouth have long seen a mixing of regional accents as naval personnel with diverse origins have settled in the area. The dockyard naval towns have historically attracted a population which is more mobile than that of other industrial towns (a demographic feature which is discussed in more detail in Chapter 3).

In Britain, as indicated earlier, there are some towns whose major role is that of a military garrison. The presence of married quarters for service personnel in the ownership of the Ministry of Defence gives to these towns a distinctive housing and social structure. In Hampshire, there are a number of such locations, where military married quarters are dominant. The county is somewhat unusual in that it houses major facilities for two services, the navy and the army. (See Bateman, Jones and Moon, 1985, for a detailed analysis of the 1981 Census characteristics of the county.) Naval personnel are much in evidence in the Portsmouth region in the south of the county, with major residential locations such as the Rowner estate near Gosport, and smaller shore bases such as HMS Mercury at East Meon and HMS Dryad at Southwick, both of which were small inland rural communities prior to the establishment of the naval shore bases. In the north and east of the county it is the army which is dominant. The garrison town of Aldershot houses the major concentration of army personnel in the UK, but there are other smaller army-dominated locations elsewhere in the county, for example Bordon some ten miles to the south. The military areas are all characterised by an age structure which is younger than that of the rest of the county, by high teenage marriage rates, and by high marriage rates in general (at the 1981 Census marriage rates were uncommonly high, since only married personnel, as opposed to couples living as common law spouses, can qualify for service housing). Mobility rates are also high, which in turn leads to a very high level of vacancy of service housing.

THE GEOGRAPHY OF DEFENCE

The chapters in this book represent an attempt to gather together analyses of many of the aspects of the geographical influence of defence activities which have been discussed above. It consciously avoids certain areas which have already received a good measure of attention by geographers, especially the discussion of the regional impact of defence spending, concentrating instead on examining areas which have been rather less well documented.

The scene of man's military defence has usually been the city. Whilst battles may be fought both now and in the past on 'battlefields', conflicts have been increasingly centred on the source of power and resources, the city. Indeed, although it has been found necessary to fortify cities for millennia, so that they might be defended, during the past half century, and especially since the

Second World War, the city itself has become the battlefield. It is of course ironic that today's military technology means that the physical defence of the city is less likely to take the form of elaborate physical defences than more remote electronic detection systems. Yet the impact on the city may still be important and the historical impact of defence is certainly still felt, often indelibly etched on the urban form. It is this impact, both past and present which is considered by Gregory Ashworth in Chapter 2 of this book. It is particularly, although by no means exclusively, the *European* city which has been deeply affected by the needs and requirements of the defence function, and Chapter 2 draws primarily on a broad view of the continent to demonstrate the importance of defence to the form of its cities.

In Chapter 3 Raymond Riley focuses on one city, examining Portsmouth as an example of a city whose morphology and land use has been fundamentally determined and directed by the past and present needs of the military. It is acknowledged that many other agents are involved in the land use process, yet it is inescapable that a city such as Portsmouth, developing as a naval port, and until relatively recently, a garrison town, should be seen as a city whose land use pattern can be explained only by reference to defence considerations. The whole process of military-effected land use patterns is seen as a national government influence on an individual urban centre, since the defence policies and the adoption of particular defence technologies were, and still are, very much the responsibility of central government.

The chapter takes a historical approach to the analysis of the impact of defence on land use, tracing the requirements of the military progressively from the erection of traditional defences through to their dismantling as military technology rendered them obsolete. At the same time, it is evident that the development of many civic facilities and their particular locations owed much to the process of land release undertaken by central government, dating from the last quarter of the nineteenth century. Conversely, there was very little evidence of land passing into the private sector until the inter-war period, when the first residential developments, both public and private, on former military land were carried out. Recent land releases have been of a more commercial nature and have included the sale of land for private housing development. This detailed case study illustrates that urban development in a city such as Portsmouth can be explained only by reference to a close analysis of the external influences of national government.

In Chapter 4, John Bradbeer and Graham Moon examine one strategy which has been adopted in the face of a growing legacy of redundant defence facilities. Many cities have traditionally re-used former defensive installations, such as castles and city walls, to promote tourist interest. Still others use artefacts associated with the defence function, the most obvious being warships, as tourist attractions, in a conscious attempt not only to illustrate the heritage of the place in question, but also to bring alive its history.

As important as the changing requirements for buildings and other defence-related facilities is the changing nature of labour demand in traditional defence towns. Many such settlements have had to adapt in a very short period of time to quite different demands for labour as the traditional artisanal skills related to defence, such as those of the shipwright, have been replaced by demands for micro-electronics experts in locations quite removed from the traditional defence towns. The question which the authors go on to address in this chapter is whether any economy which has formerly been highly dependent on the defence sector can seek a substitute in tourism. The area of so-called defence tourism is analysed in its social as well as its economic relationships to the former defence economy. It is suggested that the social order of a compliant workforce dominated by the defence sector employer and encouraged by feelings of patriotism has not been changed in any major fashion, save for the scale of the employer concerned. The dependency of the workforce is in no way lessened, yet it is increasingly evident that those employed in the emergent tourist sector are often not those who have become surplus to the labour requirements of the defence sector. The chapter concludes with a case study of Portsmouth, as a city which has seen the decline of its defence function and the increasing realisation of its tourist potential related to its historic defence role.

The social structure of defence settlements is, and always has been, distinctive. In Chapter 5, Trevor Harris examines the social structure of the specialised military town, as it emerged in the nineteenth century. Once again, the importance of external influences on the structure of the settlement is emphasised, since it was government which determined the pace with which settlements were developed and hence their eventual social form. Thus government decisions relating to expansion of a dockyard would influence the social pattern of the related settlement, determining the rate and type of growth, whilst the physical form of the expansion was greatly determined by the constraints imposed by the fortified nature of the dockyard towns. The main part of the chapter is devoted to two detailed case studies, examining the social geography of Woolwich and Sheerness during their rapid growth in the nineteenth century.

Some local economies have a very high dependence on the military through the awarding of defence contracts. In Chapter 6, Keith Grime examines the evolution of Vickers Shipbuilding and Engineering Limited (VSEL) and its impact on Barrow-in-Furness, a settlement which almost since its inception as an industrial town of the nineteenth century has been involved in the manufacture of defence equipment, including armaments, ships and submarines. Its development is seen as a conscious piece of planning by Victorian entrepreneurs, leading to the pre-eminence of one company. The dependency of that company, and in its turn that of the entire town, on government defence contracts is demonstrated, since during this century, with only a brief period of building merchant shipping, the company has increasingly specialised in the construction of armaments and warships of various kinds. Since over two-thirds of Barrow's male workforce in manufacturing and nearly half of the total male workforce have been consistently employed by the company, the level of dependency is very high indeed.

In Chapter 7, Kelvyn Jones looks at a social phenomenon which has gained little attention in the geographical literature, yet which has well defined spatial characteristics; namely the high concentration of service families in certain locations in England and Wales. Once again government policy and decisions have been crucial to the development of this phenomenon, although such distinctive localities are relatively recent features of the social geography of the country, since married quarters date only from the end of the Second World War. They are shown to be highly localised, but with a degree of concentration in southern England; three of the largest concentrations are within the county of Hampshire. Through an analysis of the 1981 Census, the characteristics of these areas are examined in detail, revealing a young, highly mobile population. The chapter concludes with a commentary on the problems which have followed from the creation of such distinctive social areas.

It is clear that many of the spatial effects of government defence policies are directly related to the economic decisions which stem from such policies. Equally, however, it can be argued that the defence policies themselves have stemmed from economic causes, the spatial impact being no less marked. In Chapter 8, Michael Asteris adopts an economist's view of Britain's overseas defence spending, tracing the global withdrawal of its defence commitment during the latter half of this century. Obviously decisions taken in Whitehall and Westminster may have a very tangible economic consequence for local economies abroad, good examples being provided by small island economies which previously housed major British defence installations. In this chapter, the economic reasons for the changing geography of Britain's global defence spending are discussed in detail.

The use of land for defence activities is almost always incompatible with its use for any other purpose. The potential for conflict between competing land uses is indeed great and nowhere is this more apparent than in Britain's National Parks. This forms the subject of the final chapter of this book by Mark Blacksell and Fiona Reynolds. The conflict was recognised at the outset by government, but it was not until the early 1970s that any real attempt to find a solution was made. The authors examine in some detail the problems of one national park, Dartmoor, which has been particularly affected by the dual demands of the military and the recreational visitor. Despite both the attention of government committees and pressure from the general public, it appears that there has been little real reduction in the requirements of the military in the national parks, neither does such a reduction seem a prospect for the foreseeable future.

Throughout this overview of the geography of defence, which often draws on historical survey to demonstrate the development of the defence role, if not dependency, one unifying paradigm emerges. The effect of central government decision-making is strong, whether it be on the original form of a settlement, the shape of its economy, or its social patterns, both past and present. The control by government can be far-reaching, and certainly is not confined to garrison or dockyard towns. The land use conflicts within Britain's national parks well illustrate this, but on a broader scale, Britain's international defence role, with its clearly defined spatial impacts, is quite obviously determined and shaped by central government. The local impact is no less strong, whether it be on the former shore bases in the Far East, the dockyard communities or the wild expanses of Dartmoor. A geography of settlements, economies and social groupings, determined by centrally controlled defence policies, has clearly emerged.

REFERENCES

Ardagh, J. (1982) *France in the 1980s*, Penguin, Harmondsworth.
Bateman, M., Jones, K. and Moon, G.M. (1985) *1981 Census Atlas of Hampshire*, Department of Geography, Portsmouth Polytechnic.
Breheny, M.J. and McQuaid, R.W. (1985) 'The M4 Corridor: Patterns and Causes of Growth in High Technology Industries', *Reading Geographical Papers*, no. 87, Department of Geography, University of Reading.
Kennedy, G. (1974) *The Military in the Third World*, Duckworth, London.
Kunzmann, K.R. (1985) 'Military Production and Regional Development in the Federal Republic of Germany', *Built Environment*, 11 (3), 181–92.
Lovering, J. (1985) 'Defence Expenditure and the Regions: the Case of Bristol', *Built Environment*, 11 (3), 193–206.
Maguire, T.M. (1900) *Outlines of Military Geography*, Cambridge University Press.
Markusen, A. (1985) 'The Military Remapping of the United States', *Built Environment*, 11 (3), 171–80.
O'Sullivan, P. and Miller, J.W. (1983) *The Geography of Warfare*, Croom Helm, London.
Peck, F. and Townsend, A. (1984) 'Contrasting Experience of Recession and Spatial Restructuring: British Shipbuilders, Plessey and Metal Box', *Regional Studies*, 18 (4), 319–38.
Schneider, J. and Patton, W. (1985) 'Urban and Regional Effects of Military Spending: a Case Study of Vallejo, California and Mare Island Shipyard', *Built Environment*, 11 (3), 207–18.
Short, J. (1981) 'Defence Spending in the UK Regions', *Regional Studies*, 15, 101–10.
Todd, D. (1980) 'The Defence Sector in Regional Development', *Area*, 12 (2), 115–21.

2

Urban Form and the Defence Functions of Cities

Gregory Ashworth

SAFETY AND THE EUROPEAN CITY

It is somewhat disconcerting for Europeans of what is significantly known as 'the post-war generation' to be reminded that they inhabit the world's most unstable continent, which for most of its history has provided the world's principal battlegrounds. Even more discomforting is the reminder that this traditional role has not been relegated to the past but that this long custom of hosting the world's major armed conflicts is likely to be maintained by it being the most important battlefront of the next such confrontation, even though on this occasion the chief protagonists on either side will not be Europeans.

If war has been a major and long-standing European preoccupation, and peace only relatively short unstable interludes between conflicts, it is not surprising that two fundamental questions have always been, 'Where is it safe to settle?' and, 'How can the security of the chosen site be enhanced?' However, from the viewpoint of the military, the important question is, 'How can towns be used to confer military advantage and be utilised as an instrument of strategic policy?'.

The importance of the defence consideration has varied through time and over space, so that a map of relative safety in Europe would emphasise zones where insecurity has played a particularly important role. In terms of external threat, Europe as the most westerly peninsula of the Eurasian landmass has been subject to almost continuous pressure through its eastern and south-eastern corridors of entry, including much of Poland and Lithuania, the North German Plain, the routes through, and north of, the Carpathians into the Danube Basin; the Bithynia/Thrace land bridge over the Bosphorous/Dardenelles; and the southern peninsulas vulnerable to seaborne entry such as the Peloponnese, southern Italy and south-east Spain.

Conversely the north and west of the continent have been relatively safe from external threat. Equally important, however, has been the incapacity of Europeans to live together without conflict among themselves which has been particularly intense in the shatter belts between the main power blocs (Cohen, 1963), one of the most persistent being the *Lotharingia* belt stretching from the Low Countries through Luxembourg, the Saarland, Rhineland, Alsace/Baden, Switzerland, to Trentino/Istria/Tirol. There are however few parts of Europe that have not from time to time proved to be a border zone and thus a battleground between nations, ideologies, feudal or tribal allegiances.

To a greater or lesser degree, defence has been a traditional urban function to be considered alongside trade and administration as a motive for initial urbanisation and choice of location. Mumford's idea of 'war as a city builder' (1961, p. 415) has been illustrated by, among others, Houston (1953) and Smith (1967) for many parts of Europe. War inevitably involves cities as they contain the political and economic means of waging it. Defence therefore is a factor shaping the urbanisation process and an influence on the creation of the internal morphology and functional structure of the city. Weber saw the city as 'a fusion of fortress and market' (1958, p. 77), while Pirenne (1949) stressed the symbolic importance of church, town hall, market and castle as representing the main facets of urban development and main structuring elements in the European urban form. It needs only to be stressed that the fourth of these has proved in practice to be not the least important, and if the nuclear fall-out shelter and anti-tank position are included with the castle then it cannot be dismissed as a relict form of solely historical interest.

This chapter will consider how the use of the city for defence has affected its morphology and subsequent functioning. The influence of defence works on the urban form is dependent on their nature and purposes. It is necessary therefore to examine more closely some of the varied defence roles of cities.

A TYPOLOGY OF THE DEFENCE FUNCTIONS OF CITIES

Towns have performed, and are expected to continue to perform many sorts of defence functions. The few broad categories outlined here are in no way exclusive, and the function of an individual settlement may change many times in the course of its history, with each change leaving a legacy in the urban form to succeeding generations. Yet it is helpful to consider briefly some of the various military roles that can be adopted, because these will impose quite different demands on the city, and even a cursory review may at the least dispel the simple idea that castle and wall are the only mark that defence has left upon the morphology of the western city.

The protected city

The most obvious and ubiquitous category is the protected city, where quite simply the city has protected itself according to its financial resources and its appreciation of the strength of an external threat, which together will determine the scale and complexity of its precautions. Constructing physical fortifications which increase the effectiveness of defence, by altering the ratio of attacking to defending forces needed to take the city, and raising it beyond the resources available to the expected aggressor, is only one alternative response. The other is the maintenance of large standing armed forces — the Spartan as opposed to the Athenian solution. It is however the cheapest in practice, whether it is the earth bank and wooden palisade of first-century London or the double stone curtain walls of fourteenth-century Carcassonne. In any event the defence function is local, with the works being locally constructed, paid for and manned. It is thus an integral part of the local urban system, dependent upon, and supportive to, the commercial and administrative functioning of the town. It was also local in another sense as it provided a defence against internal unrest of the local urban population as well as protection from external threat. The wall and its gates allowed supervision over movement in and out of the city to be exercised for local administrative, fiscal and crime prevention purposes. It was also a clear demonstration of the existence of an urban political unit with a degree of self-determination often in contradiction to the centralising policies of the state. 'The medieval city became an autonomous political entity behind the protections of its walls, whose military function was in fact second only to the symbolic expression of the will to be free' (Castells, 1983, p. 69).

The fortified strongpoint

What has been termed the protected city can be contrasted with the fortified strongpoint. Here military necessity on an extra-urban scale

Figure 2.1: The Fortress of Bourtange (Netherlands)

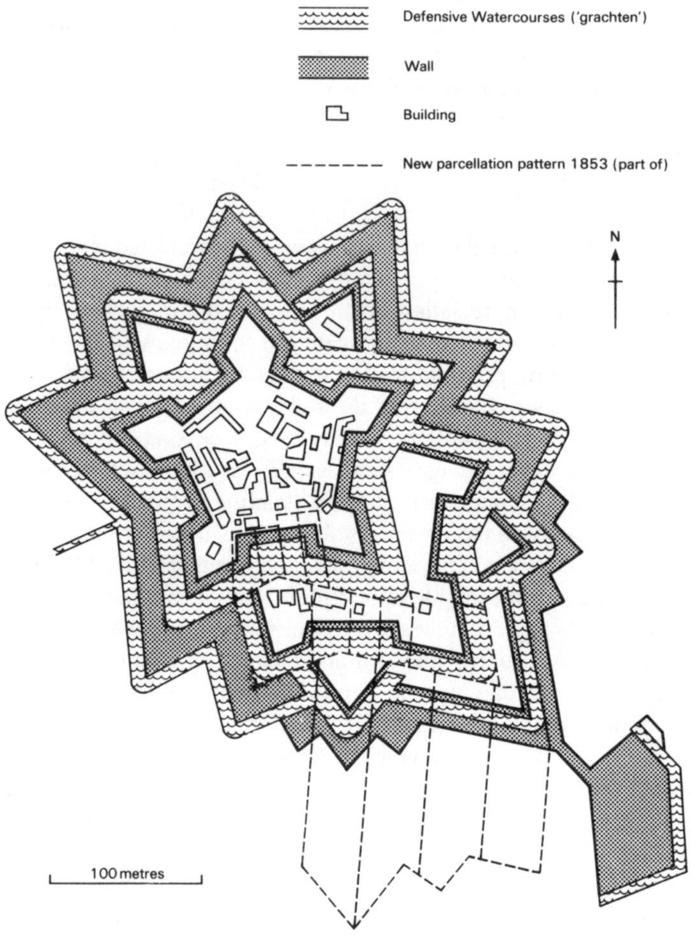

Source: Anon. (1982), Het Vesting Bourtange

takes precedence over the other functions of the town which are incidental and supportive of the defence installations, by, for example, housing and sustaining the garrison. Europe abounds in such fortress cities which were often incorporated into defence lines from the Roman *decumantes* of Rhine and Danube to the French *Maginot* line. The fortress city was only officially declared obsolete by the German Ministry of War in 1918 (Hofmann, 1977). The most cartographically dramatic examples are generally drawn from the seventeenth century when military architects such as Vauban and Menno de Coehoorn designed extensive, highly complex physical structures in response to advances in the range and effectiveness of artillery. One example from many will illustrate the type. The fortress town of Bourtange guards one of the few routeways between Germany and the northern Netherlands (Figure 2.1). It is clear that the size and internal structure of the town are completely subordinated to the requirements of defence, whose works cover an area larger than the town itself, and whose financing and purpose were not dependent on the settlement (Anon., 1982).

The city as battle terrain

'Throughout most of recorded history, the defence of the city has taken place at its periphery rather than in the streets and buildings of the town itself' (United States Army, 1976). Once the wall had fallen the battle for the town was over. However, reliance on mobile artillery, armour and the mechanisation of infantry during the Second World War led to the discovery in Stalingrad, Aachen, Arnhem, Warsaw, Caen, and elsewhere, that the built-up area itself was a defensive obstacle. Thus the degree and type of urbanisation became a critical battle terrain factor and the urban form acquired an influence on defence unsuspected by its builders. Two factors interact. The first is that urban areas are relatively richly endowed with hard surface roads which increases ease of penetration by wheeled and tracked vehicles. The second and contradictory variable is the density of buildings which provide defensive positions, and when subjected to bombardment produce a 'collateral damage' of masonry rubble that hinders mobile deployment and favours defence.

Various interpretations of the interaction of these two factors in different urban situations lie at the heart of much contemporary strategic thinking, especially about the European Central Front (O'Sullivan and Miller, 1983). Warsaw Pact tactical doctrine is believed to rely on rapid penetration by armoured and motorised units along the motorways bypassing the cities. NATO planning assumes interdiction of the through routes forcing conflict into the towns where the urban morphology favours defence (Hackett, 1978). The Braunschweig–Hannover region and the Fulda Gap between the East German border and the Frankfurt agglomeration are the most strategically critical areas in the German Federal Republic. These regions are becoming increasingly suburbanised and the question of whether suburbs with their particular building and road densities favour static defence or mobile offence is much discussed (Bruce-Biggs, 1974; Donaldson, 1979) and could in reality prove decisive.

In a Europe where such confrontations are actively prepared for, the planning of urban and suburban areas in the regions of potential future conflict assumes a military importance that is taken into account in the patterning of buildings and spaces, the use of building materials and the design of the network of roads and bridges. The urban form is therefore more than an incidental battlefield factor but can itself be influenced by the possible defence functions of cities.

The *Bastide*

This is the planned establishment of a town, generally as part of a pattern of many such plantations, as an instrument of military and associated political control of a territory. It provides both immediate protection for settlers, and also acts as a centre for a pacification programme of the area. The term has been borrowed from the many such settlements of the twelfth to fourteenth centuries which were an important element in the struggle between Angevins and Capetians for control of south western France. This use of a particular settlement form has been found previously in Hellenistic colonisation in the eastern Mediterranean; the veteran *colonia* in the frontier zones of the Roman Empire; the *castella* of reconquered Christian Spain or as part of the German 'Drang nach Osten' across Prussia, Pomerania and Poland. In more recent years variants have been found under various names in pacification programmes in Cuba (1898), South Africa (1899–1902), Malaya (1950–3) and South Vietnam (1965–75).

The actual forms of such settlements have however few common features (Figure 2.2), and, even in the case of the French archetype, Dickinson (1961) demonstrated the great variety that could result from local variations in the sites and their military significance, some not even being walled (Carter, 1983). The common features of such settlements lie in their broader locational patterns, regional distribution and reason for development rather than the details of the form.

Figure 2.2: Examples of 'Bastide' towns

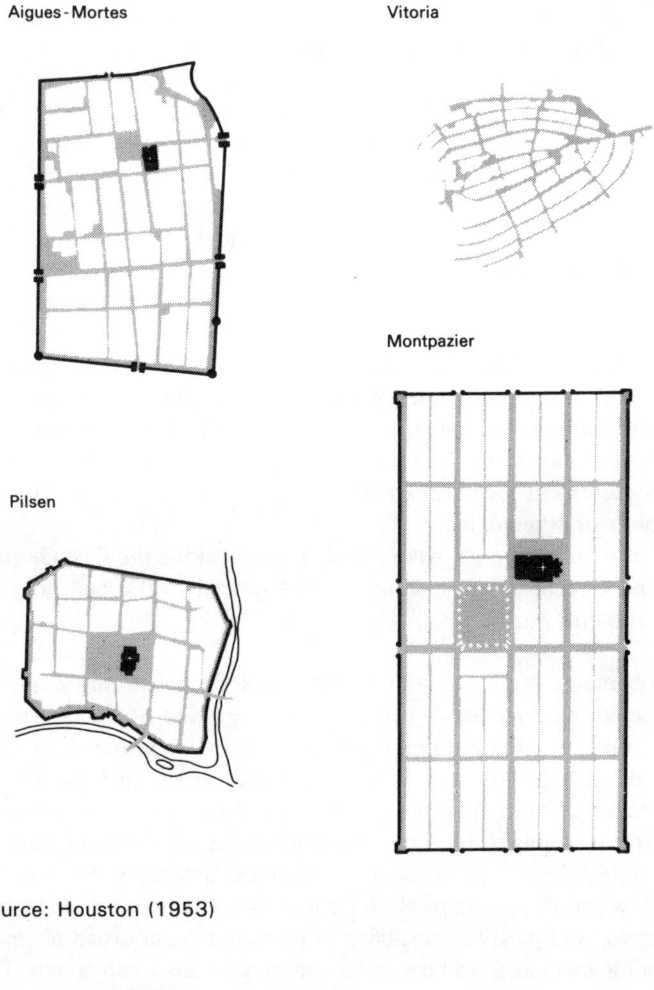

Source: Houston (1953)

The garrison town

Cities are required to provide not only defendable positions but also service facilities for defence forces. Cities house permanent garrisons, transit facilities, supply depots, maintenance arsenals and dockyards as well as parade, drill and training areas. The location of most of these is necessarily urban as they need access to transport nodes and other support services usually found in cities.

The impact of these requirements upon urban land use tends to have been underestimated in Britain where there is no tradition of a large standing army and most of the armed forces for the last 200 years were garrisoned and trained overseas. In Germany, by contrast, the armed forces have long been an important competitor for urban land. It has been calculated (Sicken, 1977) that the land requirements of the defence forces in the Federal Republic in 1972 were 423,000 ha (of which about 10 per cent is for barracks, 20 per cent for depots, and the rest for training areas), compared with 386,000 ha in the larger *Reich* of 1939. Although this is only 1.7 per cent of the country's land area, it is necessarily strongly concentrated, especially into three types of garrison town, each of which has its own requirements and planning problems (Hofmann, 1977):

(a) 'ordinary garrisons' i.e. Bundes- and Landwehr garrisons concentrated in regional centres with good access to the national road and rail network (such as Erlangen, Krefeld or Stuttgart);
(b) 'allied garrisons' located in similar cities but with a special requirement for international transport (such as Berlin, Heidelberg or Rheindalen);
(c) 'frontier garrisons' whose concentration along the East German and Czechoslovak frontier creates special traffic and policing problems such as Bad Kissingen).

One major response both to pressures on urban space and to changes in military needs has been the migration of training areas out of the city. While training was principally small unit formation drill, the parade ground was a conventional urban land use and its spectacle part of the urban scene. The need for space to manoeuvre and fire over longer distances encouraged the relocation of training areas to less densely inhabited areas. Barracks and depots have tended to follow this migration partly for convenience of access to the training areas, and partly in response to pressures from urban planners who view them as a land use to be confined to the urban fringe. The storage and handling of potentially more dangerous munitions, up to and including theatre nuclear weapons, have added to pressures to move depots out of the urban areas, and it made little sense to separate personnel from their equipment and training facilities. The resulting model of military locations in the urban region is shown in Figure 2.3.

This raises two interesting defence problems. First, training is now almost exclusively rural while the expectation is that urban environments will provide the critical European battlegrounds in future conflict. Secondly, the ability of defence forces to react has been

Figure 2.3: A model of the location of military installations in an urban region

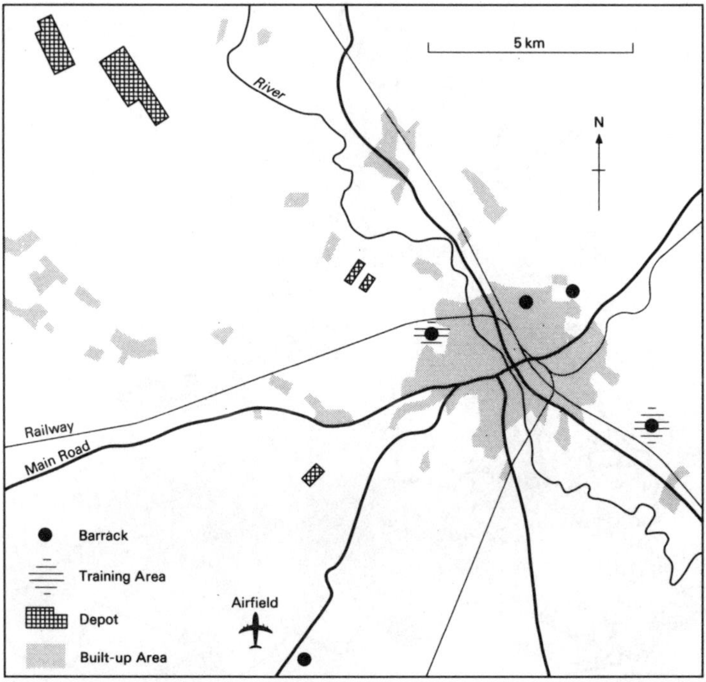

Source: Sicken (1977)

handicapped by the peripheral and scattered deployment of their installations around the city. The garrison city of West Berlin has a special international status and military importance, but it is not untypical in its pattern of peripheral military locations (Figure 2.4) which would make rapid reaction in its defence more difficult (Dunnigan, 1980).

The revolutionary city

The idea can be explored that some types of urban form are more conducive to successful popular revolution than others, or at least that the uprising of citizenry in riot or revolt against the existing formal authorities is more likely to succeed in particular urban physical

Figure 2.4: Military installations in West Berlin

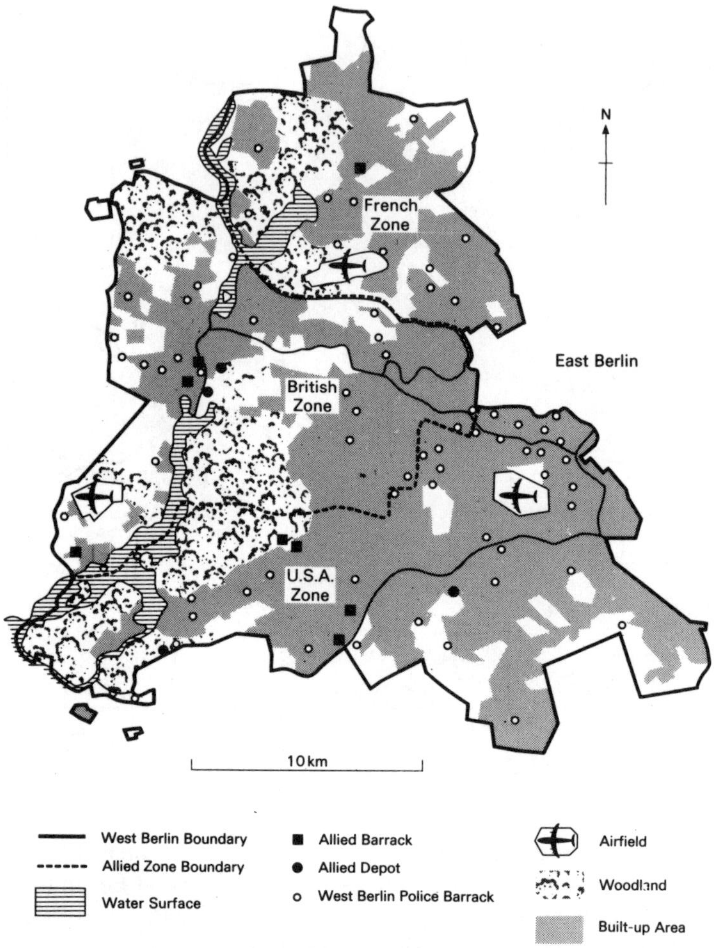

Source: Dunnigan (1980)

environments (Oppenheimer, 1964). In this sense the existence of a category of revolutionary cities may be identified.

Effective urban guerrilla warfare assumes that the ability of citizens to exploit the possibilities of their own urban environment outweighs the weapons and professional organisation of the forces of authority. A dense building structure and a pattern of narrow irregular streets with many small but interconnected spaces is an urban form favouring lightly armed irregulars, operating in small units against armoured or mechanised components (United States Army, 1972). Conversely broad avenues with long uninterrupted vistas and large open areas confer a freedom of manoeuvre on the more mobile forces of authority, and provide fields of fire for artillery and automatic weapons.

The invention of the street barricade which converts a medieval building pattern into a series of mini-fortresses has been credited to fifteenth-century Paris (Fuller, 1970). Further studies of that city's history of popular revolt have contrasted the popularly defensible close-packed quarters with the more easily policed districts of boulevards and parks. The town planning reforms of Haussmann after 1853 which opened up many of the medieval residential districts with broad radial avenues had the intention of creating an urban environment that favoured central authority over urban revolt (Harouel, 1981, p. 93), although the expropriation of housing needed for the boulevards may have instigated as much social unrest as the plan was designed to suppress. His success can be judged by the tactical geography of the suppression of the 1871 Commune, where the revolutionary strongholds (such as Montmartre, Belleville and Buttes-aux-Cailles) were in fact the districts that had been largely untouched by the sweeping changes in the town plan (Wheatcroft, 1983). If town planning here exercised a role, consciously or not, in support of the security forces, it has on occasion inadvertently rendered a similar service to revolutionaries. The planned working-class residential housing blocks of Vienna–Heilingenstadt were easily converted by their inhabitants into positions defensible even against artillery in the Civil War of 1934.

The coincidence between the growth of absolute centralised political power in many parts of Europe in the seventeenth and eighteenth centuries, and the evolution of an urban form that allowed this power to be exercised over the urban population is too close to be fortuitous. Technical change, especially the mastery of artillery, and the creation of a reliable professional army under absolutist control were at least one contributory element in the building of the baroque city that allowed these military developments to be displayed and used.

The urban revolutionary experience of Europe does not however allow a simple architecturally determinist model to be advanced. The breeding ground for revolt and the chances of its success depend more on the existence of political and social circumstances (as Castells has traced in five case studies, see Castells, 1983), and on the condition of the security forces than upon the morphology of the urban battlefield. The central area of St Petersburg in 1917 was a classic example of a planned baroque city; Barcelona, the inter-war archetype of a revolutionary city, was laid out on the broad gridiron pattern of Cerda's plan; and Budapest, architecturally one of the least defendable cities, was creditably defended for four days by a citizen militia against armoured attack in 1956.

However, the nature of the town plan remains a factor, although rarely a decisive one, in the success of urban revolution, and as such remains a consideration in the thinking of both those contemplating revolt and those charged with suppressing it. There is nevertheless a paradox, which has become evident in cities from Beirut to Belfast, that although the form of the inner city in particular renders it relatively easy to disrupt, it is also the home of the disadvantaged and potentially revolutionary population who will be the most immediate victims of such action. 'While the city is vulnerable to dislocation, anyone dislocating it also jeopardises the very population he is trying to help by revolutionary methods . . . if he seizes the city he seizes that which is at present most expendable' (Oppenheimer, 1969, p. 141).

THE INFLUENCE OF DEFENCE ON THE CITY

Destruction

An important effect of cities having a defence role that is insufficiently stressed in most accounts of morphological change is that they become targets of attack, and suffer damage as a consequence. On the regional scale the pattern of the density of urbanisation may be determined by spatial variations in security, urban deserts being found where cities were open to attack and destruction by invaders. A problem of testing any such hypothesis is that the zones of insecurity are also likely to be zones of potential commercial prosperity as both invader and trader have similar requirements. Settlements may persist in exploiting the advantages of accessibility despite the risks of sporadic destruction. Many of Europe's long-standing zones of insecurity mentioned earlier are in fact densely urbanised due to the commercial possibilities they offer. A small-scale Mediterranean example illustrates the persistent dilemma. The Pamphylian coast of Asia Minor provides good harbours on busy trade routes and a fertile coastal plain, but is equally vulnerable to attack by land along the coast and from the sea (Figure 2.5). The result has been an oscillation of settlement for 2000 years

Figure 2.5: Settlement on the Pamphylian coast

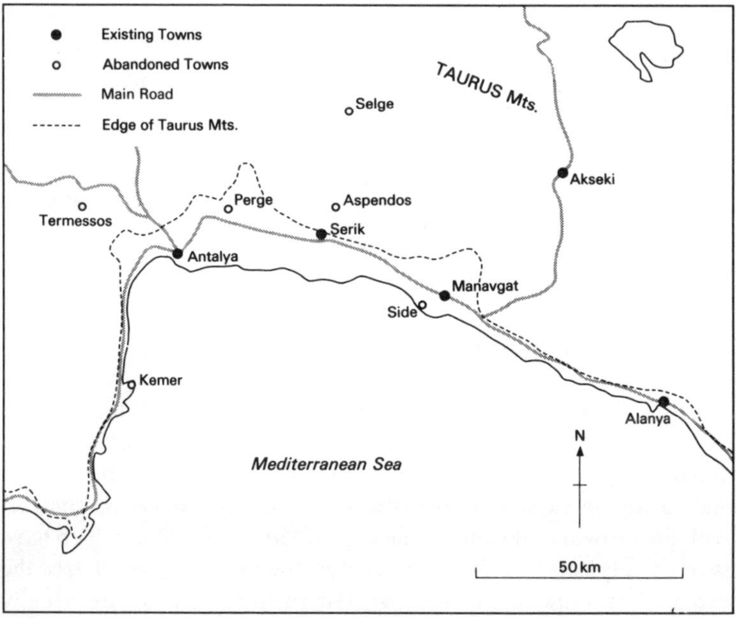

between the safer inland sites in the foothills of the Taurus Mountains (such as Aspendos, Perge, or Termessos) and the more commercially profitable coastal settlements which are periodically destroyed (such as Side, and Antalya). For most of its long urban history the citizens of the Mediterranean coast have had to respond to changes in the wider political and military situation by striking a new balance between security and economic opportunity.

While cities have long housed the main economic and political capacity to wage war, it was only with the development of the long range bomber that they became principal front line targets whose destruction is in itself a military objective. Table 2.1 indicates the extent to which the built-up areas of major cities were destroyed in the four countries most subjected to area bombing between 1939 and 1945. 'Place annihilation' (Hewitt, 1983) is not too strong a term when more than 50 per cent of the built-up area was destroyed — as occurred in Hamburg, Cologne, Dresden, Dusseldorf, Tokyo, Nagasaki, Kobe, and many smaller cities, to which we can now add Hanoi and Haiphong.

Table 2.1: Comparative figures for area bombing of cities in the Second World War

	Britain	Italy	Germany	Japan
Number of cities	*c.* 45	*c.* 50	70	62
Area destroyed (km^2)	*c.* 15	*c.* 100	333	425
Per cent built-up area	3	25	39	*c.* 50
Civilian deaths	60,595	56,796	*c.* 600,000	> 900,000

Source: Adapted from Hewitt (1983).

Restrictions on growth

Many of the most noticeable and pervasive influences of the exercise of the defence function have been negative restrictions on urban growth and development. A city wall is intended to contain the built-up area and, being an expensive investment, is slow to expand or contract with the growth or decline of the city. Examples of cities which have successively enlarged their walled area are common enough (see the example of York in Figure 2.6), but such expansions are usually separated by centuries of stability. Expansion beyond the walls incurs not only the loss of the protection they offer but may also be discouraged by the military or civil authorities, the former because it may interfere with fields of fire and provide cover for an approaching enemy, the latter out of the fear of a loss of taxation revenues or administrative control. If the demand for urban space was increasing and expansion beyond the walls discouraged, then an expected result would be an increase in the intensity of plot-use within the walls. It has been argued by Vance (1977), among others, that the higher building density found in continental European cities compared with those of Britain is a result of the survival of the city wall into the nineteenth century on the mainland while in a more peaceful and centrally controlled England it was generally obsolete, except in the Marches, by the fourteenth century.

There are, however, instances where the situation was reversed and an over-ambitious circumvallation was followed by a reduction in the town's population and its space demands, leaving the city to 'rattle around within its overlarge walls' (Vance, 1977, p. 128), as Norwich did through most of the seventeenth and eighteenth centuries. Changes in local commercial or political circumstances or a more general phenomenon, such as plague, left a land reserve within the

Figure 2.6: The fortifications of York

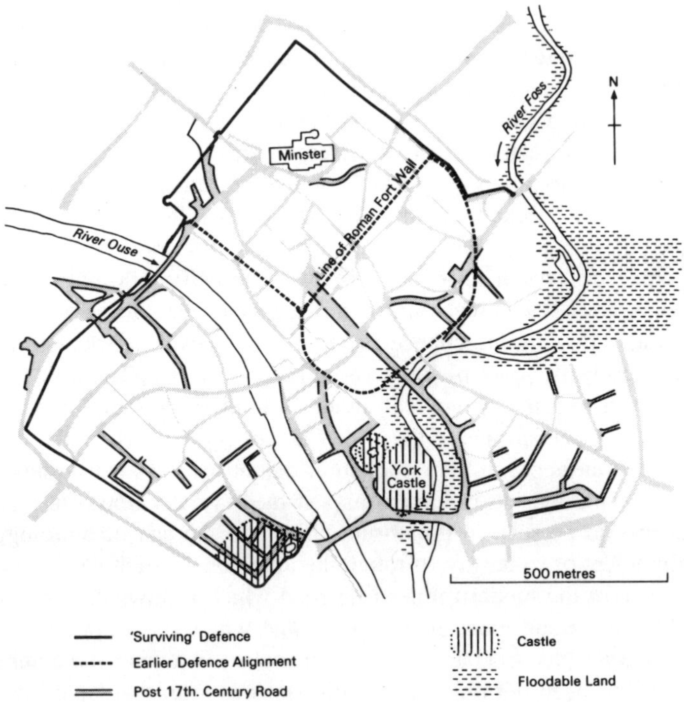

Source: Aston and Bond (1976)

walls which could be used for agricultural or even recreational purposes.

The existence of walls had functional as well as morphological effects. The wall was the limit of civic law as well as civic protection. Thus those living beyond it were literally 'outlaws' — outside the restrictions as well as the protection of civic order, taxation, guild control, or social conformity. Beyond the walls would be found, whether by choice or expulsion, trades such as tanning, and money lending and non-conforming social groups such as Jews or gypsies. City gates were thus frequently both 'break-of-bulk points' and on occasion 'free enterprise zones', which often developed as significant trade and manufacturing centres. The city gates market was a common and enduring feature of many cities. For example the main commercial activities of the city of Groningen in The Netherlands were not to be found concentrated in a central district but were, until the middle of the nineteenth century, dispersed through a ring of commercial sub-centres around the periphery of the inner city, corresponding to the 'harbours' i.e. the barge trans-shipment points where the regional canals penetrated the fortifications (Figure 2.7).

Walls and gates, even when they have lost any military or legal significance, can exercise considerable influence over the functioning of the city, merely by providing barriers and thereby channelling intra-urban circulation. In a walled city such as York (Figure 2.6) the gates or 'bars' were long regarded as unfortunate but immovable bottlenecks on vehicular traffic flows. In the 1970s, however, the situation accorded well with current traffic management ideas of 'ring and collar' allowing the chance survival of medieval defences to act as modern traffic controls on access to the inner city. The influence of the wall as a morphological divide even after its demolition can be seen in Norwich where the wall was largely derelict by the middle of the fourteenth century and either demolished or incorporated into other buildings. Its influence on post-medieval development remains clearly to be seen in the abrupt change in the age of building, the alignment of routeways through the long non-existent gates, and the course of the modern inner ring road which follows the line of the old walls along most of its length, and which has in practice reintroduced a physical barrier to movement between inner and outer city.

It has been not only the fortifications as such that have imposed restrictions on urban development, but also the requirements thought necessary for the better defence of the city. Examples include height constraints on building, restrictions on buildings too close to the inner side of the wall, and the maintenance of free fields of fire beyond the walls and bastions. These free fire zones which were needed to make the city-based artillery effective, sterilised large tracts of land around the city, preventing its use for building.

Perpignan (Figure 2.8) is an important border town and regional capital of the disputed province of Roussillon. The lines of the former defences are clearly visible as the modern octagon of boulevards. The need to maintain clear fields of fire around these defences restricted the expansion of the city until well into the nineteenth century. This has resulted in high densities of building within the octagon, an abrupt gradient in the age of building around the inner city, and the survival of a number of parks and open areas abutting the outside of the old walls; today these are welcome recreation areas for the inner city. The arrival of the railway in 1862 presented a particular problem. Even as late as this the military authorities were unwilling to allow

Figure 2.7: Groningen (Netherlands): (a) fortifications in 1826; (b) the use of fortifications in 1980

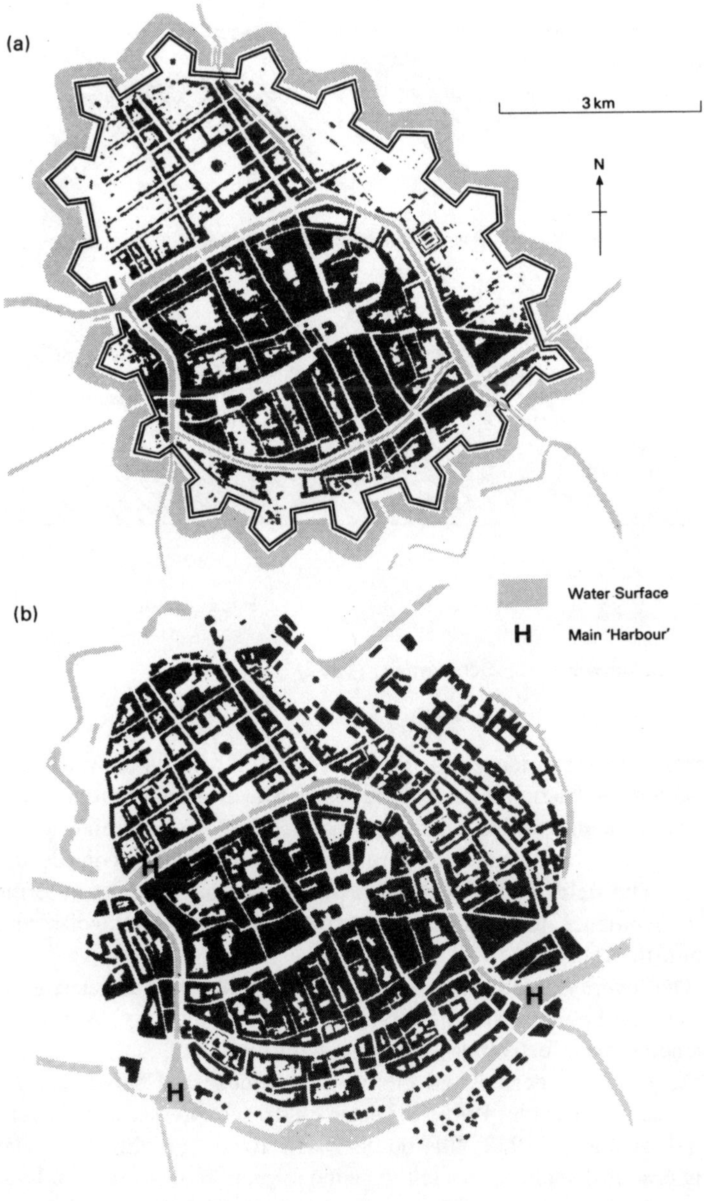

Source: Smook (1984)

Figure 2.8: The use of fortifications in Perpignan

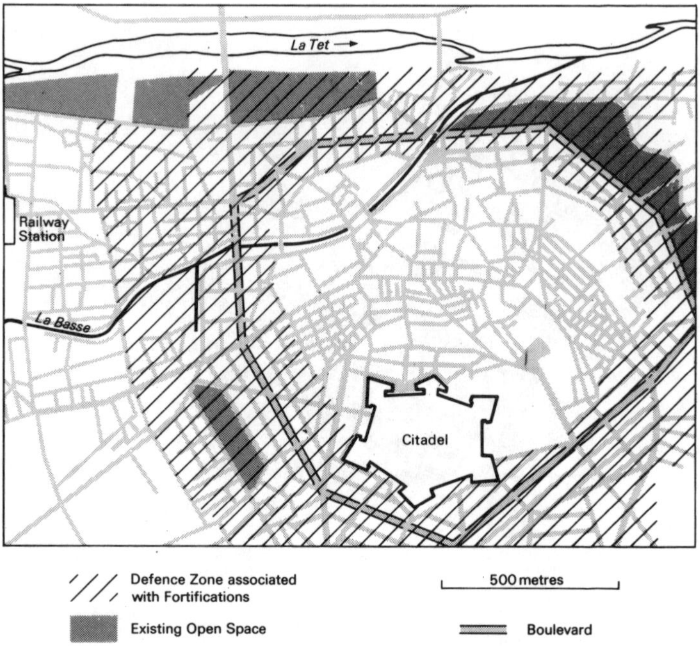

Source: Ashworth and Schuurmans (1982)

a breach in the defences for the line, or to permit its approach too close within the field of fire. The result was a railway station some 700m from the walls, which for many years was a prefabricated structure, to be dismantled in time of war and brought inside the walls. The fields of fire were thus maintained but the cost in terms of convenience to the citizens is still being paid (Ashworth and Schuurmans, 1982).

The severity of the restrictions imposed on the city was determined largely by the range and effectiveness of enemy artillery. Air attack extended this effectiveness. Some thought was given to this problem in the inter-war period, but there was a widespread belief that the city was indefensible. Prime Minister Baldwin expressed the conventional wisdom in 1932, 'the bomber will always get through'. The only practical solution was felt to be the migration of cities, or at least important functions of cities, such as munitions industries, beyond the range of a potential enemy. Only in the Soviet Union and the

Republic of China was this solution attempted on any scale. A certain reversal of thinking in the 1960s led to official programmes of civil defence against nuclear attack. In both the United States (Ziegler, 1985) and the Soviet Union (Douglas, 1983) nuclear shelter provision for at least part of the urban population was officially encouraged. Individual initiative in some countries, notably the United States, has led to defence against nuclear attack being a factor in the choice of residential location, design of homes and factories and the construction of various sorts of shelters. In Switzerland, on the other hand, there has long been an official government policy (Federal Law on Civil Defence 1962, revised 1971) for defence in the event of nuclear war in neighbouring countries which has been an important influence on regional and urban planning, including building design and residential shelter provision (Heller, 1975). In essence, however, the sorts of restrictions on building and on the functioning of cities necessary to provide an effective defence, have become so severe with the increasing destructive power of nuclear weapons, that it has become increasingly apparent that urban life as known in the West would be impossible to sustain. Policy in the United States therefore has shifted from the defence of the cities to their evacuation. A plan for the evacuation of more than 400 high risk areas, which includes most cities with more than 50,000 inhabitants, has been in existence since 1978 (Platt, 1984). After two thousand years of urban defence, the city is now recognised as being indefensible, and Douhet's prophesy of 1921, 'aerial warfare admits of no defence, only offence', appears more valid than ever.

Effects on patterns of streets and blocks

The influence of the presence of surrounding fortifications upon the patterning of the town's streets and building blocks was commented on as early as 1911: 'As a general rule the walled towns were much more regular in planning of their streets than those towns which were always open; this is more especially the case in those which received their mural girdle early, and particularly in towns of Roman foundation' (Harvey, 1911). This simple generalisation that associates a rudimentary grid geometry with fortifications does not do justice to the many variations in military requirements nor adaptions to the peculiarities of individual sites. It also does not explain the processes that shaped this patterning. Certainly the Roman walled town was constructed by military engineers to a standard design throughout the

Empire. This design was largely determined by the optimum ratio of defendable circumference to enclosed area, and by the organisational characteristics of the defending garrison whose accommodation reflected in buildings the structure of the Roman army. The result was a rectangular town with a gate in the centre of each wall, bisected by a cross of the two main streets (*decumannus* and *cardo*) which intersected at the central headquarters group of buildings.

This pattern has long been recognised in the contemporary street layout of many towns throughout Romanised Europe. One illustration from the host of similar examples of various sizes is Winchester where a medieval fortified town was superimposed upon a previous Roman settlement (Figure 2.9). It is relatively easy to recognise in the contemporary street pattern the alignment of the walls, the principal north–south and east–west streets and even the headquarters area in the present cathedral complex. However a number of questions remain, especially about how exactly the needs of defence created this particular and influential form, and about the importance of defence compared to other influences in its evolution.

The defence of the city may be conducted either by the use of the city as a strongpoint in itself, or by the urban garrison taking to the field. In the Roman case the latter was usually the intention with the wall serving only as a picket line. Indeed for the defence of the city from the walls the rectangular plan with its grid of streets has a number of serious military weaknesses. The 'Sforzinda' model (Figure 2.10), which was drawn up at the end of the fifteenth century as a theoretical blueprint and was influential in the design of many towns in the following 200 years, beginning with Palma Nova (Carter, 1983), demonstrates a more defensible city. The near circular walls are more economical of the defending manpower and allow a system of overlapping covering fire and the radial street pattern permits the 'interior lines' within the town to be exploited for the rapid deployment of the defenders. The grid pattern derives not from the requirements of defence as much as from the hierarchical organisation of the defence forces, and also perhaps the wider society of which they were a part.

Although separated in time by almost 2000 years, the military cantonments of Imperial India had many of the same characteristics, in response to the same sort of circumstances as those of Imperial Rome, and have left a similar mark upon the cities in which they were located. Such cantonments, scattered throughout the subcontinent, housing around 250,000 men in peacetime, formed a distinctive element in the town plan, with the housing, training depot, and other services being arranged according to the customary functional and

Figure 2.9: Roman defences and the present street pattern in Winchester

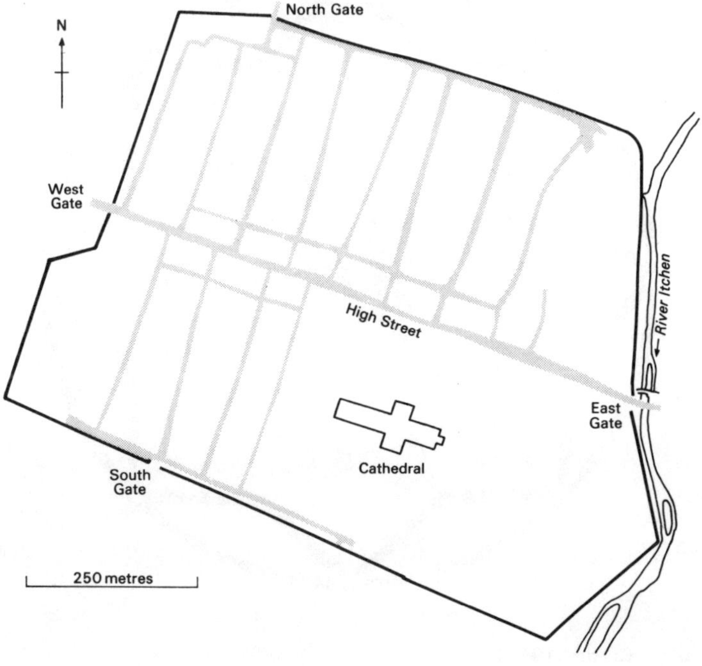

Source: Aston and Bond (1976)

social military hierarchy, forming regular patterns known significantly as 'lines'. 'The layout of the cantonment depended on the norms of social organisation in the metropolitan society, as well as the prevailing norms governing military organisation in the field' (King, 1976). The apotheosis was the Imperial capital of New Delhi where a purpose-built seat of government reproduced on an enormous scale the civil and military hierarchy of the Raj, in its processional ways, open spaces and residential districts.

The defence function was however only one of a number of processes shaping the evolution of the urban form, and the daily necessity of earning a living was, in most parts of Europe, more influential than the less frequent need for the protection of fortifications. The heavily fortified stronghold, on its natural or man-made elevation, offered protection but little space. The temptation to leave

Figure 2.10: The Sforzinda model

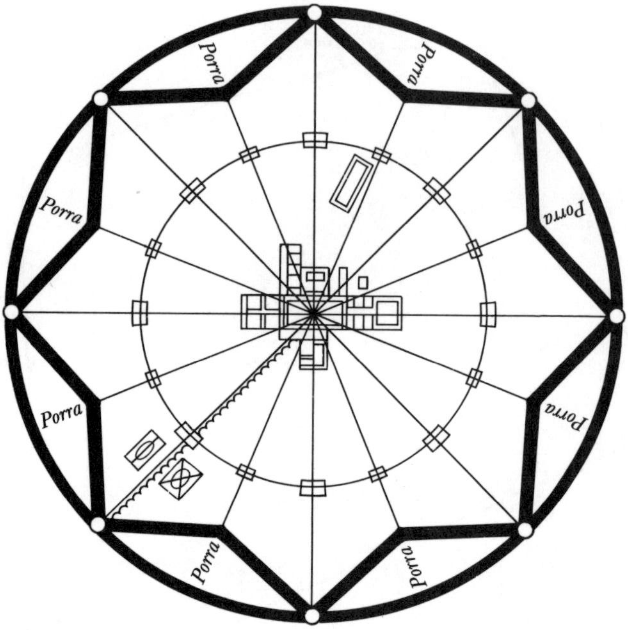

Source: Carter (1983)

the akropolis, citadel or burg to live and work outside, and generally below it, must have always been strong. In Devizes, for example, civic life, symbolised by parish church, town hall and market, developed outside the castle, and successive attempts to wall the expanding town produced a street pattern of concentric semi-circles and radial side-roads, leaving the castle only as a refuge in the event of attack (Figure 2.11). Throughout most of the Mediterranean world the choice between the security of the akropolis and the commercial convenience and space of the 'lower town' had constantly to be made. Finally it is clear that in many, if not most, fortified towns military considerations were subordinated to the commercial, and the defence works merely surrounded a town whose plan was determined by quite other considerations. The plan of Great Yarmouth, for instance, with its north–south alignment along the River Yare, its fishermen's 'rows' providing east–west access to the quays, and its broad market place, can best be explained by its site and its commercial functions rather

Figure 2.11: The defences and street pattern of Devizes

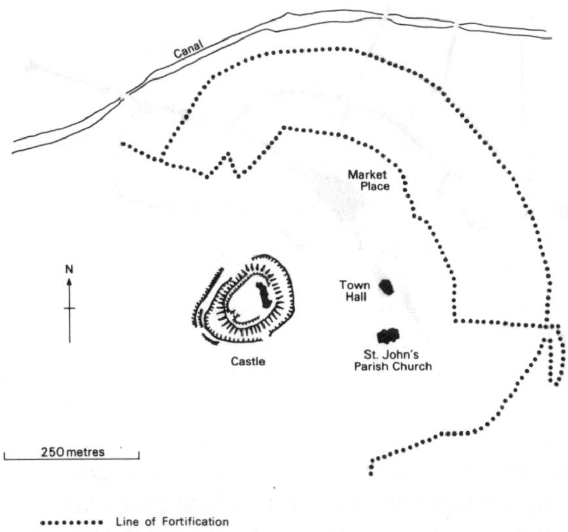

Source: Aston and Bond (1976)

than by its defence needs despite it being a walled North Sea 'frontier town' frequently under foreign attack (Hedges, 1973). See Figure 2.12.

The re-use of redundant defence works

The most widespread and positive effect of the defence function on cities is that redundant defence works can be put to other uses. Many of the changes in military technology referred to already, have successively left a legacy of relict forms in the city which can be made available for other purposes, generally after some time has elapsed between their technological obsolescence and their release by a conservative military authority. This legacy may be simply land that can be given other functions; or secondly the buildings and works can be assigned an activity quite different from that originally intended; or thirdly the defence works may be ascribed the status of historical objects to be conserved and presented as 'heritage' to residents and visitors alike.

(a) The re-use of space

One of the commonest and most useful legacies of previous defence works is the space they occupy, which may be both extensive and fortuitously located. The amount of space occupied by walls, for example, includes not merely the wall itself, but also its associated outer defence works (ditches, moats, and *grachten*), which from the seventeenth century were enlarged to include glacis slopes, counterscarps and later still bastions, redoubts and free fields of fire. The dismantling and release of a city wall therefore could provide a zone around the city many hundreds of metres wide (see for instance the case of Portsmouth discussed in the following chapter). In the case of the smaller frontier fortresses the amount of new land made available doubled the area of the town. Neuf-Brisach in Alsace had a glacis alone which was over 200m wide (Mumford, 1961).

It was not only the amount of new building land made available that presented a unique opportunity for development but equally the location within the city at the time of its release. The general reluctance of national military authorities formally to abandon their rights over fortifications, even when these have not been used for many years, or even in some cases centuries, is understandable, in that preparations for future conflicts are inevitably based on past experience, and fortifications once abandoned to other uses can not easily or quickly be resuscitated. In the Netherlands, where cities were particularly strongly fortified as part of a 300 year tradition of static positional defence which lasted until 1940, there was continual tension between city authorities, covetous of the space occupied by defence and eager to be free of its constraints, and a conservative military. Many of the larger commercial cities achieved an early victory, including Amsterdam (1837), Haarlem (1820) and Utrecht (1824), but the border towns had to wait much longer (Maastricht 1867, Groningen 1874, and Zutphen 1874), and it was not until 1875 that a general Act of Parliament enabled city authorities to dismantle urban fortifications throughout the country. The pattern in Germany, Austria–Hungary and France was similar, with the border fortress towns retaining a military function until after the 1870–1 war, and in critical areas such as Alsace, Galicia, and East Prussia, until 1918.

The important distinction in Europe was between the periphery, including Scandinavia, and the British Isles, where the fortified city had been almost entirely abandoned by the late medieval period, and the heartland of continental Central Europe where it survived until much later. The relatively late abandonment of urban fortifications

Figure 2.12: The walls and use of military land in Great Yarmouth

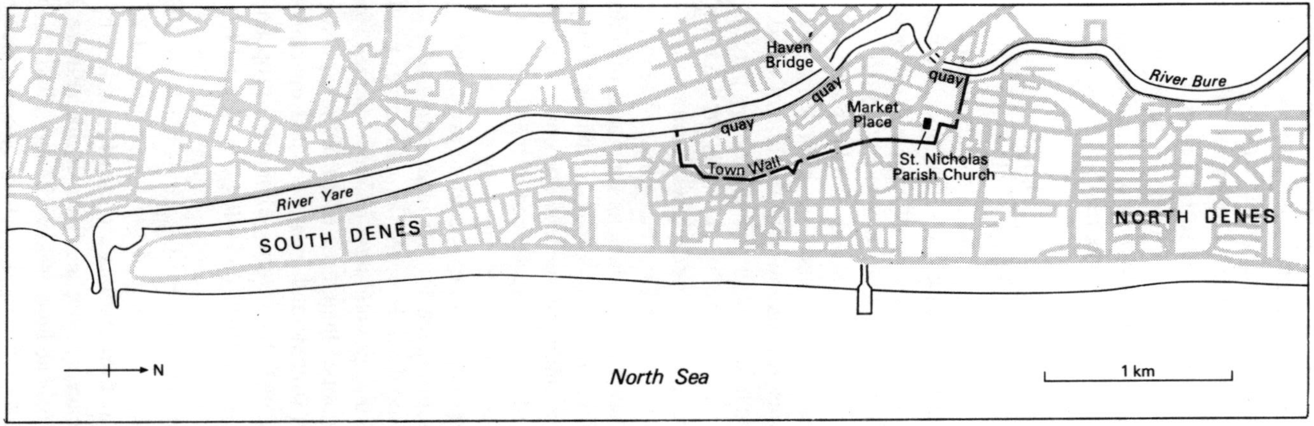

Source: De Haan and Ashworth (1984)

meant that the land was not released in many countries of Central Europe until well into the nineteenth century, by which time the pressure for expansion beyond the enclosed inner city was being felt, thus engendering in some cities the first large-scale suburbanisation. In some instances the dismantling was so far behind the expansion of the city which had already been allowed to occur beyond the walls, that land was released well within the urban built-up area thus providing a swathe of new building opportunities between the inner and outer zones of the city.

Having been presented with this unique opportunity for expansion, the problem for the urban authorities was how to utilise it. This in turn depended on the particular pressures for development in the individual town at the time of release, as well as upon the capability of the municipal authorities and private entrepreneurs in seizing an opportunity which had probably never previously occurred on that scale. The most usual result was a broad circular boulevard, or in some cases parallel boulevards, lined on both sides with new building. Only rarely was the continuity of the line of the defences broken by piecemeal incorporation into neighbouring parcels, so in most cases the morphological effect of the walls on the town plan, as a clear visual feature in the townscape was continued.

It is difficult to generalise about the categories of land uses that took advantage of the new opportunities as the needs of individual cities, and the perception of those needs by public and private developers, as well as the timing of the development, varied greatly. Much land was often left as open space and in many cities the late nineteenth century coincided with the growth of civic pride and responsibilities, encouraging public gardens, prestigious public buildings and generous provision for the landscaping of roads. In this respect the new boulevards were an attractive residential environment offering the possibilities of new homes for the wealthier classes less cramped than those of the old inner city. Later these proved to be both suitable and ideally located for conversion to office use. The old wall boulevards of many European cities became an important ring of offices and other commercial functions around the inner city.

Although spectacular examples exist, such as the Vienna *ring*, a medium-sized city will demonstrate a typical assortment of such uses. In Arnhem the old fortifications are clearly marked by their successor boulevards, except along the River Rhine (Figure 2.13). A variety of public and private land uses can be identified, including important public buildings (such as the *Musee Sacris* concert hall)

Figure 2.13: The use of fortifications in Arnhem

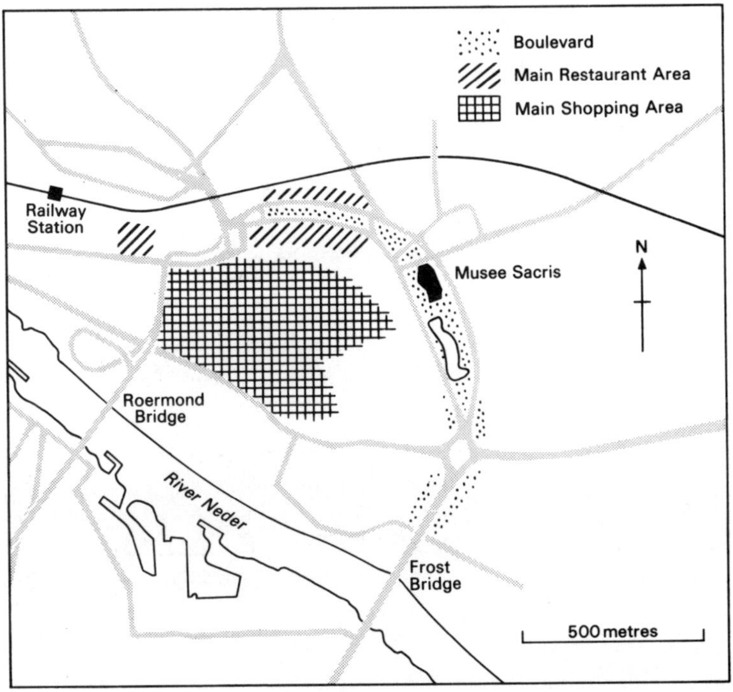

and public gardens, the agglomeration of small offices (principally financial and legal services) in the smaller buildings along the eastern boulevards, a restaurant and entertainment district along the eastern boulevards around the railway and bus station, and department store development on the edge of the main shopping district. The concentration of these land uses on the boulevard belt has accentuated the functional and formal distinction of the inner city, which is characterised by retailing and the residential districts of the town beyond the boulevards.

Although in many instances, land was released to expanding cities eager to develop it, this was not always the case. Some towns had remained content within their walls. For example the small and relatively remote settlement of Bourtange (see Figure 2.1) whose whole *raison d'être* was the defence of the frontier, had little demand for building land, and the only practical use of the area of

Figure 2.14: The fortifications of Constantinople

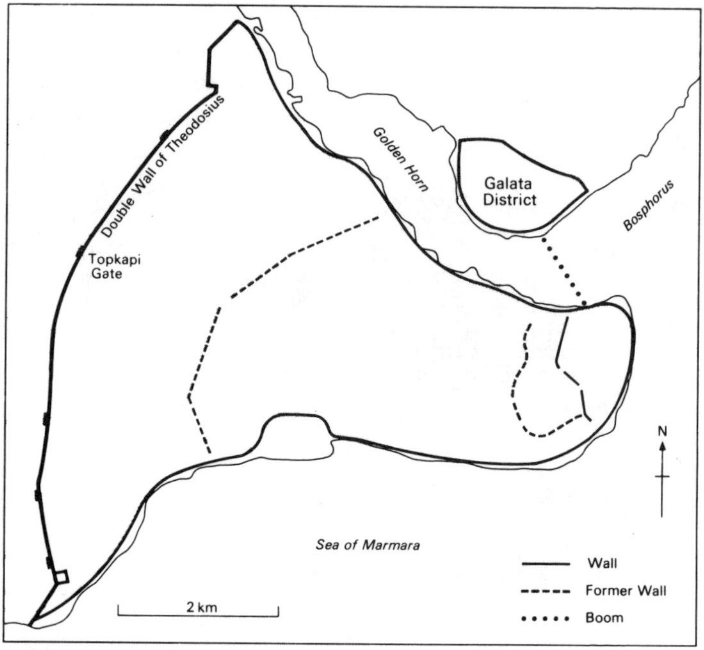

the fortifications was for agriculture. This might seem to present a difficult problem of conversion of walls and ditches into suitable workable plots. The problem was solved by the reparcellation of the land in 1853 to create saleable land holdings that included portions of wall and ditch, the former being used to fill in the latter.

A different case is where a fortification system was neither actively preserved nor demolished but simply militarily abandoned, and thus made available for informal urban uses. One of the largest examples is the 7km long double wall of Theodosius that rendered Constantinople all but impregnable for a thousand years (Figure 2.14). After the fall of the city to the Turks in 1453, the wall ceased to have a military significance, but was preserved by the inaction of the authorities and more recently by the Turkish Republic's desire to preserve Europe's most impressive fortification system without the financial resources to do more than prohibit formal development. The result is the widespread use of the space both in front of (the *parateichion*) and between the walls (the *peribolus*) for a variety of informal uses. The old ditch, when filled in, produced fertile market gardening plots in a belt 100m wide by some 2km long, conveniently located near the fruit and vegetable demands of the inner city population. The space between the double walls is used sporadically for squatter housing, including gypsy encampments, and by one of the city's most important uncontrolled markets of more than 200 selling pitches at the Topkapi Gate.

A different sort of space, offering different opportunities, was presented by the release of barracks, parade grounds and training areas. The first were usually located on scattered sites throughout the city, which provided useful infill possibilities, but the last two have generally been more important in terms of both size and location. Parade grounds were often large centrally located open spaces and associated processional ways. These contributed public open space in the heart of the city, where the need for it was greatest. Many of Europe's largest cities owe the survival of their most treasured central open spaces to their previous, and sometimes continued, use as military parade grounds. London's 'Horse Guards' or Vienna's 'Hofburg' are echoed on a lesser scale in smaller garrison towns throughout the continent; few French provincial towns for example are without their *champs de Mars*.

The larger training and manoeuvre areas were usually sited on the edge of the built-up area, and were often a potent force in the survival of peripheral open space. In the case of another coastal garrison town, Great Yarmouth, the timing of the sporadic release of military land had a considerable influence on the evolution of the urban structure over 150 years. The walled town on the River Yare (see Figure 2.12) was fronted on its eastern side by the sandy peninsula between the river and the sea known as 'The Denes', which was used mainly for military training and the recreation of the garrison. A prohibition on building in the area constrained the development of a seaside resort on the peninsula until well into the nineteenth century. Pressure from the town for the development of 'The Denes', and the decline in the importance of the garrison, led to its piecemeal release for other uses. The central section was made available between 1840 and 1870, which coincided with speculative pressure for resort development, and today this area forms the heart of the seaside resort and most of the nineteenth-century building that accommodates it. The later release of the 'South Denes' coincided with the need for more space for harbour-related activities and also for self-catering caravan holidays. Similarly the 'North Denes' was used for housing, caravan parks, and the last relic of the old garrison function of the area for the racecourse.

(b) The re-use of defence installations

Finding new uses for the existing structures saves incurring the costs of demolition and rebuilding and may also be preferred on conservation grounds. This may be difficult to achieve as military and civilian requirements are often very different. Using the city fortifications as a 'free' wall for building houses has been practically a tradition in most walled cities, bunkers and gun emplacements have been used for storage, and many a British Anderson air-raid shelter has served a generation as a garden shed. But this sort of opportunism aside, it is rare that military buildings perform new functions as effectively as a purpose-built structure. Depots and workshops have similar requirements whether in military or civilian use, but barracks present more problems. The demand for civilian communal housing is relatively easily exhausted, once the need for residential hostels of educational, judicial and social service institutions are satisfied. Conversion for family housing or hotels has been successfully attempted but is expensive, and unless the desire to preserve the building for other reasons is strong, and subsidised, rarely financially feasible.

There have been many well publicised successes. The Fredericks barracks in Leeuwarden were converted to apartments, and the Puckpool battery at Plymouth has become luxury holiday accommodation. In the last two years in the Netherlands, castles have found new uses as offices (Lochem and Voorsteden), apartments (Renswoude), conference centres (Vaals) and town halls (Ruurlo and Vorden). But these examples of successful conversion should not conceal the fact that most military installations have been replaced in the urban scene by new buildings.

The successful replacement of military by civilian uses on any scale depends upon coincidences of both requirements and timing. In Portsmouth there was the coincidence of the contraction of a major military base with an extensive network of barracks, depots and service facilities, and a major educational institution, the Polytechnic, in need of accommodation. The requirements of the two functions were not too dissimilar, some being intrinsically the same, such as the catering or sports facilities, while with others the educational requirements were sufficiently non-specific to be accommodated in barracks. But the relatively harmonious change in functions was dependent not only on the coincidences of time, place and requirements, but also on the absence of financial resources to create the purpose-built buildings which would no doubt have been preferred, and which were constructed for specialised facilities such as the library and most science departments. This experience is not unique and other examples are not difficult to find. It is possible that the whole foundation of the University of Keele, and certainly its location, were dependent on the availability of a redundant army camp.

The linear character of many defence works presents a particular opportunity for their use, as routeways provide a right of way through the city that otherwise may be difficult to secure. The use of the line of the walls as an inner ring road has already been mentioned, but in a number of cities, for example York (see Figure 2.6) or Canterbury, the walls themselves provide a pedestrian route system which combines the advantages of a pleasing elevation, attractive views of the city, physical contact with a historical relic, as well as pedestrian access.

Water defences may offer similar opportunities for navigation. Figure 2.7 shows Groningen in 1828; two different types of water surface can be identified, one for navigation (*vaarten*), and one for defence (*grachten*). The functional segregation between the two is sharp, if only because the *grachten* are by definition outside the protection of the walls and thus unsuited to harbour development, follow a circuitous course around the artillery bastions, and also were probably too shallow. A comparison with the modern situation shows that only in the southern sector was the demolition of the fortifications seen as an opportunity to improve navigation by using the straightened *gracht* as a canal with three new harbour basins. This in turn allowed the old southern canal to be reclaimed (the *Zuiderdiep*) creating a wide southern inner city ring road. The rest of the water defence system was either filled in and used for building land, notably for the city teaching hospital, or left for recreation and amenity.

(c) Defence installations as 'heritage'

The dismantling of urban fortifications in the nineteenth century provided the first large-scale public conflict between the ideas of conservation and development in many cities in western Europe. City councils and local public opinion were confronted by a series of clear-cut irreversible choices about the future use and appearance of a large part of the existing townscape. In almost every case the ultimate decision was in favour of demolition, and preservation when it occurred was usually only a result of an absence of either money or pressure for redevelopment. Nevertheless the sudden acceleration of the pace of change, on a scale not to be repeated in many cities until after the Second World War, provoked reaction. The idea of preserving aspects of the built environment as historical artefacts received a substantial stimulus, which led to the establishment of pressure groups dedicated to slowing the rate of change, and which placed the issue of urban conservation permanently on the council planning agenda.

Defence installations have some characteristics that render them ideally suited to become 'heritage'. They are frequently, especially in the case of fortifications, sufficiently robust to have survived the ravages of time. The innate conservatism of military authorities allows many installations to pass directly from active defence use to historical monument without an intervening period of neglected obsolescence. Finally, and probably most significantly, military artefacts are inevitably imbued with the strong human emotions generated by war, and therefore exercise a particular fascination on the imagination. It is not surprising therefore that conserved defence installations can be found throughout Europe fulfilling simultaneously two functions, viz. *being* 'heritage', and *housing* 'heritage', so that the castle museum is one of the most ubiquitous features of the urban scene.

The relative importance of this function depends not only on the national or international significance of the defence heritage but also on the size and alternative functions of the town. In the smaller fortress towns the entire settlement is an entity both legally, being defined as a whole as a monument, and functionally as the preservation and presentation of military history becomes the principal occupation of the town. Bourtange has never had other important urban functions, and has now become in effect an open-air museum whose object is to recreate for visitors the atmosphere of an eighteenth-century fortress town even if this does involve the expensive replacement of the previously demolished bastions. The cycle is thus complete, from construction for defence, through demolition and re-use, to preservation and finally reconstruction as 'heritage'. The scale of the post-artillery defence works renders the seventeenth-century fortress particularly prone to this pattern, witness Willemstad (Netherlands), Neuf-Brisach (France), or Fredericia (Denmark). There are examples from both earlier periods such as the medieval reconstructed city of Carcassonne in France, or the fortress state of San Marino, and even later periods although these are rarer, such as the preserved monument towns of Sonderborg, Denmark (mid-nineteenth century) and Dien-Bien-Phu in Vietnam (mid-twentieth century).

The small size and monofunctional character of these towns renders them atypical, and in terms of planning policies and priorities relatively non-controversial. Most of Europe's defence heritage is to be found in large, multifunctional cities where its role in the urban economy and in the evolving townscape is neither as clear nor as inevitable.

The attempt to transform the Royal Naval dockyard city of Portsmouth into the 'flagship of England's maritime heritage' will be examined in Chapter 5, where the implications of this important step, from the preservation of defence artefacts to the marketing of history as a part of urban tourism, will be discussed. It need only be stressed here that this metamorphosis is a result of relatively recent management decisions which have selected elements from within the wide range of obsolete defence installations and artefacts (including, in this case, ships), for the re-creation of a sample of historic episodes stretching from the sixteenth to the twentieth centuries for sale to tourists (Windle, 1980). Unlike the situation in the small fortress towns these decisions have spatial implications for the definition and delimitation on the ground of the 'tourist–historic city' within the city as a whole (Ashworth and De Haan, 1985). Defence monuments can make two important morphological contributions to this spatial differentiation. First, castles by their size and elevation, and surrounding open space of bailey and parade grounds, can be focusing elements, marking a clearly visible centre to the historic district (for example, in Norwich). Secondly, the city wall can be an enclosing element separating the tourist–historic city from other functional areas, such as the modern commercial city. This is particularly noticeable where the city has recently expanded beyond its fortifications, so that the wall divides the old from the new, or in the case of the Mediterranean 'akropolis town', the upper from the lower, as, for example, Bergamo in Italy. The action radius of the tourist and the protected zone of the conservation planner, can be neatly defined by this clear morphological divide.

CONCLUSION

It is clear from this review of the experience of European cities over two millennia that the relationship between the defence function and urban form is neither simple nor one-sided. It varies with the many different sorts of defence roles that cities perform, as well as in response to the evolution of military technology, engineering, organisation and tactical thinking. This particular link between form and function has to be redefined in each city in response to the circumstances of place and time.

Given the importance of security in what remains an unsafe continent in an unstable world, it is not surprising that defence considerations have been important in the choice of individual urban sites, the nature of the national or regional urban system, the pace and character of urbanisation, and, not least, the form and structure of the city itself. Defence, however, is not just a historic process explaining aspects of the contemporary town plan by reference to a turbulent past, and Europe's prosperous modern cities of concrete and glass are as much military positions under imminent threat of attack as ever. Such influences have been both negative constraints, including on occasion annihilation, but have also included, intentionally or otherwise, the positive endowment of the city with the gift of land, buildings and 'heritage'.

At the heart of the matter, however, remains the paradox that the city is both the object of attack or defence through its concentration of productive capacity, essential services and symbolic values, as well as being simultaneously a means of conducting those operations as a fortress, strongpoint or battle terrain. Ultimately therefore, the most important influence of defence upon urban form is that, 'the decision to attack or to defend a city may be tantamount to a decision to destroy it' (United States Army, 1976).

REFERENCES

Anon. (1982) *De Geschiedenis van de Vesting Bourtange*, Stubeg, Hoogezand, Netherlands.

Ashworth, G.J. and Schuurmans, F. (1982) *Perpignan: Commercial Activity in the Central Area*, Veldstudies, Reeks no. 4, Geografisch Instituut Rijksuniversiteit Groningen.

Ashworth, G.J. and De Haan, T.Z. (1985) *The Tourist–Historic City: a Model and Initial Application in Norwich (UK)*, Veldstudies, Reeks no. 8, Geografisch Instituut Rijksuniversiteit Groningen.

Aston, M. and Bond, J. (1976) *The Landscape of Towns*, J.M. Dent, London.

Bruce-Biggs, B. (1974) 'Suburban Warfare', *Military Review*, 54 (6), 3–10.

Burtenshaw, D., Bateman, M. and Ashworth, G.J. (1981) *The City in West Europe*, Wiley, Chichester.

Carter, H. (1983) *An Introduction to Urban Historical Geography*, Arnold, London.

Castells, M. (1983) *The City and the Grassroots*, Arnold, London.

Cohen, S. (1963) *Geography and Politics in a Divided World*, Random House, New York.

De Haan, T.Z. and Ashworth, G.J. (1984) *Modelling the Seaside Resort: the Example of Great Yarmouth*, Veldstudies, Reeks no. 7, Geografisch Instituut Rijksuniversiteit Groningen.

Dickinson, R.E. (1961) *The West European City*, Routledge & Kegan Paul, London.

Donaldson, S. (1979) 'City Fight: Modern Combat in the Urban Environment', *Strategy & Tactics*, 77, 15–24.

Douglas, J.D. (1983) 'Strategic Planning and Nuclear Insecurity', *Orbis*, 27, 667–94.

Douhet, G. (first edn 1921, English edn 1942) *Command of the Air*, Coward-McCann, New York.

Dunnigan, J.F. *et al.* (1980) 'Berlin '85: The Enemy at the Gates', *Strategy and Tactics*, 79, 4–14.
Fuller, J.F.C. (1970) *The Decisive Battles of the Western World*, ed. J. Terraine, Paladin, London.
Hackett, J. (1978) *The Third World War*, Sphere, London.
Harouel, J.-L. (1981) *Histoire de l'Urbanisme*, Presses Universitaires de France, Paris.
Harvey, A. (1911) *The Castles and Walled Towns of England*, Methuen, London.
Hedges, A.A.L. (1973) *Yarmouth is an Ancient Town*, Great Yarmouth Borough Council, Great Yarmouth.
Heller, H. (1975) 'Zivilschutz und Raumplanung', *Plan*, 7/8, 15–18.
Hewitt, K. (1983) 'Place Annihilation: Area Bombing and the Fate of Urban Places', *Annals of Association of American Geographers*, 73 (2), 257–84.
Hofmann, H.H. (1977) 'Zur Einfuhrung', in Hofmann, H.H. (ed.), *Stadt und Militarische Anlagen*, Forschungs und Sitzungsberichte, Band 114, Akademie für Raumforschung, Herman Schroedel Verlag, Hannover.
Houston, J.M. (1953) *A Social Geography of Europe*, Duckworth, London.
King, A.D. (1976) *Colonial Urban Development*, Routledge & Kegan Paul, London.
Mumford, L. (1961) *The City in History*, Penguin, Harmondsworth.
Oppenheimer, M. (1969) *Urban Guerrilla*, Penguin, Harmondsworth.
O'Sullivan, P. and Miller, J.W. (1983) *The Geography of Warfare*, Croom Helm, London.
Pirenne, H. (1949) *Medieval Cities*, Princeton.
Platt, R.H. (1984) 'The Planner and Nuclear Crisis Relocation', *Journal of American Planning Association*, 50, 259–60.
Sicken, B. (1977) 'Historische Entwicklung im Stradtraum', in Hofmann, H.H. (ed.), *Stadt und Militarische Anlagen*, Forschungs und Sitzungsberichte, Band 114, Akademie für Raumforschung, Herman Schroedel Verlag, Hannover.
Smith, C.T. (1967) *An Historical Geography of Western Europe Before 1800*, Longmans, London.
Smook, R.A.F. (1984) *Binnensteden Veranderen: Atlas van het Ruimetelijk Veranderingsproces van Nederlandse Binnensteden in de Laatste Anderhalve Eeuw*, De Walburg Pers, Zutphen.
United States Army (1972) *Combat in Built-up Areas*, Field Manual no. ST 31–50–171, Infantry School, Fort Benning, Georgia.
United States Army (1976) *Operations*, Field Manual, 100–5, Washington D.C.
United States Army (1977) *The Tank and Mechanised Infantry*, Field Manual No. 71–1/2, Washington D.C.
Vance, J.E. (1977) *This Scene of Man*, Harpers College Press, New York.
Weber, M. (1958) *The City*, Heinemann, London.
Wheatcroft, A. (1983) *World Atlas of Revolution*, Hamish Hamilton, London.
Windle, R. (ed) (1980) *Records of the Corporation 1966–1974*, City of Portsmouth.
Ziegler, D.F. (1985) *The Geography of Civil Defence*, in Pepper, D. and Jenkins, A. (eds) *The Geography of Peace and War*, Blackwell, Oxford.

3

Military and Naval Land Use as a Determinant of Urban Development — The Case of Portsmouth

Raymond Riley

That economic and ecological influences are but partial explanations of urban land use patterns is not now a compelling issue, and indeed it is over three decades since Form (1954) identified the role of organisation complexes as a determinant of the spatial sorting process. It is undeniable that estate agents, property developers, the larger industries, businesses and utilities, individual home owners, together with local government agencies, all with differing goals and values, combine to render the rationale of land use change a highly complex notion. Yet comprehensive though it may be, Form's model underplays the impact of central government activity, which in some instances is a crucial explanatory strand. Perhaps because the insular nature of Britain has proved to be defensive in itself, the phenomenon of the strongly defended town is not one that has occupied a central position in urban studies. While recognising that such towns are special cases from which generally applicable conclusions cannot be derived, they nevertheless demonstrate the way in which forces quite beyond local control, such as the threat of war or changes in weapon technology, can influence land use, very much in the manner of the present day large corporation taking decisions in distant headquarters on international issues leading to the closure of a branch plant (Watts, 1981).

Since garrison towns are components of national defence strategy, the appropriate government departments have traditionally been granted powers which transcend the wishes of local authorities, commerce and individuals, although there is now more of a dialogue than formerly obtained. A number of towns were designated as garrisons as early as the fifteenth century, but the use of land for

Figure 3.1: Model of the evolution of a fortified garrison and Royal dockyard town

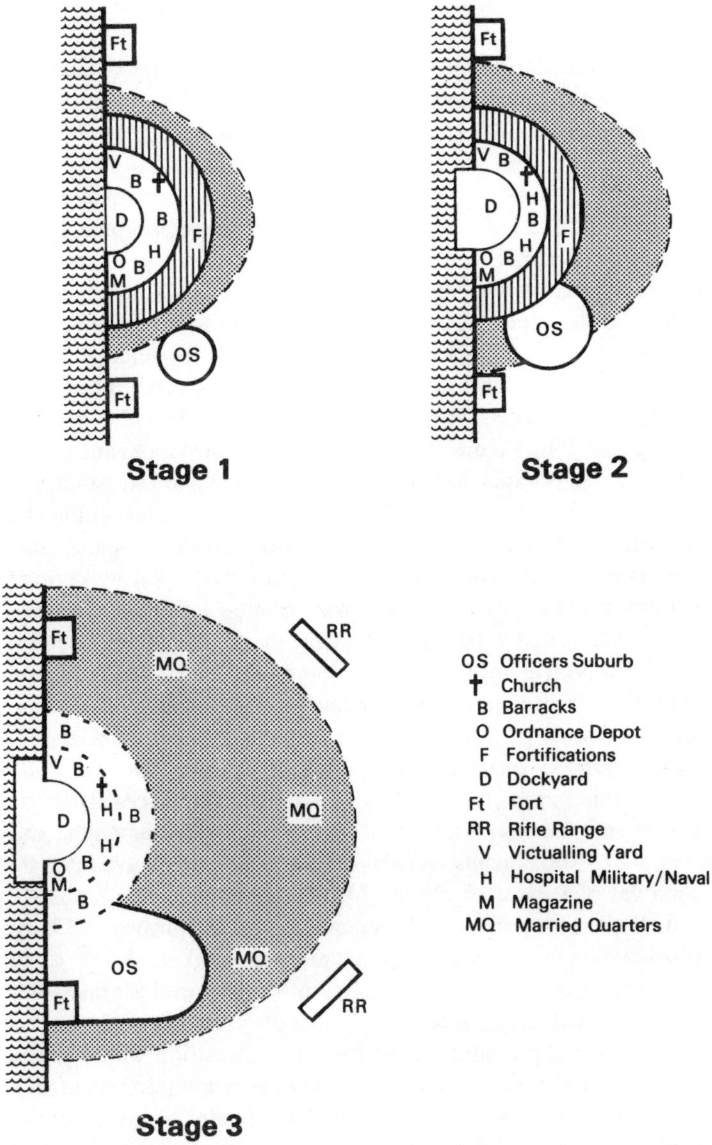

military purposes in such settlements reached its peak in the nineteenth century, when the friction of distance was still sufficiently powerful to ensure that the full panoply of necessary services was tightly compacted. A typical garrison included extensive barracks, an ordnance depot, a hospital, a church, separate and often quite palatial accommodation for senior officers, and a cluster of substantial houses rented by married officers. A fortified garrison would have substantial earthworks, ramparts and moats, together with open space beyond to offer the gunners an uninterrupted field of fire. Land for these functions could, until mid century when many urban areas expanded spatially at an unprecedented speed, account for as much as half the total built-up area.

Where a garrison was also a Royal dockyard, a victualling depot and a magazine might be expected, in addition to a naval hospital and a church; since a dockyard must be coastal, its defence would be assisted by the establishment of forts on the shore well beyond the inner fortifications. These features are illustrated in schematic form as stage 1 in Figure 3.1. Subsequently, the dockyard rather than the garrison expanded, following the switch to steam-driven vessels, and this was achieved by the purchase of land within the fortifications and by the reclamation of ground from the sea. At this second stage the officers' suburb was encroached upon by civilian population growth. The third stage was ushered in by the introduction of sophisticated artillery, rendering the fortifications useless, their demolition triggering land use change as Crown land came on to the market. Improvements in weaponry called for the construction of rifle ranges, at peripheral sites because of population pressure, and later married quarters were similarly located for the same reason. In this period further dockyard expansion, necessitated by the arrival of iron warships, was engineered by reclamation, and naval shore establishments were built on the land made available by the removal of the fortifications. Military barracks were similarly located. Were the garrison subsequently to be withdrawn, military premises would be disposed of on the open market. At all three stages of the model Admiralty permission was required for tidewater development, and should it be thought that the consequential vessels' movements would prejudice naval operations, sanction would not be granted, with negative results on land use. It is the purpose of this chapter to examine the extent to which this model of government-induced land use change has application to Portsmouth, and simultaneously to consider the impact of such changes that were effected on competition for land.

MILITARY AND NAVAL LAND USE IN PORTSMOUTH TO MID NINETEENTH CENTURY

While Portsmouth existed as a settlement prior to 1496, its subsequent development almost entirely hinged upon Henry VII's decision in that year to declare the town both a garrison and a Royal dockyard. The monarch's perception of the strategic value of the site was confirmed by later rulers and governments, giving rise to constant elaboration of the defences. Southsea Castle, the first angle bastioned fort in the country, was completed in 1544, and by the 1690s the original town's defences had been rebuilt by De Gomme in a manner similar to the great continental fortress towns, making Portsmouth the most heavily defended garrison in Britain (Corney, 1983). The dockyard itself was regarded as being of secondary importance, and was not only located outside the town itself, representing a conflict with the model, but also was enclosed only by an earthen bank surmounted by a wooden palisade. The loss of the dockyard was obviously considered less of an issue than the need to secure the political symbolism that the town represented as an instrument of foreign policy. In this there are overtones of the way in which political and ecclesiastical influences dominated economic considerations in the pre-industrial city (Sjoberg, 1965). A further coastal defence work, Fort Cumberland, was constructed in the 1740s, and rebuilt between 1794 and 1820 (Saunders, 1967, p. 148), to inhibit a landing in Langstone Harbour. In the same decade fortifications more than a mile in length, known as Hilsea Lines, although of a less comprehensive character than those at Portsmouth, were thrown up along the northern tip of Portsea Island to offer additional protection against light mobile guns. The appearance of a second coastal fort beyond Southsea Castle, and the scale of Hilsea Lines, neither of which is predicted by the model, are attributable to the configuration of the local coastline and to the location of the town and dockyard on an island.

Modifications were undertaken to De Gomme's fortifications in mid eighteenth century, but more far-reaching land use changes flowed from the decision to erect round the dockyard fortifications even larger than those at Portsmouth. Begun in the 1770s and completed in 1809 (Masters, 1964), the ramparts and outworks were set well to the east of the dockyard wall on agricultural land, extending for a distance of three-quarters of a mile (see Figure 3.2). By comparison the fortifications of Portsmouth which encircled the town were some one-and-a-third miles in length. More important

Figure 3.2: Military land use in Portsmouth and Portsea, 1860

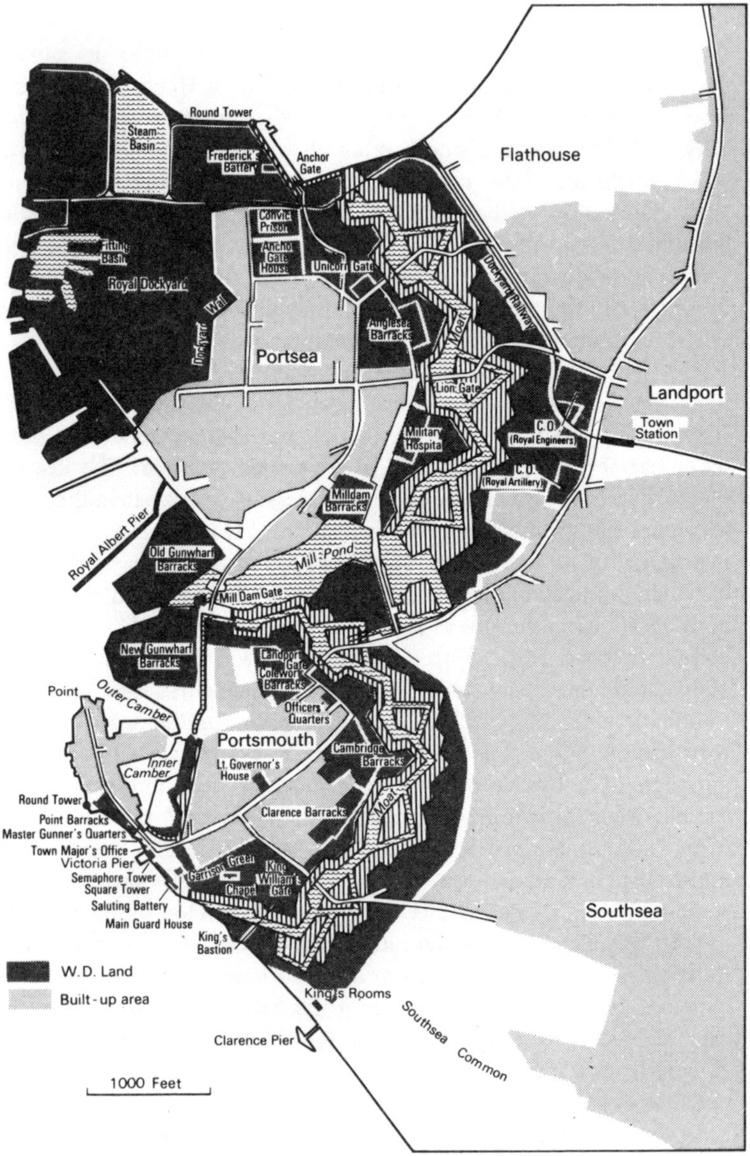

was the sheer width of the works. Angle bastions projected from the ramparts to ensure that the entire face of the outer walls could be raked with defensive fire from some other point. Separated from the angle bastions and their linking curtains by a wide moat were large V-shaped ravelins, themselves surrounded by moats. Beyond the latter was an earthen glacis sloping gently down to the natural surface of the surrounding land. The Portsmouth ramparts and outworks were almost everywhere approximately 300 yards wide, but those at Portsea (the dockyard settlement) varied between 375 and 450 yards in width. In the case of both towns the width of the fortifications was at least half as great as the longest distance within the ramparts. Small wonder that contemporary topographers (Hollingsworth, 1825) and railway guides (London, Brighton and South Coast Railway, 1853) waxed lyrical on the size and complexity of these structures whose area was actually greater than that of the towns they surrounded. Doubtless because their extent was less obvious to travellers and since their rural setting did not cause them to enclose a settlement, Hilsea Lines failed to attract such attention. Yet land purchased in 1813 by the Crown to the south of the Lines on Portsea Island and to the north on the mainland was so extensive that it gave the Board of Ordnance control of some 364ha, that is, half as large again as the combined area of Portsmouth, Portsea, their fortifications, the dockyard in its 1860 form, and Southsea Common (see Table 3.1). The justification for the size of the area annexed was that building construction in the vicinity of the ramparts could be controlled; should these buildings 'get into the possession of an Enemy they could be turned into a means of annoying the works' (Howell, 1913, p. 143). However, since the land other than that on which the fortifications and barracks were built was leased for agriculture, the effective impact on land use was small. By comparison, Crown land surrounding the militarily powerful Fort Cumberland was of modest proportions.

Inside the fortifications the most obvious indication of the function of both Portsmouth and Portsea was the presence of large barracks. Portsmouth was host to Colewort Barracks opened in 1680 and enlarged in 1828, Cambridge Barracks dating from 1825 and rebuilt 1856–8, and Clarence Barracks opened in 1753 and enlarged in 1770 and 1824. In addition there was the military hospital of 1834, Garrison Chapel, Grand Parade, Governor's Green, the Lieutenant Governor's House and officers' quarters in High Street. At Point, immediately outside the town walls, Point Barracks were constructed in 1847 to house the gunners serving on the Round

Table 3.1: Military and naval land use in Portsmouth,* Portsea* and Southsea in 1860

	Fortifications		Barracks and depots		Dockyard		Civilian area		Total
	ha	%	ha	%	ha	%	ha	%	ha
Portsmouth	38.8	55	9.2	13	–		22.6	32	70.6
Portsea	48.5	36	13.6	10	41.5	31	31.3	23	134.9
Southsea Common	53.4	97	–		–		1.5	3	54.9

* Ward boundaries not used since these follow the moats, thus delimiting neither the civilian towns nor the fortifications.

Source: Ordnance Survey 1:10560, 1870; *Collins' New Map of Portsmouth, Portsea, Landport and Southsea with the Dockyard and Public Establishments*, c. 1860.

Tower and Long Battery overlooking the entrance to the harbour. These military functions accounted for more than one-third of the area of the town within the fortifications. Barracks in Portsea were rather more muted, possibly because of the later date of the fortifications. Milldam Barracks were completed c. 1820, as was the Garrison Hospital, although substantially enlarged in 1853, and Anglesea Barracks and the Garrison Prison were both first occupied in 1848. However, Portsea, the dockyard town, had two large ordnance depots. The gunwharf was created from reclaimed ground south of the dockyard in 1662, and although its area was far in excess of any of the barracks mentioned, such was the Navy's need of guns, ammunition and associated equipment that New Gunwharf was built between 1797 and 1814 to the south of the original, once again on made ground. In order to secure a supply of flour for ships' bread and biscuit, in 1744 a corn mill — the King's Mill — was constructed between the two gunwharves, its tide pond doubling as a source of water for the moats. Following the contemporary notion that convicts should be required to earn their crust, many hundreds were employed in the dockyard, being accommodated in insalubrious hulks in the harbour, until 1852 when a spacious convict prison was opened in northern Portsea. Not surprisingly, the dockyard, the very *raison d'être* for Portsea, was substantially larger than the town it had spawned. Notwithstanding, the true scale of government ownership is not manifest until allowance is made for the fortifications themselves. As Table 3.1 indicates, the Portsmouth ramparts and outworks alone accounted for more than half the surface of the town, giving the Crown control of two-thirds of the total area. Despite their absolute size, the Portsea fortifications were restricted to one-third of the town's surface, but in total the government could lay claim to no less than three-quarters of the settlement. Arguably Portsmouth and Portsea were no less company towns than those which were satellites of railways and steelworks.

Outside Portsmouth and Portsea, two barracks were established as adjuncts to particular military functions. Troops whose task it was to man Hilsea Lines were housed in Hilsea Barracks, originating in 1756 and enlarged in 1794 and 1854, when a hospital and a church were included. Small barracks were set up at Tipner when in 1813 a magazine was built on the ideally isolated peninsula, all of which came to be owned by the Crown. A third barracks, at Eastney, was established for the Royal Marines on 60ha of farm land purchased in 1845 (Howell, 1913, p. 26), incorporating a hospital, a church, sizeable recreation grounds, and a little later, swimming baths. In addition, two small forts were constructed facing on to the sea. With Fort Cumberland to the east, the Eastney site totalled some 83.6ha, only slightly smaller than the area of the Portsmouth and Portsea fortifications. The relatively late completion of Eastney Barracks in 1867 ensured that they were sited peripherally, as predicted in the model for rifle ranges, but since they were not associated with a specific defensive outwork, the premises must conflict with the model. With the purchase of the land for Eastney Barracks, apart from one small section, the War Department then controlled the entire south coast of Portsea Island, for the Board of Ordnance had purchased Southsea Common in 1785 to provide artillery with a clear sight of the waters of the Spithead. Since the northern tip was similarly owned, and a substantial portion of the Portsmouth Harbour foreshore occupied by the dockyard and Tipner, had it not been for the absence of military land giving on to Langstone Harbour, Portsmouth Island would have come close to being encircled by Crown property.

The extent of the fortifications had an important impact on transport routes. Egress to and from Portsmouth and Portsea on the landward side was controlled by the provision of five town gates, the approach to four of which was by narrow road, bridge and drawbridge. As though to emphasise military control, the town gates were shut between the hours of midnight and 4.00 am, but this seems only to have interfered with the operations of the night soil carriers (Gates, 1928, p. 52). Fringing the glacis was a ring of roads whose spatial form was entirely determined by the shape of the glacis itself, a pattern which in Portsmouth has persisted unchanged. On the eastern side of these roads edging the Portsmouth glacis, five blocks of substantial terraced houses were built by developers Thomas Croxton and John Williams, who appreciated the then novel advantage of a pleasing uninterrupted view over the glacis to the elm trees growing on the inner banks of the ramparts, thus obscuring the reality of the town of Portsmouth beyond (Riley, 1972). By 1830 these terraces housed 22 of the 78 nobility and gentry listed for Southsea (Pigot, 1830), suggesting that the fortifications had a role in the location of the first upper middle class residential area outside the old town. Even though the Portsea glacis was more extensive than that at Portsmouth, and elm trees similarly obscured the town, the social stigma attaching to the dockyard and its workmen's houses prevented the emergence of a middle class area.

If the glacis helped determine adjacent road configuration and the beginning of an officers' suburb, Crown ownership of Southsea

Common gave rise to similar results on a larger scale. Seafront development for more than a mile to the south east of the Portsmouth glacis was prevented, with the consequence that not only did the main coastal road follow an inland path, but effectively the suburb of Southsea was unable to reach the sea in the early years of its growth. Moreover, the existence of the Common, coupled with views of the Spithead, made the plots bordering the government land very desirable for expensive housing, which developed quickly in the 1840s and 1850s, giving a distinctive wedge shape to this middle-class area (Bateman, 1974, map 3.3). When hotels arrived in the 1860s as Southsea's resort function burgeoned, they too found they had to take up sites behind the Common. Despite its large size, the area of open land represented by the Common constitutes only a minor modification of the model since its function was essentially that of an extended glacis, and its length determined by local geography. However alluring properties adjacent to the Common may have been to officers of the garrison and the Navy, they never constituted the core of the officers' suburb. It was increasingly the detached villa that came to be the householder's goal, and here an especially skilful developer was on hand to take advantage both of the new trend and of the growth in the armed forces apparent in Table 3.2. Thomas Ellis Owen, who was an architect and a builder to boot, purchased land to the east of the glacis terraces, and until his death in 1862 erected 106 villas and 54 terraced houses, a hotel, assembly rooms and, at his own expense, a church, creating a middle class community living at what was then a very low density (Riley, 1980). In 1851 some 47 per cent of the heads of household in Owen properties were army and naval officers and, attracted by the ambience, those with private incomes played a strong supporting role; in the same year 24 per cent of heads of household were property owners, fundholders and annuitants (Riley, 1980, p. 16). Whatever Owen's capacity as an urban gatekeeper, it is arguable that without the demand from the officer class for his and his imitators' houses, central Southsea would never have become the largest middle class enclave in present day Portsmouth.

Inevitably, naval control of the harbour and its traffic was a powerful influence upon tidewater land uses. In some instances refusal of sanction caused development to occur elsewhere. Thus the effective blocking of the London & South Western Railway's proposal to build their line from Southampton in the early 1840s along the western edge of Portsea Island caused the company to join forces with the London, Brighton & South Coast Railway to create

Table 3.2: Armed forces employment in Portsmouth, 1841–1981

	1841	1881	1911	1931	1961	1971	1981
Working population	17346	51487	101733	97076	113910	110990	107590
Forces	2834	7881	23252	20786	11060	10910	10050
Forces as per cent working population	16.3	15.3	22.8	21.4	9.7	9.8	9.3

Source: Census Reports.

the route that now exists (Course, 1969, p. 6). More often there was a negative impact on land use. Following the improvement of the Camber wharf in Portsmouth by the Corporation, ocean liners began to call in the 1840s (Gates, 1928, p. 63). An attempt by the Corporation to extend the railway to the Camber in 1858 also proved abortive since the line would have breached the fortifications, and although a dry dock was opened in 1863, lacking a rail link even medium-sized docks were out of the question. Surprisingly, no line was laid down when the fortifications were removed, perhaps because of naval objections to commercial shipping, and the Camber never became more than a miniscule handling point. Unquestionably the negative impact on land use proposed by the model has had real application.

While there are deviations from the model flowing from Portsmouth's insular nature, the clear separation of the dockyard from the old town of Portsmouth, and from the establishment of barracks outside the fortifications, there is considerable evidence in support of the proposals made in stages 1 and 2. Moreover, the construction of the Steam Basin in the dockyard between 1843 and 1848, together with associated engineering shops, smithy, foundry, timber stacking ground and two docks on made ground (Riley, 1985b), meshes well with stage 2 of the model, although it should be observed that no land was acquired from Portsea at the time.

THE INNER FORTIFICATIONS DISMANTLED

It had been known since the sixteenth century that if a trajectory could be made to rotate during flight, accuracy would be much improved, but the introduction of the necessary spiral rifling in gun barrels required the use of sophisticated machine tools not available until mid-nineteenth century. William Armstrong's 40 pounder, which came into service in 1859, incorporated both rifling and a breech loading mechanism which doubled the range of artillery to a distance of 8,000 yards. Since other nations could be expected to develop the same technology, above all France, whose armour plated warship *La Gloire*, launched in 1859, was more advanced than anything possessed by the Royal Navy, fresh defences became crucial. The Royal Commission on the Defence of the United Kingdom reporting in 1860, recommended that a string of six forts be built to the north of Hilsea Lines along the ridge of Portsdown Hill to supplement a further five whose construction had begun in 1852 to the west of Gosport, and that four sea forts be erected to protect the Spithead approaches. The Portsdown forts were completed in 1868 (Saunders, 1967, pp. 150–1), but the Spithead forts were not declared ready until 1880 (Temple-Patterson, 1967, p. 14, pp. 16–17). The sea forts clearly played no part in urban land use and, indeed, the Portsdown forts and their 573ha strip of land were so far removed from the built-up area that they represented a loss to agriculture rather than to urban functions. Despite the subsequent northward march of Portsmouth, land in the vicinity of the forts has largely remained agricultural or waste, absolving the Crown from having prejudiced development.

The new developments may have had a minimal impact on urban areas, but their corollary was of outstanding significance for central Portsmouth since the greater part of the Portsmouth and Portsea fortifications were now irrelevant. Demolition of all but those overlooking the harbour entrance began almost immediately, although the last sections of the Mill Pond were not filled in until 1876 (Gates, 1928, p. 132). The reasons for this celerity are unclear, but contributory considerations are likely to have been the need for brick rubble as backing for the new docks and basins being constructed in the dockyard between 1867 and 1876 (Riley, 1985b, p. 22), the pressure to provide barrack space for the growing garrison, and the decision to lay out extensive recreation grounds to help reduce the rigours of service life. That the land might be sold off for non-military purposes seems not to have been a central issue.

The first changes following demolition involved the road system. There was some realignment and widening of roads that had breached the fortifications, but more importantly, it became possible to lay down a number of new links that greatly eased traffic flows between constituent parts of the town. Park Road was built in 1875 over the Mill Pond between Landport and southern Portsea, where it was met by Alexandra and St George's Roads — effectively a single thoroughfare — from Southsea, opened in 1877. The third fresh artery was that between the northernmost Southsea terraces and Queen Street, Portsea — St Michael's and Anglesea Roads — a route which a century later proved easy to widen as part of the city's inner ring system. Within this road network some 70 per cent of the area was retained for military and naval use, as Table 3.3 indicates, although it is clear from Figure 3.3 that around the old town of Portsmouth such uses had a virtual monopoly. Clarence Barracks were greatly extended to form Victoria Barracks between 1880 and 1897, the gunwharf annexed land reclaimed from the Mill

Figure 3.3: Land uses in the former Portsmouth and Portsea fortifications, 1910

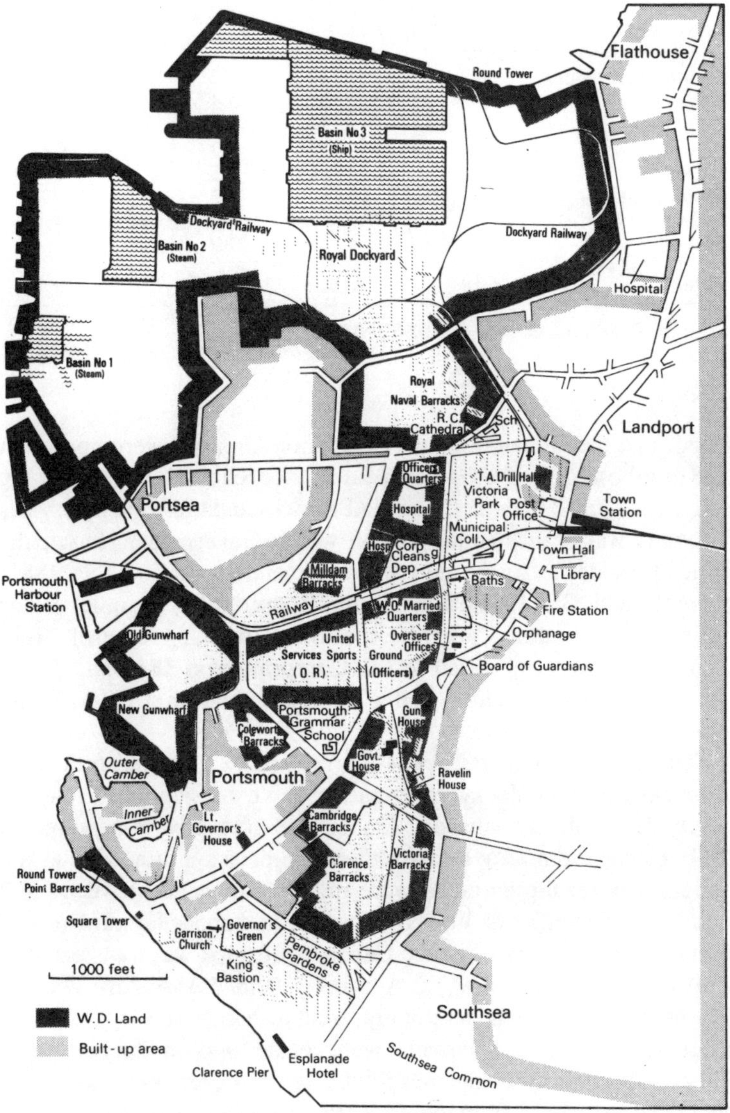

Table 3.3: The re-use of land occupied by the Portsmouth and Portsea fortifications, 1910

Function	ha	%
Service barracks	20.7	28
Service recreation grounds	15.1	21
Service residences	5.5	7
Dockyard	10.4	14
Civic park	7.0	9
Civic centre	4.3	6
Ecclesiastic	3.5	5
Commercial	3.5	5
Railway	3.3	4
School	0.7	1
Total	74.0	100

Source: Ordnance Survey 1:10560, 1910.

Pond, and the United Services Recreation Grounds were opened in 1881, followed by the Garrison Recreation Ground adjacent to the sea. Sandwiched between Victoria Barracks and the United Services Grounds was a substantial plot on which Government House, the official residence of the garrison commander, was built in 1882, together with Gun House and Ravelin House (1891) for other senior officers. Exceptions to this continued military control were Pembroke Gardens, leased to the Corporation in 1886 and put to good use as tennis courts, and a small area sold in 1879 to Portsmouth Grammar School.

The situation at Portsea was more complex. To the north, land was taken into the dockyard as part of the extension work referred to above, while the adjacent Anglesea Barracks were acquired in 1891 by the Admiralty as a result of the decision to accommodate sailors ashore; the barracks were greatly expanded between 1899 and 1903. The officers' mess obtained further space for gardens and tennis courts in 1908 when the Garrison Hospital was transferred to Portsdown Hill, becoming the Admiralty-funded Alexandra Military Hospital. These events did not represent a change of ownership, but elsewhere in Portsea inroads were made into military control. Firstly, the railway companies jointly secured permission to extend their line in 1876 to Portsmouth Harbour station. A direct link with the sea, formerly denied because of the sanctity of the fortifications, with ferries carrying holiday-makers to the Isle of Wight, was the obviously lucrative justification for the scheme, although it was somewhat tempered by government insistence upon the construction of sidings to the gunwharf and a viaduct to the dockyard as part of the agreement (Course, 1969, pp. 16–17). The extension was achieved without the wholesale destruction of dwellings so typical of such projects in many other towns (Kellett, 1979), and in fact the buildings destroyed were practically all within the gunwharf. Secondly, the Corporation purchased ground from which Victoria Park was fashioned in 1878, an enlightened act in the light of adjacent population density. Further acquisitions by the Corporation allowed the construction of the Overseer's Offices in 1879, a free library in 1883 in what had been the house and garden of the officer commanding the Royal Artillery, the public baths, also in 1883, and the Guildhall, completed in 1890, largely in the grounds of what had been the residence of the colonel commanding the Southern District Artillery (Gates, 1928, p. 170). The Corporation continued to develop amenities in the locality by putting up a fire station in 1894, a building for the Board of Guardians in 1900, a Municipal College in matching architectural style to the Guildhall in 1908, and stables for the cleansing department. Despite the diversity of these activities, civic land accounted for only 15 per cent of the new land available. Thirdly, the churches seized the opportunity to augment their influence. A Presbyterian church was consecrated in 1880, followed by St Michael's in 1882, the Roman Catholic cathedral in 1887, together with an associated school, and in 1896 a Congregational church. Fourthly, a string of retail premises, some offices and the General Post Office (in 1883) opened on Commercial Road, reflecting the area's position as the focus of the borough of Portsmouth. In keeping with its new orientation, the civic centre contained only two forces-related functions, a naval orphanage (1876) and a territorial drill hall (1901).

It is predicted in stage 3 of the model that the removal of the fortifications would lead to much of the land being sold on the open market, yet in practice almost three-quarters of the land remained in the control of the Crown, even if it was put to somewhat different uses. As a consequence land uses were apparently aberrant. For instance, it is difficult to believe that market forces would have led to the allocation of the large open spaces of the United Services Recreation Grounds in such close proximity to the historic core of the old town. A further notable feature was the institutional control of much of the land that passed out of the hands of the War Department. This certainly enabled the Corporation to create an identifiable and cohesive civic centre, including a park, at a location central to contemporary needs (the borough's previous town hall had been in the High Street of the old town of Portsmouth, a position decidedly peripheral by 1900), without having to redevelop a previously inhabited area. This fortuitous advantage was something few towns could boast, and that it should exist was due entirely to previous government ownership of the land. Although no documentary evidence in support of the view is available, the restriction of retailing and offices to a small area, half of which was in any case donated by the War Department to the Corporation and then leased (Gates, 1928, p. 164), and, ecclesiastics' residences apart, the total absence of dwellings, suggest that very little of the land ever appeared on the market, and that negotiations were conducted almost wholly between Whitehall, the Corporation, the church and the railway companies. The process is in a sense more redolent of post-war central area redevelopment than of urban metamorphosis in the late nineteenth century.

Just as technological change in artillery power was responsible for the obsolescence of the fortifications, and therefore in part for the land uses following their removal, so the introduction of armour-clad warships heralded new developments in the docks and basins necessary to accommodate them. Propeller-driven ships were slimmer than their paddle-driven counterparts, while increasing length allowed heavier guns to be carried. These issues could not be ignored, given the perceived threat of invasion by France, and between 1867 and 1876 the Admiralty carried out extensive modifications to the dockyard, which trebled its area. Half the new ground, some 40ha, was reclaimed from the harbour, as predicted by the model, the remainder by the acquisition of land. Earlier landward growth by the dockyard had impinged upon Portsea, but the principal thrust of this extension work, which took the dockyard very nearly to its maximum extent, was the conversion of land beyond Portsea in the parish of Landport. One-quarter of the new area derived from the former fortifications, the residue from what was agricultural land between the built-up edge of Landport and Portsmouth Harbour. In other words, the scale of this extension was far greater than that mooted in stage 3 of the model. There was admittedly little impact upon existing settlement, but unquestionably in the absence of the extension, developers would subsequently have pushed the housing margin of Landport to the shoreline. In addition the public wharf at Anchor Gate was subsumed within the dockyard, but in fairness the Admiralty donated to the Corporation land which in 1871 became Flathouse Wharf (Gates, 1928, p. 100), a facility still operated by the City, its location nevertheless externally determined. The sophistication of the new weaponry had an impact outside the dockyard, for not only did gunnery training become a lengthy process, but it also involved many more personnel. The Admiralty therefore economically used the spoil from the new docks and basins to create Whale Island out of the mud flats of the harbour as a gunnery school, the work being completed in 1895. Horsea Island to the north emerged between 1886 and 1888 by the amalgamation of two existing islands for use as a torpedo testing range. While these islands, like the ground reclaimed for the dockyard, added to the area of Portsmouth, and to that in service control, they can hardly be regarded as falling within the notion of land use competition since they were created by the Admiralty for Admiralty use, and as such add a complexity to urban land use models.

Developments in military weapon training were responsible for the establishment of extensive rifle ranges at Tipner and at Eastney beyond the Royal Marine barracks. Their location on the then urban periphery reflected the siting of civic amenities, equally heavy consumers of land, such as isolation hospitals and cemeteries, although in this case the land was already in War Department hands. New weaponry also gave rise to the construction at Hilsea on existing Crown property of a major ordnance depot, with its own railway system linked to the main line network. With the completion of Whale and Horsea Islands, military and naval land use in Portsmouth reached its apogee, some 767ha (or 30 per cent of the borough's surface) being so utilised in 1910. Fortifications constituted by far the largest component of the total, as is apparent from Table 3.4, despite the removal of the works at Portsmouth and Portsea; this was largely due to the generous expanse of land purchased to protect the rear of Hilsea Lines, but which was retained even though in military terms it was superfluous. No provision is made in the model for the importance of these fortifications. The spatial distribution of land uses shown in Table 3.4 is mapped in Figure 3.4. Despite the continued strength of service personnel until mid twentieth century (see Table 3.2), there were no further major incursions into civil territory. On the contrary, the subsequent trend was in the opposite direction.

Table 3.4: Military and naval land uses in Portsmouth, 1910 and 1986

	1910		1986	
	ha	%	ha	%
Fortifications	346.8	45	–	–
Barracks, depots	175.2	23	101.4	24.5
Dockyard	114.5	15	122.1	29.5
Experimental stations	63.0	8	84.0	20.0
Rifle ranges	46.4	6	16.5	4.0
Recreation grounds	16.0	2	39.6	9.5
Married quarters	5.5	1	51.9	12.5
Totals	767.4	100	414.5	100

Source: Ordnance Survey 1:10560, 1910.

FROM MILITARY TO CIVIL LAND USE

The process of the release of Crown land effectively began in the 1870s, with the creation of a civic centre, as we have seen. Many of the subsequent exchanges also involved the Corporation, certainly in Southsea where the shape of resort functions were more a result of War Department and municipal interaction than of private initiative. On the sea front a small plot of land near Lumps Fort was leased to the Corporation in 1875 for recreation purposes, and in 1884 the entire expanse of Southsea Common followed, albeit with a moratorium on building construction. Since the Common had previously been levelled by convict labour this was an important acquisition for a town eager to capitalise on its tourist assets. Ownership of the Common did not pass to the Corporation until 1923; that the conveyance contained a clause forbidding permanent buildings (Riley, 1972, p. 3) ensured the preservation of an outstandingly attractive swathe of greenery, even though this might not have been in the forefront of the solicitors' minds at the time. Also in 1923 the borough purchased the land between Lumps Fort and Eastney Barracks, again putting it to recreational use, while Lumps Fort, bought in 1933, became a tranquil rose garden. With the possession in 1933 of part of Long Curtain, a section of the remaining fortifications, and of a further part of Pembroke Gardens for use as a bowling green, the Corporation controlled a strip of land some two miles in length, between Old Portsmouth and Eastney Barracks, unbroken save for the brief intervention of an Owen terrace opposite South Parade Pier. It is sufficient to point to Owen's development at the

Figure 3.4: Military land use in Portsmouth, 1910

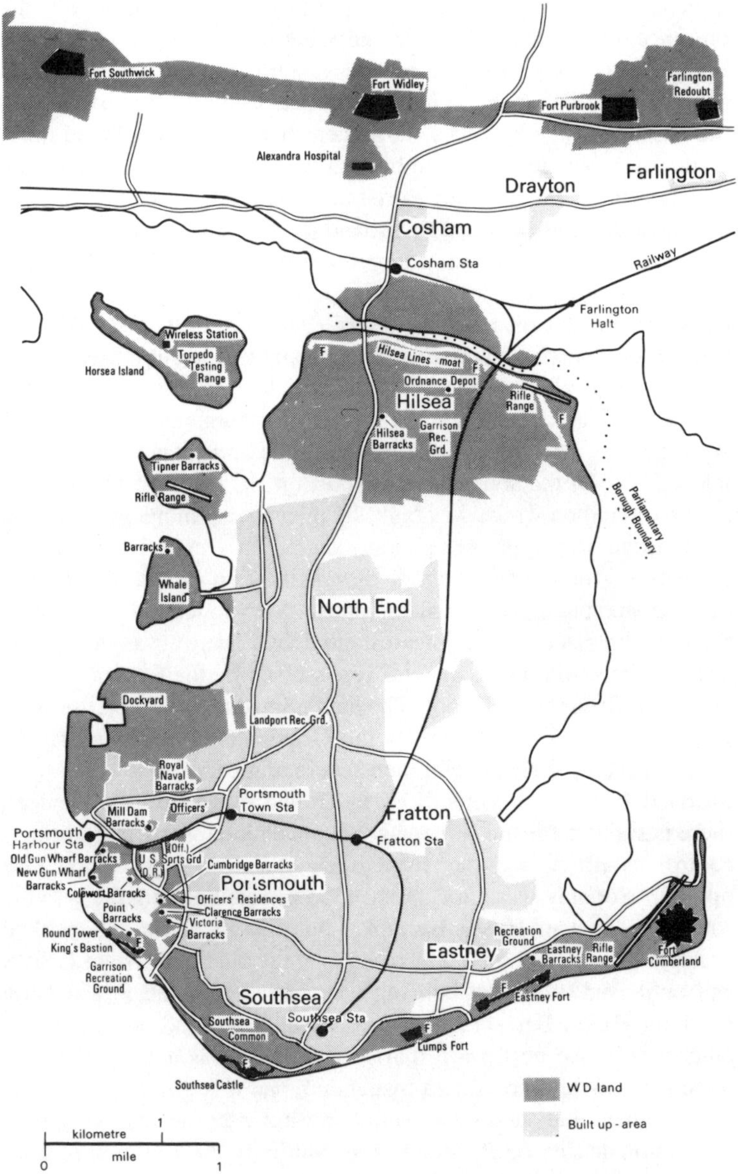

one point not formerly owned by the Crown to demonstrate what would have happened to Southsea's sea front in the absence of government control. In part offsetting this advantage, however, the presence of Eastney Barracks adjacent to the beach may have inhibited the development of the eastern end of the sea front (Ashworth, 1979, p. 80). It is not unreasonable to suppose that in the absence of the barracks, large detached houses similar to those further west would have been built in the inter-war period. The sale of Cambridge Barracks to Portsmouth Grammar School in 1926 extended the tradition of Crown land passing into institutional use.

In the inter-war period, competition for land at Hilsea began to reach the stage when there were financial advantages accruing to the Crown from the disposal of assets. Between 1929 and 1930 the Corporation purchased the East Bastion and Curtain at Hilsea Lines, together with all the land to the south, for the construction of a second road link to the mainland and of a municipal airport. The West Bastion was bought at the same time and its moat converted into a lido. To the south of West Bastion, in 1926 the city bought a strip of land on which was built the then largest municipal housing estate in an archetypal peripheral location on a main tram route, a recreation ground and a school. It was the first instance of former defence land being put to residential use. Very much in keeping with the prevailing social ethic, a substantial area nearby was designated as allotments, although part was repossessed by the Crown in 1940 as a naval firefighting school. The land immediately behind the West Bastion was sold off to Portsmouth Grammar School as a playing field. Arguably these developments were of the kind that would have obtained had the land not been in Crown ownership, and indeed there is support for the somewhat unconventional view that military control at Hilsea was far from being the dead hand of popular opinion. Not only was land conveyed to private building firms to the south and west of Hilsea Barracks, but also there was no marked break in the date of house construction at the old boundary of Crown and civil land, although housing was forced to come to a halt on reaching Hilsea Barracks and the recreation ground to its east. In other words, the northward march of the city was not substantially impeded by War Department ownership, and it is difficult to sustain the argument that such ownership contributed to the relatively high population density on Portsea Island. Similarly the sale of almost all War Department land on the mainland immediately to the north of Portscreek to private developers in the early 1930s, and to the Corporation in 1944, conflicts with received wisdom on the restrictive role of Whitehall.

The events of 1939–45 followed by the Cold War ensured that military and naval strength was maintained at a high level, and no further modifications to Crown landholding were effected. However, the decision to withdraw the garrison in 1960, reflected in the data on forces personnel enumerated for 1961 and after shown in Table 3.2, ushered in a period of change at least as important as that witnessed three decades earlier. Whereas at the latter time substantial open spaces were transferred, now it was the military, but not naval, barracks themselves together with the remaining fortifications that were redundant. Further, the age of the barracks implied that many were within the old towns of Portsmouth and Portsea, their demise allowing a welcome diversity of land use. The transfer of Point Barracks and the fifteenth century Round Tower to the city in 1960, and the following year Square Tower, of similar antiquity, and Southsea Castle, in addition to the remainder of Long Curtain in 1962, provided a marvellous opportunity to open up these historic military artefacts as tourist attractions, a strategy which has been tastefully achieved. In the light of both the income generated and the aesthetic contribution to the environment, gratitude rather than complaint now seems a more appropriate sentiment in respect of former military presence. Of the sizeable Clarence Barracks, almost all of which was bought by the City in 1967, the splendidly baroque northern barrack block has been retained as the City Museum and Art Gallery, while smaller adjacent premises house the City Records Office; but by far the largest area has been devoted to middle class housing, known as Pembroke Park, and the Centre (now Crest) Hotel. These land use changes, together with the construction of further expensive housing elsewhere within the old town, have been responsible for the emergence of a distinctive social area now attractive to those very social groups who had begun to leave in the post-Napoleonic period. The erection of a small number of houses in Pembroke Park as naval officers' married quarters meshes with the ambience of the locality, and can hardly be a serious contribution to land use competition. That Colewort Barracks was sold to the CEGB as a coal store for their adjacent power station appeared to conflict with the changes on the Clarence Barracks site, but with the end of electricity generation, the land has been sold for middle class housing, matching those developments to the east. The plot containing Government House was transferred to Hampshire County Council in 1973 as part of the expansion programme for Portsmouth Polytechnic. On the site of Government House now stands the Polytechnic Library, but the other residences and surrounding trees remain to enhance an environment heavily influenced by its former ownership.

Following its close naval associations, Portsea has retained most of its barrack accommodation, the exception being the army's Milldam Barracks which passed into the hands of the Polytechnic in 1972. Indeed, in the late 1970s the dockyard actually expanded southwards along the eastern side of Unicorn Road on residential land that had been badly damaged during the Second World War and never redeveloped. Portsea was, and is, a working-class town. Redevelopment has taken the form of municipal housing, and it is tempting to speculate on the nature of the housing that might have been built had the RN Barracks, now HMS Nelson, been declared surplus to requirements. Although no longer in military occupation, Eastney Barracks still stands, in the absence of an alternative use, although the officers' mess is used as the Royal Marines Museum. Despite the withdrawal of the garrison, not all military land is available for sale as a consequence of the demand for married quarters by the services. This has occurred at Eastney where an extensive area of other ranks' married quarters was laid out for the Navy at the eastern end of the recreation grounds in the 1960s, arguably a site that might have been attractive to private and municipal housing schemes alike. This pressure manifested itself in the early 1980s and middle-class dwellings were constructed on three small plots. In the same area, the Corporation purchased the rifle range and contiguous land in segments between 1969 and 1975, and there are plans to develop part of it as a caravan park, which is indicative of the low level of competition for land on the peninsula. Beyond is Fort Cumberland, regarded as the best preserved example of an eighteenth century fort in Europe, now in the hands of English Heritage, whose intention it is to open it up to the public. The peripherality that has caused its survival may militate against its becoming such a source of popular attraction as the fortifications at Portsmouth and Southsea. Present day military land and remaining fortifications are mapped in Figure 3.5.

Crown land at Hilsea, which had been reduced by four-fifths in the inter-war period, contracted still further after 1960. The southern portion of the ordnance depot passed into Council ownership in 1962, and was designated as an industrial estate, one of several established contemporaneously by the City to take advantage of low local wage costs, the availability of space to offer firms, and a location in the south east of England (Riley and Smith, 1981). It

Figure 3.5: Military land use in Portsmouth, 1986

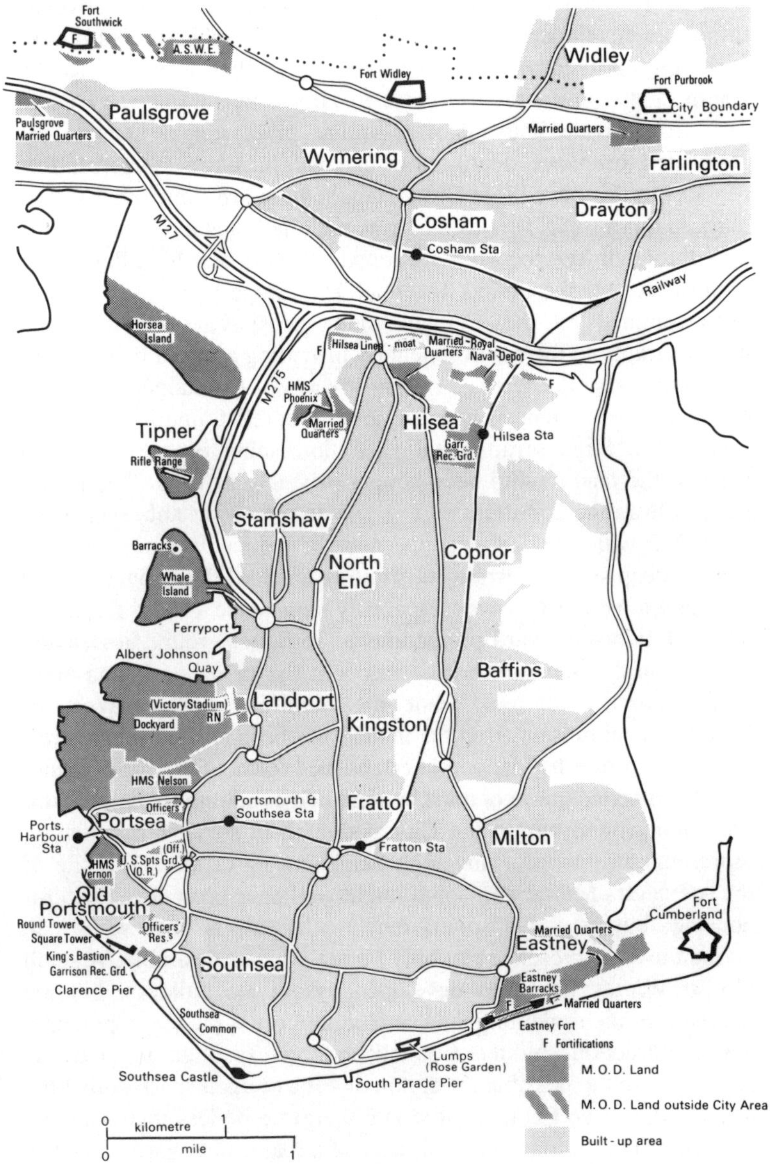

was an inspired move, for a decade later the M27 was constructed within a few hundred metres of the site. Hilsea Barracks themselves were sold to the City in 1970, two-thirds of the area being conveyed to private developers between 1971 and 1973, middle-class houses springing up to form Gatcombe Park. Somewhat belatedly, Rugby Camp, a wartime structure close to Hilsea Barracks, was sold in 1982 for private housing in a similar price range. Outside the attenuated ordnance depot, now a naval furniture store, all that remains of this once large Crown landholding are some other ranks' married quarters, a Territorial Army drill hall, and a recreation area now the Civil Service Sports Ground, on part of which have been built offices for the Inland Revenue. The ramparts themselves have been retained by the Council, quite sensibly, since they add immeasurably to the environment by providing a raised belt of trees in an otherwise flat terrain, fronted by a well maintained moat. To the south west, Tipner Barracks now lie derelict among the serendipity of a large scrap metal yard flourishing on surplus naval vessels, the land having been bought privately in 1964. The proximate rifle range continues in use, albeit somewhat abbreviated by the M275 which passes over the neck of the small peninsula.

The steep sloping terrain constituting much of the Crown land on Portsdown Hill was never especially conducive to development, although two southward projections on to flatter ground at Drayton and Paulsgrove have been used respectively for officers' and other ranks' married quarters, while the Admiralty Surface Weapons Establishment (absent from the model) has been located on the crest of the hill. Since they lie within established tracts of private housing, both the married quarters must be regarded as adding to the pressure on building land within the City, although in social terms neither represents an unconformity with neighbouring estates. The site of the Alexandra Military Hospital might well have been developed for housing, but as the hospital, much enlarged, is now wholly in civilian use, its presence can only be regarded as desirable. A small plot at Widley has been developed by private builders, but the purchase of the remaining land, including Fort Widley as a potential tourist attraction, by the Council, has not resulted in land use change, with the possible exception of 47ha of open space converted to a municipal golf course. It would therefore be less than accurate to suggest that military control has had a major untoward influence in the area.

The military retreat charted above has resulted in a very substantial amount of territory falling into the hands of other, principally municipal, users, leaving a small and tenuous outpost at Hilsea to carry the flag. The foothold at Eastney Barracks seems unlikely to hold out for very much longer. Portsmouth now has assumed the role it has always possessed in the public eye, that of a naval base, not a garrison town. At the same time Crown landholding has been reduced to 415ha, or 10.5 per cent of the City's surface. As Table 3.4 indicates, the dockyard is now the largest single element of external control, a situation likely to be further confirmed following recent decisions to close the gunnery school on Whale Island (HMS Excellent), and the gunwharf (HMS Vernon). Moreover, Horsea Island has effectively been relegated to the role of a dyke for the North Harbour reclamation project. It is not therefore unreasonable to expect that government land might be reduced to 288ha, or 7.3 per cent of Portsmouth's surface area in the near future. One result will be that the peripherally located married quarters, a relatively new direction in naval life, will assume a position of greater importance than that harsher and more evident landscape feature, the barracks.

It will be recalled that Admiralty control of shipping movements and government sovereignty over the foreshore together combined to thwart municipal efforts to establish a port complex in the mid nineteenth century. These sanctions remained in force and their constraining influence on land use was evident in the Ministry of Defence objection to the 'shore-line' road proposed in 1953 for Portsmouth Harbour (Horton, 1979, p. 14), and Townsend-Thoresen's decision to operate their car ferry from Southampton rather than Portsmouth in 1967 was at least in part the result of Admiralty misgivings. However, in the wake of the run down of the Navy a more relaxed attitude has come to prevail. The first tangible evidence was the approval of the Council's scheme to construct the Albert Johnson Quay to the north of the small Flathouse Quay in 1968. The 'shore-line' road was resuscitated, receiving Ministry support in 1968, and the notion eventually manifested itself as the M275. The construction of the M27 itself was assisted by the reclamation of a 182ha polder from the Harbour, utilising Horsea Island, no longer a torpedo testing base, as one of the dykes (Birch, 1973); Ministry agreement to the scheme was thus partly responsible for the establishment by IBM of their UK administrative headquarters within the polder. Yet these developments pale into insignificance against the implications for harbour shipping movements of a roll-on/roll-off ferry terminal (opened in 1976), which by 1979 was handling one million passengers a year and had replaced Southampton as the south coast's second ranking passenger port after Dover. Moreover, the site had important cost advantages to operators springing from the naval responsibility for dredging and for the provision of a free harbour-control service (Riley and Smith, 1981, p. 147). Positively to influence tidewater land use was one thing, but to assist it financially was verging on the revolutionary; in the harsh winds blowing presently from the Treasury, the arrangement is under scrutiny.

CONCLUSION

The external environment is now recognised as an important determinant of economic and urban geography (Dicken and Lloyd, 1981; Massey, 1984; Massey and Meegan, 1979). The example described is an extension to this thrust in the sense that it illustrates the manner in which international political events, strategic considerations and the evolution of weapon technology are capable of transcending those political and socioeconomic parameters which normally control human activities. It has been demonstrated how in Portsmouth military and naval priorities were of first importance, and how civilian land uses had perforce to mesh into a predetermined spatial pattern, very much in the fashion of an urban population coming to terms with pockets of uninhabitable terrain. Present-day land uses on the fringes of the old towns of Portsmouth and Portsea are very largely determined by past government decisions, as is the entire southern edge of Portsea Island, and indirectly, the core of the middle-class suburb of Southsea. Because for a long time they were distant from the built-up edge of the town, military operations at Hilsea, Tipner, Portsdown Hill, and to some extent at Eastney, have had a more muted impact, allowing a restatement that the principal weight of government policy has been experienced in those areas built-up in the nineteenth century. It follows therefore that, if anywhere, it is in the central areas where military control of land had its greatest influence on the civilian population by limiting the area of land available. Yet the urban population reacted to the problem by spreading into areas outside the old towns, such as Landport and Southsea, making it difficult to agree with those who argue that substantial military land ownership itself caused high population density. Thus the pleasant open spaces and congenial ambience of much of Portsmouth and parts of Portsea and Southsea have not necessarily been achieved through past hardship. This should not obscure the undoubted parlous influence of Admiralty dictates upon efforts to establish Portsmouth as a commercial port, at least until coexistence became the watchword in the 1960s.

The empirical evidence advanced is generally supportive of the proposals set out in the model of the development of a fortified garrison and dockyard town. There are, inevitably, a number of distortions, even allowing for Portsmouth's island site. Firstly, and most obviously, the separation of the garrison from the dockyard led to the establishment of two settlements rather than the monostructure proposed. Secondly, the model inaccurately gauges the scale of both military and naval activities, making no provision for the construction of barracks and depots outside the inner fortifications, for the extent of the Hilsea fortifications, for the outer ring of Palmerstonian forts on Portsdown Hill, or for the extent of the landward expansion by the dockyard. Thirdly, the dismantling of the inner fortifications did not lead to a major change of ownership since much of the surface was retained for military use. Fourthly, very little superfluous Crown land has come on to the market, rather the greater part has been purchased by the City Council, suggesting that lines of communication, so powerful that third parties were largely excluded, were set up between Whitehall and the City at least as early as the 1870s. Certainly from 1967 onwards regular meetings were held between the Council and representatives of the armed forces to expedite the transfer of land to the City (Ashworth *et al.*, 1979, p. 84). Yet in spite of substantial purchases by the Council, the majority of housing that has been put up on former military property has been by private interests. Fifthly, the model is silent on the impact on land use of the presence of large numbers of servicemen. Unable to influence the property market by virtue of life in barracks, they contrived to leave their mark on both manufacturing and retailing through a notable consumption of alcohol. It was no accident that there were two breweries in the old town of Portsmouth with a collective area equal to that of Clarence Barracks, and that there were more than 100 breweries in the borough in the 1860s, when there was one drinking place for every 68 persons living in Old Portsmouth (Riley and Eley, 1983, p. 7). Sixthly, the whole question of the Admiralty's policy of encouraging the dockyard to aim for self-sufficiency, which had an important negative effect on local manufacturing, is not addressed. The kind of production that might have been expected close to a commercial shipbuilding yard failed to materialise, as did the middle class deriving from the ensuing profit (Riley, 1976). The consequence was that Portsmouth entered the twentieth century with a very narrow civilian manufacturing base, led by the clothing industry staffed largely by sailors' and soldiers' wives working in factories located in what was the suburban housing area in the 1880s (Riley, 1985a). That the Crown paid no rates on its extensive landholding until 1860 (Gates, 1928, p. 90), causing the level of payment to be relatively high, must have adversely affected purchasing power, and therefore retail provision. Finally, while recognising that military land may revert to civilian use, the model makes no allowance for the recent dramatic reappraisal by the Navy of what constitutes tidewater land use prejudicial to its operations, eloquently demonstrating once more the propensity of central government to influence land use patterns in towns harnessed to the defence of the realm. The shortcomings of the model emphasise the less predictable spatial effects of national policy pursued in this cause.

ACKNOWLEDGEMENT

The author is grateful for the considerable assistance rendered by Mr C.R. Tozer of the Portsmouth City Council Estates Department in the compilation of data for this chapter.

REFERENCES

Ashworth, G.J. (1979) 'Leisure', in R. Windle (ed.), *Records of the Corporation 1966–74*, Portsmouth City Council, 70–81.

Ashworth, G.J. *et al.* (1979) 'Planning, the Economy and the Environment', in R. Windle (ed.), *Records of the Corporation 1966–74*, Portsmouth City Council, 82–102.

Bateman, M. (1974) *Atlas of Portsmouth*, Portsmouth Polytechnic.

Birch, B.P. (1973) 'Winning Land from the Sea at Portsmouth', *Geography*, 58, 152–4.

Corney, A. (1983) 'The Portsmouth Fortress', *Journal of the Royal Society of Arts*, CXXXI, 578–86.

Course, E.A. (1969) *Portsmouth Railways*, Portsmouth Paper no. 6, Portsmouth City Council.

Dicken, Peter and Lloyd, Peter E. (1981) *Modern Western Society*, Harper & Row.

Form, W.H. (1954) 'The Place of Social Structure in the Determination of Land Use: Some Implications for a Theory of Urban Ecology', *Social Forces*, 32, 317–23.

Gates, William G. (1928) *Records of the Corporation 1835–1927*, Charpentier, Portsmouth.

Hollingsworth (1825) *The Portsmouth Guide*, Portsmouth.
Horton, S. (1979) 'Politics and Administration', in R. Windle (ed.), *Records of the Corporation 1966–74*, Portsmouth City Council, 1–19.
Howell, A.N.Y. (1913) *Notes of the Topography of Portsmouth*, Barrell, Portsmouth.
Kellett, J.R. (1979) *Railways and Victorian Cities*, Routledge & Kegal Paul.
London, Brighton and South Coast Railway (1853) *Official Illustrated Guide*.
Massey, Doreen (1984) *Spatial Divisions of Labour*, Macmillan.
Massey, D.B. and Meegan, R.A. (1979) 'The Geography of Industrial Reorganisation: the Spatial Effects of the Restructuring of the Electrical Engineering Sector under the Industrial Reorganisation Corporation', *Progress in Planning*, 10, Part 3.
Masters, Betty R. (1964) *Portsmouth: A Brief Outline of its Development*, Portsmouth City Council.
Pigot & Co. (1830) *National Commercial Directory*.
Riley, R.C. (1972) *The Growth of Southsea as a Naval Satellite and Victorian Resort*, Portsmouth Paper no. 16, Portsmouth City Council.
Riley, R.C. (1976) *The Industries of Portsmouth in the Nineteenth Century*, Portsmouth Paper no. 25, Portsmouth City Council.
Riley, R.C. (1980) *The Houses and Inhabitants of Thomas Ellis Owen's Southsea*, Portsmouth Paper no. 32, Portsmouth City Council.
Riley, R.C. (1985a) 'The Influence of the Clothing Industry upon a Regional Economy: The Portsmouth Case', *Acta Universitatis Lodziensis Folia Geographica*, 6, 145–61.
Riley, R.C. (1985b) *The Evolution of the Docks and Industrial Buildings in Portsmouth Royal Dockyard 1698–1914*, Portsmouth Paper no. 44, Portsmouth City Council.
Riley, R.C. and Eley, Philip (1983) *Public Houses and Beerhouses in Nineteenth Century Portsmouth*, Portsmouth Paper no. 38, Portsmouth City Council.
Riley, R.C. and Smith, J.-L. (1981) 'Industrialisation in Naval Ports: the Portsmouth Case', in B.S. Hoyle and D.A. Pinder (eds), *Cityport Industrialisation and Regional Development: Spatial Analysis and Planning Strategies*, Pergamon, Oxford, 133–50.
Saunders, A.D. (1967) 'Hampshire Coastal Defence since the Introduction of Artillery', *The Archaeological Journal*, 123, 136–71.
Sjoberg, G. (1965) *The Preindustrial City Past and Present*, Macmillan.
Temple-Patterson, A. (1967) *'Palmerston's Folly' The Portsdown and Spithead Forts*, Portsmouth Paper no. 3, Portsmouth City Council.
Watts, H.D. (1981) *The Branch Plant Economy: A Study of External Control*, Longman.

4

The Defence Town in Crisis: The Paradox of the Tourism Strategy

John Bradbeer and Graham Moon

INTRODUCTION

For many centuries the activity of defence has been a potent factor in the creation of the urban form. As the preceding two chapters have shown, both in their physical nature, and in their design, towns and cities have been strongly affected by the demands of defence, and the fixed engineering feats and building works which have traditionally constituted defensive systems have acted both to constrain and direct the urban form. Inevitably in doing this, the defence systems have themselves come to occupy a significant and overt position in the outward manifestation of the urban form of many cities. This manifestation is historically persistent, with the contemporary city containing relict reflections of the defensive approaches of past eras.

Examples of this persistence abound, particularly in European cities where a lengthy tradition of urbanism has been much influenced by the defensive function (Curl, 1969; Burtenshaw *et al.*, 1981). A well-known example is the medieval fortress town of Carcassonne, where the outward manifestation of a form of urbanism based on the medieval conception of defensive needs is clearly evident. Other important examples from more recent periods include the fortification works constructed by Vauban (Rosenau, 1959), and the influence on the Parisian townscape exerted by the 'Grands Boulevards' of Baron Haussmann. The retention of these relict formations in the midst of a dynamic and contemporary urbanism emphasises the importance which the defensive role has played in urban history.

The presence of these monuments should not, however, be taken to imply that the urban arena is static in its function or appearance.

The exigencies of economic change within a particular mode of production, and the varying roles which local agencies play in the mediation of those exigencies, mean that the outward form and internal organisation of the city is constantly changing. The defence town is not isolated from these forces. Among the many changes which may occur are alterations in the conceptualisation of the role of defence, and, by extension, the need for the paraphernalia of defence-oriented urbanism. Thus, the ravelins, walls and moats constituting fixed defensive systems may become outmoded. In addition, the industrial plant and residential infrastructure, for example the barracks and supply yards which sustain a particular strategic and economic construction of defence, may also become redundant. In both cases however a relict formation is left within the urban system, providing a powerful illustration of the impact of the changing nature of defence on the city.

In this chapter attention is focused on this change and the consequences which it poses in terms of the need to restructure the local economy. Drawing on recent work on industrial change under late capitalism, a perspective is developed which seeks to incorporate a socioeconomic analysis of the changing defence economy. A trend from the visible to the invisible both in terms of defensive plant and defensive industry is noted and its impact on the traditional defence-oriented town examined. Attention then shifts to the need to restructure and the difficulties posed by this eventuality. The problem is seen as being, at root, one involving the need to re-use redundant space, redundant manpower and redundant plant. There have been many local and national state responses to this problem. Here just one will be considered: the superficially attractive solution of developing the tourism potential of defence heritage. A critique of this strategy will be developed, drawing attention to its role in perpetuating economic dependency and reconstructing a glorified and partial view of urban history. The chapter concludes by illustrating some of these contentions through a case study of the partial restructuring of Portsmouth's local economy from a defence to a tourism basis.

THE CHANGING DEFENCE ECONOMY

It is clearly evident that, even within the last twenty-five years, defensive needs and indeed the nature of defence have changed. In fact there is evidence that superpower politics and the spectre of nuclear war mean that defence is, in reality, redundant. As Openshaw and Steadman argue: 'For the UK, nuclear war means national suicide' (Openshaw and Steadman, 1985, p. 123).

In drawing back from this unfortunately realistic scenario, it is possible to discern an underlying theme which determines changing defence needs and their manifestation in urban localities. This theme involves close analysis of the social relations of production (Wright, 1976; Massey, 1984), and the way in which these have structured the development of the defence town. A suitable, though somewhat superficial starting point for the analysis is the recognition that, in broad terms, the technology involved in the attack function to which defence responds has evolved to the extent that defence is no longer against a visible threat. Indeed attacks can now be delivered from hundreds, even thousands of kilometres away from a target.

In the past then, an enemy would have been expected to be visible or at least nearby. Defence against this threat involved the need to find, fortify and then hold a commanding position. This task required a clear geographic vision and was often best accomplished through the development of a particular location which might confer strategic dominance — for example a harbour entrance or an elevated area dominating surrounding lowland. An equally clear form of urbanism developed in such situations and is witnessed by a myriad of medieval towns with defensive systems emphasising the natural advantage of site. These sites with their associated developments, in addition to making sound strategic sense, also contained a clear reflection of past social relations. Under the feudal mode of production the visual manifestation of domination was an important aspect of social control. The feudal landlord could be seen in his expected position of domination occupying a location which was, often literally as well as figuratively, elevated.

This theme of the visual signature of power within defence urbanism continued under mercantile and imperialist capitalism. Through this period some towns ceased to be worth defending, others ceased to be defensible. These settlements were the victim of twin forces: economic change rendering them functionally obsolete or so large as to be unprotectable, and economically fuelled technological change making existing defences inadequate. As a consequence some towns lost their visible defences, whilst, in other cases, defences became fossilised. For some towns, however, a geostrategic significance was maintained. Such settlements tended to assume a more global importance, representing the bases from which the military might of empire could be despatched in the quest for the continued profit accumulation. It is these towns which even today might be thought of as 'defence towns'.

It is ironic that the imperialistic aspects of capitalism provided the means by which the visual defence economy reached perhaps its most developed form, as it was also the changing requirements of the capitalist economy which caused the decline of that form. There were two forces which led to this situation: the inability of capitalism to sustain the all-important imperialist system, and the immensely successful quest for ever greater profit by the defence industry. While the former issue was undoubtedly important, with the loss of empire being paralleled by a lesser need for overtly demonstrable military might, it was the latter factor which was of crucial importance.

This goal of profit accumulation required, as will be argued below, changes in the organisation of production within the defence industry. At this juncture, however, it is sufficient to note that the outcome of these changes was the perfection of weapon systems which rendered any reliance on visible defence systems redundant. The consequence for the geography of defence was that it ceased to take a spatially concentrated, highly visible form, but became dispersed and often subterranean; the individual defence town, with its specialised urbanism, became a relict feature in the military–economic context.

As suggested, in addition to an analysis of the political-economic context within which the physical entity of the defence system can be sited, an examination of the changing organisation of production must also be set out. Thus, account must be taken of alterations in the nature of work and social relations of production for those who provide the military equipment necessary for defence. Naturally the changes which have been evident in this context cannot be divorced from the points made above. Indeed, in terms of the geography of the contemporary defence industry, the two are inextricably connected. This inter-connectivity has become particularly marked because of the relative success experienced by the defence industry as a crucial component of the capitalist system.

The recent geography of defence industry, like defence itself, has been marked by a tendency towards de-concentration, although at first glance this is not always evident. At one time some defence industries had clearly defined and relatively well-known locations, such as the Royal dockyards and the Royal ordnance factory. This state-owned defence industry is, however, no longer of major importance within the sector, and, indeed, had only been so to any extent during the imperialist phase of capitalism. The expansion of private sector defence industry has meant that two locational tendencies within the industry as a whole have emerged. In the case of state-owned defence industries there have been closedowns and rationalisations, with Chatham and, less recently, Pembroke losing Royal dockyard status, and job losses in the Royal ordnance factories scheduled for 1986. This situation, of course, is one of fewer plants and concentration; it is however only part of the picture. The current status of the private sector within British defence industry means that new locations have emerged away from those traditionally characteristic of defence industry.

It is possible that the dispersal of operations which has taken place is a response to strategic necessity: the capability required to take out, on a first strike, a dispersed set of locations is obviously far greater than that required for a limited set of targets. In reality, however, a more plausible explanation for the dispersal of the defence industry is the requirements of free-market capitalism. The perceived necessity for competition within the capitalist system, fostered extensively in the USA and more recently in Britain, has meant that the position which was enjoyed by the state within the defence industry has been seen as grossly inefficient. That position has been challenged and opened up to competition through the encouragement and facilitation of private sector activity. Private firms have bid successfully for defence industry contracts, and the new geography of the defence industry is the geography of the location of successful bidders (Breheny and McQuaid, 1985).

Given the contract potential of proximity and the powerful inertia exerted by the long established state-owned defence industries, it is not surprising that one manifestation of the geography of the new defence industries is an only slightly de-concentrated version of the past, with clusters of defence contractors located within a few kilometres of the old sites. A second locational preference represents a more radical shift and is a reflection of the changing technological construction of defence. Defence is no longer a heavy industry; it is now the cutting edge of nuclear physics, biotechnology, space science, laser technology, and micro-electronics. The shift to high technology means that the new geography of defence is that of other high technology firms. As Keeble (1976) has shown, this is mainly in the Thames Valley, South Hampshire and Silicon Glen.

The inevitable consequence of this change in industrial character is that the relations of production within the industry are also changing (Braverman, 1974). In the past the defence industry, like many other industries, was noted for being pre-eminently a place of employment for skilled artisans. These people, respected for their skills and employed in highly specific jobs, were involved in the industrial manufacture and repair of the equipment of war. They were employed in industrial conditions close to the object of their labour, in such jobs as plate-making, keel-laying and rope manufacture. Now such jobs have been automated, abandoned or contracted-out to private sector firms, and the skilled artisans are largely unemployed or de-skilled. What has occurred is a fragmentation of the defence industry into two classes: a low grade clerk sector maintaining stores records using automated means, and a high grade white collar developmental sector concerned with the enhancement of the technology of defence/attack. The former is usually still to be found in the defence town, the latter, as has been argued above, can be and usually is elsewhere. The all-important skilled artisan is no longer needed in anything like the numbers once employed.

The growth of this private sector defence industry, together with the changing requirements of the military, has facilitated the creation of large tracts of redundant space in the traditional defence towns. Notwithstanding the debatably justifiable retention of some land to maintain military secrecy, this land represents an important but often, albeit temporarily, unobtainable resource for the people of the defence towns; it also acts as a memorial to the loss of a town's key function.

To summarise this section, the physical and morphological context of defence has changed; it is now decentralised and dispersed, whereas once it was centralised in symbolic locations redolent of feudal or imperial power. The nature of the defence industries has also changed. It is no longer necessary to be near the army or navy; it is more functional to be near to the microelectronics industry. This process of industrial change has had two clear impacts. First, workforce needs have changed so there now exists a redundant yet highly specialised ex-defence labour force. Second, industrial buildings in many of the traditional locations have become redundant. These buildings, together with the physical paraphernalia of defence (barracks, old ships), represent a concentration of historic but redundant defence heritage in precise geographical locations.

RESTRUCTURING THE DEFENCE TOWN ECONOMY

There is a clear theoretical indication that there is a need for restructuring in the local economies of the defence towns. This is particularly the case for those towns which dominated Britain's defence during the imperial heyday. With some exceptions these towns today possess a much reduced defence function.

The withdrawal of defence-based industry from a town can leave an economy without the prop which has been central to that economy for a considerable period. One of the characteristics of defence industry in the past has been that it has been loath to permit the development of substantial competing industries in its vicinity. It might be argued that it has preferred instead to maintain a monopoly position in the labour market with the result that the local economies of the defence towns are often extremely dependent. The consequences of 'pulling out the plug' can thus be fairly extreme.

The local state, as the bearer of the brunt of any reaction to the loss or reduction of the defence function, is likely to be at the forefront of any moves towards restructuring. Given the limitations on local fund raising and spending, appeals to central government for regional or localised aid are tactics which are much in use. Examples in recent years include the attraction of ferry companies to disused naval dockyards at Sheerness and Pembroke Dock, and the declaration of the only non-metropolitan 'Enterprise Zone' in southern England at Chatham. The prime aim of these and other attempts at restructuring has been to try to provide at least some possibility of re-employment for those whose jobs have been lost when defence interests pulled out. The employment issue is thus central in any analysis of the post-defence economy.

Attempts to attract new industry, however, bring with them problems. First, the trends within industry as a whole are precisely the trends which have led to the changes in the defence economy. Few industries are any longer the mass employers which would be needed to re-employ the numbers made redundant by the closure of a defence plant. In addition, new industry has little use for the skills developed in the traditional defence economy. These skills are those of the craftsman rather than the twentieth-century scientist. Second, the industry which is able to respond freely to the welcoming overtures of the desperate burghers of the abandoned defence town, is typically the branch plant of the high technology multinational company. As noted in the previous section, this is precisely the sector of industry (in both its assembly and research and development forms) to which defence has tended to move; it is highly unlikely that the high technology concern would itself be willing to reverse this process. This sort of industrial concern is seldom overly keen to site a new plant on a decayed, heavily developed site, redolent of outmoded industry. Green field locations are preferred on the urban fringe or in 'New Towns'.

Undeniably the defence town is, in one way, functionally a suitable site for high technology industry. It usually possesses a highly compliant and weakly unionised workforce. However, those few who possess the necessary scientific skills demanded by high technology industry are usually willing to move to a job, and remain within the same defence industry — albeit away from the defence town. Those who remain have unsaleable skills or no skills. This factor, together with the perceived poverty of the environment, means that new technology industry cannot generally be regarded as providing a worthwhile future for the ex-defence town. Even situations which superficially contradict this analysis, in fact offer confirmation. For example, IBM, arguably the most prestigious high technology firm in the world, have their UK headquarters in Portsmouth where the defence function has been much reduced since its heyday. IBM, however, is not providing employment for redundant dockyard workers, or even to any great extent people who are actually resident in Portsmouth itself. Rather, they employ new technology professionals from the suburban regions of Greater Portsmouth.

Paradoxically it is, however, the perceived poverty of the redundant defence environment that is held to offer one way out of the dilemma of the loss of *raison d'être* in the defence town. It is the redundant space, rather than the redundant people, of the defence town which provides the possibility for restructuring. That the loss of the defence function creates redundant space cannot be open to contradiction; evidence is widely available and was illustrated in the previous chapter. This situation is a recognised consequence of the more general industrial decline of contemporary Britain (Anderson, Duncan and Hudson, 1983). In the case of the defence town examples of abandoned defence works, rope-walks, warehouses, hangers, dry docks, barracks, ramparts, even whole forts can all be identified.

These relict features are undoubtedly unpleasant to look at when abandoned or divorced from their function. To adapt them to suitable modern uses is often also problematic and expensive. Some successful or semi-successful examples exist: a significant part of

Portsmouth Polytechnic is in ex-service buildings; Park Hall Camp at Oswestry provides retail units; and Fort Wallington at Fareham has been subdivided into small industrial units. These cases are infrequent. The conclusion must be that defence buildings are most effectively used for the purpose for which they were designed. When this outcome is impossible, the next best alternative is to fossilise them in an apparent reconstruction of their intended use. Taking this course involves recognising and developing the tourist potential of such features.

DEFENCE AND TOURISM

Defence as a recognisable and organised enterprise, of course, far pre-dates the development of tourism. By the time that the Grand Tour, often taken as the origin of modern tourism, became popular defence was already a long established and significant state activity. As suggested above, a specific form of defence urbanism had evolved and the functionality of defence for the economy was clear. Some nascent early links between defence and tourism can, however, be distinguished as early as the start of the nineteenth century. These links were particularly fuelled by the Napoleonic Wars and the patriotism which they engendered. The garrison and naval towns became places of resort for local elites, the presence of the fleet in Torbay contributed substantially to the growth of Torquay; and, at the end of the war, many army and navy officers retired to the newly established seaside resorts of southern England. Indeed many of them secured their futures through investing in property in the new resorts.

Through the nineteenth century technological progress and the growing inadequacy of the visual defence system meant that defence became a progressively more secret activity. Links with tourism were discouraged. Few tourists were as favoured in their travels as the composer Joseph Haydn, who wrote enthusiastically of a trip to Portsmouth which included a tour of the dockyard. A change in attitudes began to be evident by the mid nineteenth century. The zenith of imperial power was marked by a nationalism which led tourists to wish to bask in the reflected glory of great armies and navies. Social attitudes to conflict also changed as mass mobilisation and conscription meant that more people came to have a personal stake in conflicts. The introduction of the practice of burying the dead in individual rather than communal graves added war cemeteries to the list of sites to be visited.

There is, therefore, a pedigree which links defence to tourism. The exploitation of this linkage following the change in the nature of the defence economy has been problematic. Tourism has not, in reality, played much part in the re-use of defence establishments or defence industrial plant. Picklecombe Fort, a nineteenth-century fortress guarding the entrance to Plymouth Sound has been converted into luxury holiday apartments; Fort Regent on Jersey has become a sports centre, as has Calshot Flying Boat Station; while part of the former naval dockyard at Pembroke Dock has become a ferry terminal for crossings to Ireland. Much of the tourism potential of defence lies instead in the promotion of an often unique industrial archaeology and architecture. Thus, interest is fostered in the development of defensive systems, the intricacies of military architecture, and most recently and most strikingly in defence equipment. On retirement from active service, fighting vehicles, aircraft and ships are preserved as tourist attractions, others are rescued from scrapyards, crash and wreck sites through the enthusiasm of volunteer workers. Unlike buildings, defence equipment is essentially mobile, and thus can frequently have little historical association with its place of display. Operational bases, such as the Fleet Air Arm Museum at Yeovilton and the Royal Naval Submarine Museum at Gosport, are one type of location where the equipment can remain in context; another is the defence town.

TOURISM, DEFENCE, THE STATE AND CAPITAL

Defence tourism in the defence town is, at root, the presentation of a reconstruction of the defence town in its heyday. This is usually taken to be a classic example of what Cohen (1979a, 1979b) has termed 'overt tourist space'. The tourist is offered a reconstruction of a period of history; that reconstruction has been substantially sanitised and cleaned up to remove any of its unpleasant connotations, and the tourist recognises that process. In some cases, however, what is offered is 'covert tourist space' where the synthetic nature of the experience is not recognised and reality is assumed.

There are superficial justifications available for the pursuit of this strategy of defence tourism; it places history in context, it provides local employment. Yet it can be more accurately seen as a means of social control, diverting the public from more disruptive forms of behaviour (Kaplan, 1975). In a wide ranging attack on contemporary manifestations of tourism, especially the 'great men [*sic*], famous places, major events' variety, Horne (1984) develops this theme of the deliberate representation of the past. Tourism, he argues, is playing a key role in the legitimation of the status quo with the past being constantly re-examined and re-interpreted in the light of the present. Monuments (and defence monuments are a particularly clear example) play an important role in this process. Aided by the carefully guided imagination of the tourist, a dreamland, or a suitable construction of reality emerges. As Horne (1984, p. 34) argues: 'each generation turns the monuments of earlier generations to new purposes and creates new monuments out of what had previously seemed everyday objects, thus creating a new dream to match the world view of a new social order.'

Defence tourism in the 1980s can be clearly seen in the context of Horne's work. The economy is weak and social cohesion at times collapses; with the exception of the Falklands adventure, which itself clearly fits the analysis, there seems little justification in the epithet 'Great' Britain. The nineteenth-century expansion of empire, based on strong armies and powerful fleets, and victory in two world wars, offers the striking contrast of certainty, success, strength, unity of purpose and discipline. To capital and the state the promotion of these ideals is a welcome civil antidote to present problems.

Tourism is therefore far more than just a valid and attractive potential strategy for the re-use of the redundant defence towns. It legitimates a contemporary view of history, and draws attention away from current evils. The analysis can, however, be extended yet further. The promotion of defence tourism is crucially and inextricably bound up with the reproduction of the existing structure of social relations in the defence town.

The social relations of production in the defence town are, like those of the 'company town', predicated to the needs of the employer. This involves the maintenance of a culture of subservience and deference (Piepe, Prior and Box, 1969) in which a virtue is made of economic dependency. This facet is emphasised in the case of the defence town through the linkage to patriotism and the glory of the protection of the realm. A shift of emphasis in the local economy from defence to tourism, particularly to defence tourism, makes no difference to this dependency. In fact where it occurs in the same location, the nature of the dependency is very similar.

The defence function relied on patriotism for its continuation, and so defence-based tourism requires that the public retains an interest in the past successes of the patriotic feeling. Where the economy once depended on a single big employer, now it depends on a fragmented, competing group of smaller employers. Both however have the same interests: a compliant workforce and a consumer market with a worldview dominated by patriotic glories. The Falklands War has undoubtedly facilitated an increased patriotism that has benefited defence tourism, while the domination of the home tourist market by the elderly (for whom past military glory may seem more immediate) is another contributory factor. Elements of the compliant workforce, once employed on a daily basis according to the number needed, are now employed on a seasonal basis and often with fewer benefits. For the local state, inextricably bound up with the interests of capital the result is the same; the workforce is dependent and it is conservative; overt or radical change is not in its interests.

Restructuring the defence economy towards tourism is not however a clear-cut example of moving from one form of dependency to another. The dependency persists and in its nature it is somewhat similar, yet its internal relations change. Tourism provides seasonal and low paid manual work; much of its employment potential has traditionally relied on the exploitation of female labour. This contrasts considerably with the traditional structure of defence labour with its largely male workforce employed in either a skilled tradesman capacity or as unskilled manual workers. While the latter may find some situation in tourism, the former do not. The situation which develops is therefore one where those who fall through the net which tourism was expected to provide are precisely those who were once crucial to the defence system. The restructuring of the defence town towards tourism thus not only involves the legitimation and reproduction of the status quo, it also de-skills and marginalises the creators of its heritage.

DEFENCE AND TOURISM: A CASE STUDY

Many of the contentions outlined above have drawn on the case of the naval town. This is inevitable as it is the naval town which has often been best placed to develop tourism functions in conjunction with existing seaside developments. As an illustrative case study, Portsmouth provides an excellent example. Considerable reductions in the naval presence in the city in the post-war period have been accompanied by a gradually growing emphasis on the tourism function.

Tourism in Portsmouth has, until recently, largely been confined to the resort satellite of Southsea. The early growth of this resort during the nineteenth century has been discussed by Riley (1972, 1980), but there is little work on the late nineteenth century period which saw the resort grow into a fairly typical English south coast seaside resort. Defence played a part in the early growth, both through the constraints on the direction of development, and through the generation of demand for houses from serving and retired naval and army officers. The role of defence in the consolidation period is however unclear, although boat trips to view the fleet were undoubtedly an attraction, adding extra interest to the sea voyages which formed an important part of the Victorian and Edwardian visit to the seaside.

Until the middle of the twentieth century, Portsmouth remained pre-eminently a dockyard town. Tourism co-existed with the dockyard and offered some employment to the wives and families of dockyard workers and serving and retired ratings and petty officers (NCOs). The local authority was only marginally involved, running such enterprises as beach trading and the maintenance of sea-front promenades and gardens. The promotion of Southsea as the resort town was part of a deliberate attempt to separate the tourism and defence functions. Portsmouth, with its naval connections, was perceived to lack tourist appeal.

During the 1950s Southsea began to experience problems. Foreign holidays became more popular and, even within the UK, other holiday destinations grew in importance. Portsmouth and Southsea, with its schizophrenic attitude to tourism was left behind. The south coast as a whole lost its place as the leading region for home-based holidays to the south west; it later fell to third place behind Wales. At the same time, the car replaced the train as the main mode of holiday travel, allowing tourists both a wider range of destinations, and also the possibility of making day trips. Further changes included the declining popularity of the traditional guest house and bed and breakfast establishments in favour of the caravan, chalet and self-catering apartment. Many established resorts found it difficult to adapt to these new trends, Southsea being no exception.

In the early 1960s the first sign of a renewal of the link with defence occurred. A study commissioned by the City Council in 1963 from the British Holiday and Travel Association recommended the development of the resort. A concentration of facilities at Eastney and a consolidation of a 'leisure and recreation corridor' along the eastern and southern coasts of Portsea Island were urged. As part of this initiative Clarence Pier was reconstructed following wartime damage and neglect, and Southsea Castle and the Old Portsmouth fortifications purchased from the Ministry of Defence.

Vested interests, however, inhibited any major change in the tourism agenda. A powerful group of local hoteliers and guest house owners attempted to mediate the changing economic context of tourism and preserve the existing situation. They were able to resist proposals for new, modern hotels and self-catering complexes and, although they were less successful in preventing the residential development of prime sea-front sites, they fought a hard rearguard action for the traditional seaside holiday.

It was business capital which provided the catalyst for new developments when they finally came. The first new hotel to be built in the city for over sixty years was opened in 1969, on land released by the Ministry of Defence. Built with assistance under the Development of Tourism Act, its owners emphasised that they were aiming to attract the businessman rather than the traditional tourist. In the same year the city played host to the Annual Conference of the Trades Union Congress. This again was a deliberate attempt to emphasise business tourism, but it was a logistical nightmare which exposed the limitations of the city for such a function. The blow to the city's prestige was so substantial that no large conference has since come to the city. The 1987 Institute of British Geographers Annual Conference will be the largest since the TUC Congress.

Significant reductions in dockyard employment, and the threat of more, made the City seriously embark on a programme of economic diversification during the 1970s. Attempts were made to attract, first new manufacturing employment, and then new office employment. In both cases some success was met, although, as suggested earlier, neither development effectively came to terms with the issues of redundant space and redundant dockyard craftsmen. Tourism was given a marginal role, with the major initiative being a review of street furniture and townscape aesthetics on the sea-front (Portsmouth City Council, 1969).

Tourism in the city was at this time in a state of stagnation. A major collaborative study by the Polytechnic Department of Geography and the City Council was suppressed by the latter, apparently because of its political sensitivity. The results suggested gradual decline. Period visitors fell from 150,000 in 1963 to 130,000 in 1973; 68 per cent of the visitors were over 45 compared to only 49 per cent for Britain as a whole (Ashworth and Bradbeer, 1973). Such results undermined the position of the powerful hotel and guest house owners lobby noted above, particularly since the number of day visitors was increasing rapidly. With period visitor spending estimated at £5.7 million and falling, and day visitor spending at £2.6 million and rising, decisions clearly had to be made. The report recommended a more positive attitude to day visitors, but the hotel lobby won.

The incorporation of the defence theme made little progress at this time; it figured only marginally in the hoteliers' concept of the traditional seaside holiday. Significantly perhaps, local government reorganisation saw the creation of a Department of Leisure Services which brought tourism together with museums, thus introducing an awareness of history into the minds of the leisure decisionmakers. Also significant was the creation and successful promotion of the continental ferry port (Riley and Smith, 1981). This brought more tourists to the city, although they were, and remain, a largely passing trade. It was also one of the first occasions when defence interests were regarded as secondary in the interests of restructuring the local economy. Indeed, the view of the Navy in port which was once problematic, is now a selling point for the ferry companies.

The economic recession and the major cuts in dockyard employment in the early 1980s led to a rethinking of the place of tourism in the local economy. Encouraged by a newly appointed deputy director of Leisure Services, who later succeeded to the directorship, it became accepted that tourism had a significant role to play in revitalising the economy, and that tourism meant more than the traditional seaside holiday. The importance of the day trip was recognised and promoted, and particular emphasis placed on the defence heritage of the town. This abrupt shift of emphasis was thus largely a response to crisis. It also contained an element of nostalgia and opportunism, for there was a recognition that tourism could be coupled with the preservation of the city's extensive collection of naval and military relics. There was a strangely sudden realisation that the city had one of the few examples of major nineteenth-century fortifications in Britain, and, with HMS *Victory*, the Naval Museum and the Royal Marines' Museum, the nucleus of attraction for a unique tourist experience.

The genesis of the defence tourism solution was completed by two events; both occurred in National Maritime Heritage Year (1982) which underlined their importance. First and foremost the Tudor warship *Mary Rose* was raised from the Solent. Second, in an echo of the imperial past, the fleet sailed to the Falklands, won victory, and returned triumphantly. A fuller discussion of these two events and the meanings to be drawn from their linkage as cultural manipulation of history is provided by Wright (1985) who also points out that: 'In this age of nuclear millenialism an antique Tudor war-machine certainly makes a more decorous curio than any Cruise missile' (p. 166).

The publicity generated by the raising of the *Mary Rose* confirmed the view that naval and military heritage was a major tourist attraction. In 1979, the City Planning Department prepared a report on the siting of the ship when it was raised, and outlined the substantial benefits that might accrue from its display. Although the ship was eventually displayed in the dockyard, rather than the originally planned museum at Eastney, the themes which were identified in the 1979 report formed the cornerstone of the new defence tourism. As well as dramatising Tudor social life and the place of the ship in maritime history, an important theme was to be the power and influence of the monarchy and the development of the British navy. This represented a clear attempt to re-interpret an event which had received little attention in the history books (the ship sank before battle had been joined). The *Mary Rose*, rather than the result of the battle, became the focus of attention, and an emphasis was placed on the precursor of Britain's hearts-of-oak and long period of naval supremacy. Such was the perceived certainty of the success of this strategy, that the city engaged in lobbying to ensure that HMS *Warrior*, the Royal Navy's first ironclad, would be located in Portsmouth after restoration. The popularity of day trips to see the *Mary Rose*, and the likelihood that the same will apply to the *Warrior*, has created an atmosphere in which Portsmouth feels it has a prior claim to house all the major naval artefacts in Britain. To enhance this claim, a programme is now under way to raise from the Solent the wreck of the *Indefatigable*, a captured eighteenth-century man-of-war.

The departure and return of the Falklands' battlefleet provided contemporary legitimation for the defence theme. The history which the city was promoting so assiduously was shown to be also a living part of its present. The defence theme and the tourism theme came together in a dramatic one-off presentation. More people watched the ships depart than had seen the Jubilee Review of the Fleet in 1977. The publicity of the return, particularly that of HMS *Invincible* and HMS *Hermes*, firmly linked Portsmouth with naval might and British success.

Defence tourism in Portsmouth is clearly suited to the worldview of the ruling city councillors. The opposition of the hoteliers' lobby has been largely overcome, and the city is firmly promoting itself as a monument to the great British military and naval past. The contradictions within the defence tourism package are largely ignored: with the exception of occasional suggestions for a defence-based theme park, the lack of employment prospects for the former craftsmen of the dockyard is not noted. The re-interpretation of history continues apace and, perhaps in a subconscious recognition of the important place assumed by tourism in the local economy, new opportunities are eagerly seized. Thus, despite being some 20 kilometres from the planning headquarters for the D-Day operations, the city attached itself firmly to the fortieth anniversary celebrations and constructed a costly and prestigious new museum in a sea-front site adjacent to Southsea Castle. Tourism literature now promotes the city as forming part of the 'Solent Stronghold' — an encapsulation of the defence-tourism linkage.

CONCLUSION

There has been surprisingly little written on the changing fortunes of the defence town in recent years. The local peculiarities of economic change in these towns perhaps makes it difficult to generalise about their experiences. Certainly they have developed an economic structure and, more interestingly, a cultural nexus which demands new and incisive research.

Defence and tourism are unlikely bedfellows; indeed it seems strange that, in the eyes of some at least, tourism should be viewed as the saviour of the abandoned defence town. Both however, are predicated to an element of dependency in the economy. Both are dependent on controls external to the local economy — the whims of the Ministry of Defence or the tourist public — and both demand the maintenance of a particular structure of social relations. They are not so dissimilar.

REFERENCES

Anderson, J., Duncan, S. and Hudson, R. (1983) *Redundant Spaces in Cities and Regions*, Academic Press, London.

Ashworth, G. and Bradbeer, J. (1973) 'The Southsea Story: a Report on Tourism to Portsmouth City Council', unpublished mimeo, Department of Geography, Portsmouth Polytechnic.

Braverman, H. (1974) *Labour and Monopoly Capital: the Degradation of Work*, Monthly Review, New York.

Breheny, M.J. and McQuaid, R.W. (1985) 'The M4 Corridor: Patterns and

Causes of Growth in High Technology Industries', *Geographical Papers*, no. 87, Department of Geography, University of Reading.

Burtenshaw, D., Bateman, M. and Ashworth, G. (1981) *The City in West Europe*, Wiley, Chichester.

Cohen, E. (1979a) 'Rethinking the Sociology of Tourism', *Annals of Tourism Research*, 6, 18–35.

Cohen, E. (1979b) 'A Phenomenology of Tourist Experiences', *Sociology*, 13, 179–201.

Curl, J. (1969) *European Cities and Society*, Hill, London.

Dartington Amenity Research Trust (1979) 'Defence of the Realm: an Interpretive Strategy for Portsmouth and the Surrounding Region', *DART Report 59*, Dartington, Devon.

Horne, D. (1984) *The Great Museum: the Re-presentation of History*, Pluto, London.

Kaplan, M. (1975) *Leisure: Theory and Policy*, Wiley, New York.

Keeble, D. (1976) *Industrial Location and Planning in the UK*, Methuen, London.

Massey, D. (1984) *Spatial Divisions of Labour*, Macmillan, London.

Openshaw, S. and Steadman, P. (1985) 'Doomsday Revisited', in Pepper, D. and Jenkins, A. (eds) *The Geography of Peace and War*, Blackwell, Oxford.

Piepe, A., Prior, R. and Box, A. (1969) 'The Location of the Proletarian and Deferential Worker', *Sociology*, 3, 239–44.

Portsmouth City Council (1969) *Seafront Review*, City Architect and Development Departments, Portsmouth.

Portsmouth City Council (1979) *Site for the Mary Rose*, Portsmouth City Planning Department, Portsmouth.

Riley, R.C. (1972) 'The Growth of Southsea as a Naval Satellite and Victorian Resort', *Portsmouth Paper 16*, Portsmouth City Council, Portsmouth.

Riley, R.C. (1980) 'The Houses and Inhabitants of Thomas Ellis Owen's Southsea', *Portsmouth Paper 32*, Portsmouth City Council, Portsmouth.

Riley, R.C. and Smith, J.L. (1981) 'Industrialisation in Naval Ports: the Portsmouth Case', in Pinder, D.A. and Hoyle, B.S. (eds) *City Port Industrialisation and Regional Development*, Pergamon, London.

Rosenau, H. (1959) *The Ideal City*, RKP, London.

Wright, E. (1976) 'Class Boundaries in Advanced Capitalist Societies', *New Left Review*, 98, 3–41.

Wright, P. (1985) *On Living in an Old Country*, Verso, London.

5

Government and the Specialised Military Town: The Impact of Defence Policy on Urban Social Structure in the Nineteenth Century

Trevor Harris

Since their inception in the sixteenth century the Royal Naval dockyards have, under the control of central government, combined to form a military-urban system (Harris, 1982a). The dominance of dockyard establishments in the economy of the adjacent townships has resulted in the system being comprised almost entirely of 'specialised' towns and, as the major employer of labour, the actions of government have dominated the development and affairs of these towns. The dockyards span some four centuries and are long-standing participants in the military-industrial complex in which the level of well-being of many industrial concerns and townships depends upon the issue and distribution of government-funded defence work. Indeed, it was through the naval dockyards that direct state intervention in major weaponry in this country was introduced and the dockyard-urban system was an early precursor of government involvement via defence expenditure in urban and regional development.

The origins of the naval dockyards date from the time of the Tudors when technological advances in armament and ship design radically altered naval architecture to produce the first of a line of specialised warships (Naish, 1958). Thereafter, the dual role of the merchant ship could no longer be maintained and the task of constructing and maintaining a specialist naval fighting force fell to the only institution capable and in a position to perform such an undertaking: the state. During the early sixteenth century, therefore, dockyards were established by government on the Thames at Deptford and Woolwich, at Portsmouth, and at Chatham on the

Medway. As the Royal Navy grew in size and complexity, so did the shore establishments necessary to construct, maintain and provide for the fleet. Further dockyards were established as circumstances dictated, as with the short-lived yard at Harwich, at Sheerness in 1667, and those at Devonport in 1691 and Rosyth in the early twentieth century. The choice of location for the siting of the yards was based as much on strategic considerations as on the physical attributes of the sites themselves. These conditions changed through time, however, and though the substantial fixed investment at these locations did favour their continued use for many centuries, only Devonport, Rosyth and Portsmouth continue as functional yards.

A number of issues arise with respect to the involvement of government in the dockyard towns over such a long period. Primary amongst them is that throughout this time the yards operated under the direct control of central government. The management, formulation of policy and the allocation of resources to the dockyards was heavily centralised within government. The management structure was strictly hierarchical and policy decisions and resource allocation to the dockyards which emanated from the executive in government filtered down to the yards through intermediate agencies. Both the executive and the intermediate agencies were located in London. Very little responsibility rested with officials at the dockyard establishments. One outcome of this long-standing relationship was the development of a specialised military-urban system in which the interdependence of the various dockyards and townships was founded upon the specialised military activity of the yards and the pivotal centralised control of government. Importantly, in its role as urban manager, the policies, decisions and allocation of resources which emanated from government were largely determined by the demands of national defence and far removed from local or regional economic considerations.

A second related issue is that the determinants of government policy and the allocation of resources toward the dockyards were tied to questions of national defence and to the defence budget. The naval dockyards came into being with the specific purpose of servicing the logistical requirements of the Royal Navy and, inevitably, it is to events surrounding the navy that the development of the dockyards must be related. As now, policy decisions were primarily based on this country's relations with foreign powers. The fortunes of the dockyards and adjacent townships rested heavily upon the vagaries of foreign affairs and, especially from the early nineteenth century, on the aspirations of the political party in power concerning public expenditure on defence. Furthermore, technological change has played an important role in the development of the dockyards particularly with respect to the adoption of radical, but invariably more expensive, defence technology.

The importance of this military-industrial link to the dockyard towns lies in the extent to which the towns were 'specialised' and dependent upon government and the defence budget for their prosperity. The impact of such a dependence can be seen in the morphology of the dockyard town and in its population composition and residential patterns. As a result of this centralised control many features of the dockyard town are replicated throughout the dockyard-urban system. Despite the symbiotic relationship between government and the dependent dockyard towns, however, government was very reluctant to become embroiled in the running of the towns themselves and only Sheerness achieved 'pseudo-company' town status (Harris, 1984). That the dockyard communities were dependent on the decisions of government and the funding of work from the defence budget is clearly demonstrated by the employment structure of the towns. The devastating effect which the withdrawal of such funds had on the towns, as in the event of dockyard closure or military redeployment, graphically illustrated this point.

A fourth issue stems from the considerable involvement of government in the dockyard localities with respect to the construction of extensive fortifications. Due to the need to defend the dockyards from sea-borne or land-based attack, government had long surrounded the yards with a variety of defences (see, for instance, the discussion of Portsmouth in Chapter 3). The imposition of bastion-trace fortifications around several of the dockyards and townships during the eighteenth century, however, produced an urban morphology more akin to the fortified towns of continental Europe than to those found elsewhere in Britain. These bastion-trace defences resulted in a process of urban colonisation and had a major impact on socio-spatial variation within the dockyard towns. The residential clustering of dockyard workers according to occupational skills and workplace affiliations in the towns during the nineteenth century was considerably facilitated by the colonising process which enabled clear social patterns to emerge in the dockyard towns.

This chapter examines the impact of government defence policy on the urban and social structure of naval dockyard towns in the nineteenth century. The period of the mid nineteenth century was an important time in the development of the dockyard town. The populations of the fortified towns were fast outstripping the available space within the restricting girdle of the defences and the resulting colonising process shifted the centre of gravity away from the older dockyard settlements to new residential and commercial centres beyond the fortifications. At the same time, the industrial dockyard base of the towns underwent great technological change which had far-reaching effects on the towns. Not least, the impact of government defence policy on the development of these urban communities can be seen as fundamental many years before the full extent of the defence-driven military-industrial complex came to the fore in the twentieth century.

THE HIERARCHY OF CONTROL

The importance of organisations and institutions in urban development have been variously considered (see, for example, Williams, 1982). The management structure which controlled the network of dockyard establishments comprised essentially three parts, each of which conforms closely to the trichotomy of decision-making levels hypothesised by Herbert (Herbert and Smith, 1979). The structure was hierarchical with the policymaking executive, comprising initially the monarch and his close advisers and subsequently parliament, cabinet and the prime minister of the day, forming the pyramidal apex. The executive determined both overall policy and the level of funding toward the dockyards and, in so doing, government had early assumed an urban managerial role (Pahl, 1977). Such resources consisted principally of funds for the repair, construction, supply and maintenance of the navy and were commensurate with the level of activity anticipated in the yards by the executive.

From the executive came the policy and orders upon which the immediate agencies controlling the dockyards and Royal Navy, the Admiralty and Navy Boards, were to act. These two boards, later combined to form the Board of Admiralty, formed the lynch-pin connecting the dockyards and Royal Navy with the policymaking executive. It was these bodies which disseminated instructions to the various branches of the navy and dockyard system. In general, the Navy Board controlled and organised the civilian side of the Royal Navy and principally the dockyards. The active or sea-arm of the Royal Navy came under the direct control of the Lord High Admiral and the Admiralty Board to whom the Navy Board was officially subservient. In matters relating to the civilian management of the navy, the Admiralty Board worked through the Navy Board but retained for itself direct control over fleet and ship manoeuvres. The allocation of resources to specific yards, especially the determination of employment levels, was generally undertaken by these Boards based upon postulated work schedules. The level of employment in the dockyards was a vital element in the prosperity of the dockyard towns and, along with the presence of military and naval personnel, had a major impact on the supporting tertiary sector. In determining the specific allocation of resources to the various yards, the Admiralty Board and especially the Navy Board undertook the role of 'gatekeeper' in which they channelled resources within the dockyard system and exerted a major influence on the fortunes and development of the dockyard locations.

At the lowest level of the administrative structure, the day-to-day management of the dockyard establishments up to 1832 was in the hands of 'Resident Commissioners' and thereafter, Admiral Superintendents. They were directly responsible to their colleagues on the Navy Board for the efficient functioning of the dockyards and for implementing the commands which filtered down through the system. Under each Resident Commissioner were five principal officers who were responsible for the daily control of the yard, its work and the workforce. Despite the considerable problems of communication between the dockyards and the Navy Board in London, which involved at least a day's journey even to reach Chatham in the late eighteenth century, and considerably longer for the yards at Portsmouth and especially, Devonport, the Resident Commissioners were delegated little freedom of action. Power over the dockyards was securely based in the Navy and Admiralty Boards, situated, like their political masters, in London.

THE DETERMINANTS OF GOVERNMENT POLICY

The major determinant bearing upon events in the dockyard-urban system was that of war or the threat of war. The alternating cycle between war and peace was a fundamental trend upon which the dockyards had grown from the earliest years. Employment in the dockyards fluctuated sharply from peacetime levels to much higher levels needed to meet the naval demands of an emergency. Upon the conclusion of hostilities, however, severe retrenchment inevitably followed in the government's haste to reduce expenditure to peacetime levels. The effect on the dockyards and townships was immense. Up to the mid nineteenth century, however, the general trend within this cycle was marked by an overall increase in the number of workmen employed in the various yards. From about 1850 this pattern was increasingly influenced by other factors, notably that of rapid advances in ironclad steamship and armament technology, which contributed to large upswings in dockyard employment toward the end of the nineteenth century. The implementation of new technology, as with the decision to go to war, necessitated decisions by government as to where and when to implement new shipbuilding and ship repair programmes with concomitant dockyard extension schemes (Pollard and Robertson, 1979; Lyon, 1977; and Sandler, 1967).

Whilst international relations were a major factor determining government policy toward the Royal Navy and the dockyard system, it was not the sole influence. Party political views on the level of defence expenditure were particularly relevant. Certainly during the nineteenth century, political and, increasingly, financial constraints were imposed upon the Admiralty by successive governments with consequent implications for activity in the dockyards and for the workforce (Briggs, 1897). Such constraints were not directed solely at the Admiralty but at most departments of state, though the armed services were, as now, in the position of preparing to counter potential threats whose real danger may be open to debate. During time of war or hostilities, however, budgetary constraints were invariably laid aside and funds were more readily forthcoming (Briggs, 1897, p. 108).

THE DOCKYARD TOWNS AS 'SPECIALISED' TOWNS

All the dockyard towns were 'specialised' in that the employment structure of the town was dominated by naval shipbuilding, repairing and support activities. Many examples exist of the specialised township, not least because of the legacy which closure or contraction of the indigenous industry has bequeathed to their dependent communities (see, for example, Smailes (1943) for an early discussion of the position). However, dockyard towns were additionally 'specialised' since almost without exception they possessed other defence-related activities which added to the economic dependence of the township on the state. Only in rare exceptions, as in the corset-making industry in Portsmouth, did manufacturing activity occur outside the auspices of government (Riley, 1976).

An extension of the specialised town is the phenomenon of the 'company' town in which the community is dependent on a single company which, for economic or philanthropic reasons, takes an active role in the creation and development of a settlement and in the provision of services and facilities. Whilst the Admiralty and dockyard authorities had representatives on local dockyard town committees, they were there to represent the interests of government rather than participate extensively in local affairs. Only in the case of the 'pseudo-company' town of Sheerness did a reluctant government provide extensive accommodation and facilities for its civilian workforce and this was forced upon them by the difficulties encountered in attracting workmen to the yard (Harris, 1984).

FORTIFICATIONS AND THE URBAN COLONISING PROCESS

Morphologically, the dockyard towns may be divided into two groups based upon the extent of fortification as a component of the urban plan (Harris, 1982a, pp. 186–213). The imposition of fortifications around some dockyards had a major influence on socio-spatial variation in the dockyard town. All dockyard locations were protected by fortifications in one form or another though some yards were considered sufficiently exposed to amphibious attack to warrant extensive land defences. Deptford, Woolwich and Pembroke Dock were defended by fortified positions covering sea and river approaches but these were at some distance from the yard itself. At Chatham, Sheerness, Portsmouth and Devonport, however, the yards were surrounded on the landward side from the mid eighteenth century by an extensive array of fixed bastion-trace defences constructed to within just a few hundred metres of the dockyard. Included within the fortifications were the settlements immediately adjacent to the dockyards. Surrounding the fortifications was the glacis or 'killing ground', a wide tract of open land upon which building was prohibited for fear of interfering with the field of fire from the defences. The conflict of interests between the Board of Ordnance, responsible for the fortifications, and the local inhabitants was a feature of the fortified dockyard town. Whilst the Board sought to maintain an obstacle-free glacis, the inhabitants residing outside the walls naturally sought accommodation as close to the dockyard as possible. As the population of the dockyard towns expanded, especially during the nineteenth century, the constraining defences placed increased demands on the existing housing stock within the defences. The density of population in these towns during the first half of the nineteenth century placed them amongst the most densely populated towns in the country. Building land within the defences was scarce and plots became smaller and narrower and the buildings taller. The settlements within the restraint of fortifications at Brompton, Portsea and Plymouth Dock soon expanded to the fullest extent possible and further settlement had to take place outside the fortifications and beyond the glacis. Thus began the colonising process so characteristic of the fortified dockyard town. The extensive building programme which took place in these settlements during the mid-years of the nineteenth century created colonies on the periphery of government-owned land. The movement of residents out of the older congested urban cores to these colonies led to a considerable filtering down of housing in the mother settlements, whilst facilitating the grouping of dockyard artisans to form new residential neighbourhoods. Such clusters also existed in the unfortified dockyard town where, as at Woolwich, government ownership of land in the towns similarly influenced urban and social patterns.

In view of the importance of fortifications on social patterns in the dockyard town, two case studies, those of Woolwich and Sheerness, representing the unfortified and the fortified dockyard town respectively, are used to examine the impact of government defence policy on the social geography of the dockyard town.

THE SOCIAL GEOGRAPHY OF THE UNFORTIFIED DOCKYARD TOWN: WOOLWICH

Woolwich is acknowledged as the mother of British naval dockyards and, with its extensive military garrison, can claim to have been one of the foremost military towns in the country. In the early eighteenth century Defoe referred to Woolwich as being 'a town on the bank of the . . . [Thames], wholly taken up by, and in a manner raised from, the yards and public works, erected there for the publick service' (Defoe, 1948). A century later the town remained dominated economically and physically by the military and naval establishments. Population growth in Woolwich during the nineteenth century was closely correlated with the vicissitudes of government defence spending. Between the years 1801 and 1811 the military and naval demands of the Napoleonic War brought about a population growth in Woolwich of some 75 per cent. (See Figure 5.1.) During

Figure 5.1: Population of Woolwich and Sheerness, 1801–71

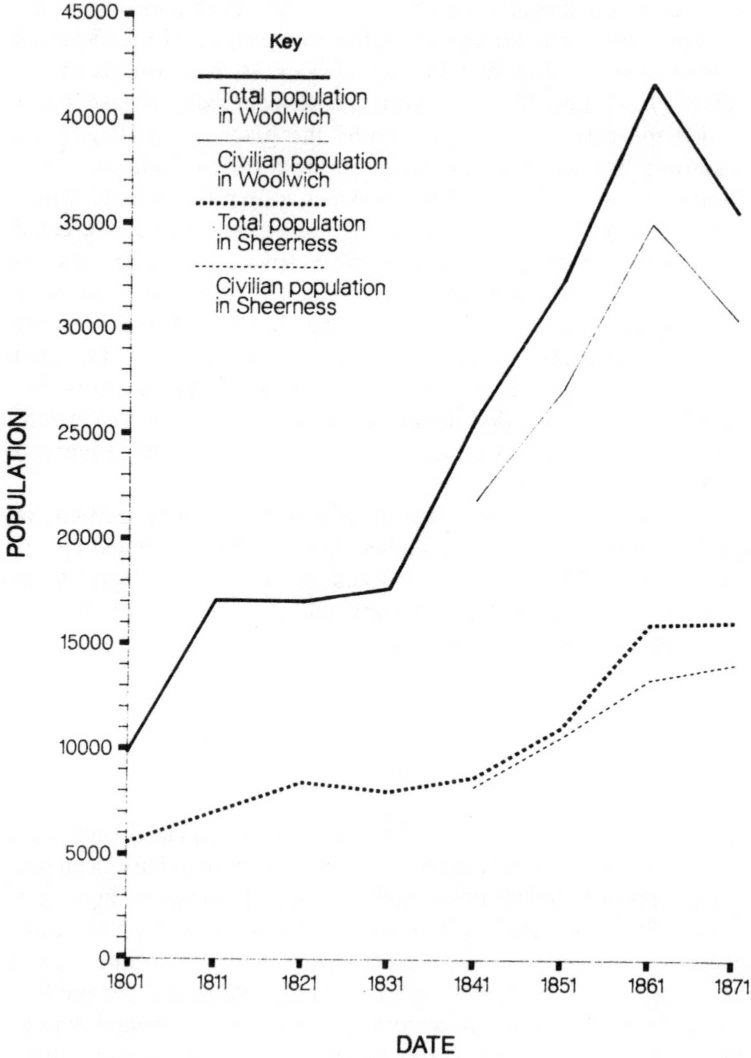

Figure 5.2: Housing in Woolwich, 1801–71

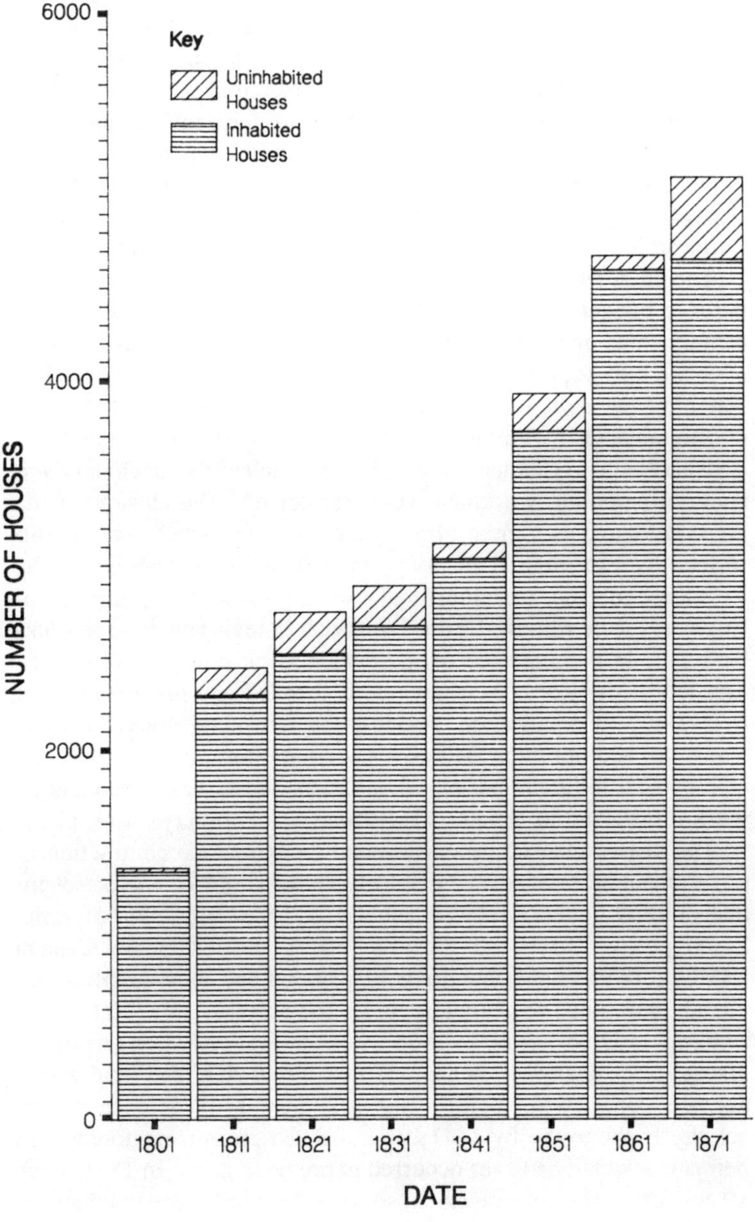

the following decade, however, in the wake of the severe retrenchment in the dockyard and armed forces following the Treaty of Vienna in 1815, the population of Woolwich registered zero growth. In 1821, following extensive out-migration resulting from the cessation of hostilities six years earlier, some 9 per cent of the housing stock was uninhabited. (See Figure 5.2.) Not until the 1830s and the construction of the dockyard steam factory extension, increased activity in the Royal arsenal, and a greater military presence, did the population of Woolwich return to its previous rate of growth. Between 1831 and 1861 the population more than doubled as the Crimean War boosted dockyard and military activity in the town.

The vulnerable dependence of Woolwich on government and the defence budget, demonstrated in the early years of the nineteenth century, was particularly poignant when, due to the inability of Woolwich to cope with the site requirements of the new breed of warship, the yard was closed by government order in 1869. The closure coincided with the completion of the first stage of the dockyard extension at Chatham to which yard much of the machinery and some officers and workmen were transferred. The closure of the dockyard came as a great blow to the township which was hit still further by extensive reductions, for reasons of economy, in the workforce of the Royal arsenal. At the same time, the Royal Engineers were removed from Woolwich to their new base at Chatham and, in consequence of the dockyard closure, the Woolwich division of the Royal Marines was disbanded and its personnel of over 1,000 men dispersed amongst the remaining dockyard divisions. In addition, the Military Clothing Store, which provided employment for a number of women in the town, was closed and its work transferred to Pimlico (*The Times*, 22 February 1869, p. 5).

The distress caused by closure and the wholesale contraction in government defence-related employment in Woolwich was so severe that in 1869 government consented to aid the emigration of some 2,500 persons from the town on board naval ships to Canada (HMSO, 1869). Some hundreds of workers and their families had already emigrated to Australia under the auspices of a 'Relief and Emigration Fund' set up in 1868 when the first reductions from the arsenal and dockyard began. Whilst Woolwich had undergone defence contractions before, the withdrawal of defence-related activity in the town, by 1871, was of much greater magnitude and permanency than had ever occurred in previous years. In 1871, over 10 per cent of the housing stock, some 400 houses, were uninhabited and, from a projected population of 41,000, based on the growth rate of the previous three decades, the town slumped to 30,000 (see Figures 5.2 and 5.3). As a result of these reductions, the tertiary sector in the town was badly depressed and many shopkeepers were forced out of business (*The Times*, 1 September 1869, p. 10).

From 1841, when such information first becomes available, the institutionalised military component in Woolwich was substantial, comprising between 14 and 16 per cent of the total population of the town. In reality, this figure underestimates the military presence, for a large number of military personnel resided not in barracks but in private accommodation in the town. For instance, Rawlinson (1851) estimated that some 500 Royal Marines lived with their families in the town. In 1871, 4 per cent of the population were military personnel living in private accommodation. The extent of military personnel in the town, therefore, approached some 20 per cent of the total population and, with their dependants, formed a substantial sector of the inhabitants. Such a presence certainly boosted the tertiary sector of the community.

As in other dockyard towns, this military presence was reflected in the composition of the civilian population. Perhaps surprisingly for a town dominated by male-employing industries, females comprised 50 per cent of the civilian (as opposed to total) population. Such a figure is characteristic of most military towns and in 1851 Rawlinson drew attention to the problems which this element of the population posed to the dockyard town;

> but there is still a large class, consisting of . . . wives and children of soldiers, who by the regulations of the service cannot be sent with their husbands, or fathers, to the foreign stations when they go on duty; and of the widows and children of these same soldiers who die, leaving nothing for their families. The aggregate of these form a pauper population which presses heavily upon the poor rate, and among whom, crowded as they are in small ill-ventilated dwellings, disease in its most fatal form is always found to prevail (Rawlinson, 1851, p. 46).

The dockyard employed just over one-third of the active male civilian workforce in the sub-district of Woolwich dockyard and, as in the case of other dockyard towns, was the major source of employment in the town (Figure 5.3). In reality, this proportion was likely to be much greater given the large number of labourers (15.5 per cent of the male workforce) whose place of work was unspecified in the census schedules. A large number of these were

Figure 5.3: Employment structure of Sheerness in 1871 and Woolwich in 1861

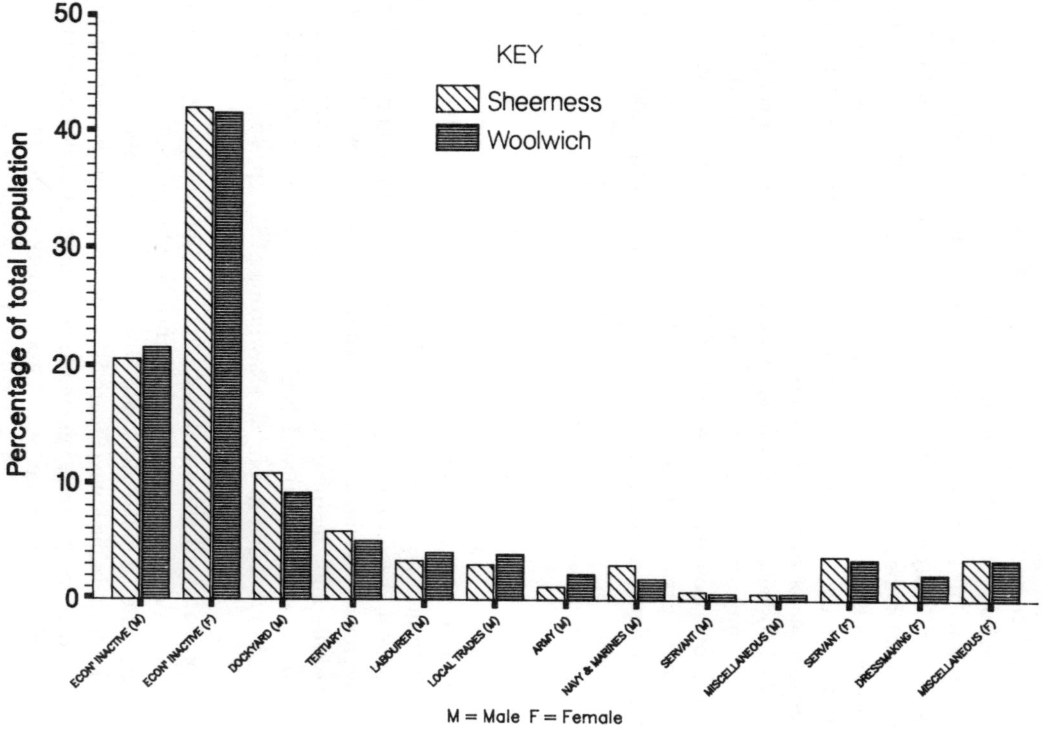

Figure 5.4: Birthplace of Woolwich residents, 1861

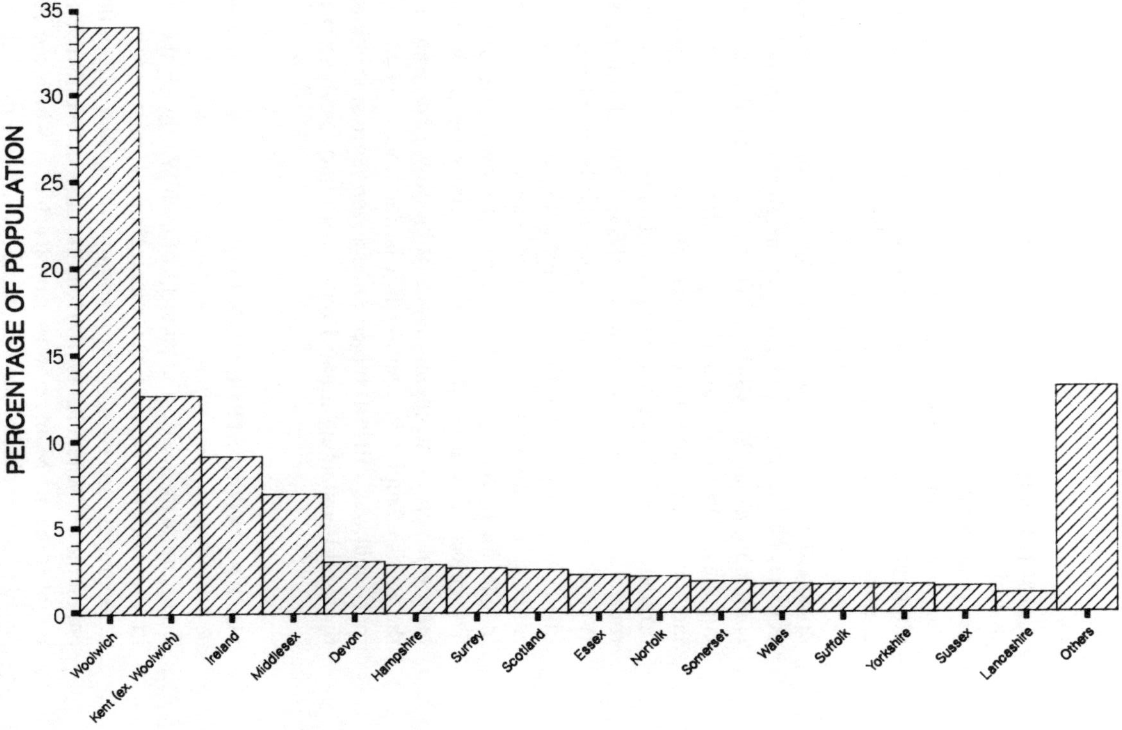

undoubtedly employed in the dockyard. The tertiary sector formed the second largest economic activity for civilian males, as well as providing employment for many females. Employment opportunities for females in the dockyard towns were severely limited, extending only to domestic service, dressmaking, laundry work and the tertiary sector. Females were employed in the Government Clothing Store in Woolwich and some had obtained employment in the arsenal, though by 1872 all females had been dismissed (Vincent, 1890, p. 357).

The population of Woolwich in 1861 was more cosmopolitan than that of most dockyard towns, with native born comprising only 33 per cent of the population (Figure 5.4). This may be a reflection of the town's proximity to London and the busy River Thames, although its position at the nexus of a number of counties may confuse the census-derived picture here slightly. Certainly, the origins of migrants in Woolwich mirrors those found in other dockyard towns and can be grouped broadly into four categories comprising, in order of importance, neighbouring counties, counties containing naval dockyards, maritime and coastal areas and inland counties. The ready availability of travel by ship did much to facilitate movement to the dockyard towns and, indeed, many migrant ships from Ireland stopped at Devonport and Portsmouth en route to London (Ravenstein, 1885). The Irish presence in Woolwich, being the second largest contributor of migrants to the town, was greater than that in other dockyard towns and probably reflects the importance of the metropolis and the Thames as a magnet for Irish emigrants in the period following the Great Famine. The presence of a number of foreign-born residents in Woolwich, however, represents the influence of the Royal Navy and its role in the British Empire for, although it is not always stated whether an individual was a British subject, many were born at locations around the world containing a naval base or military establishment.

SOCIO-SPATIAL STRUCTURE IN 1861

To examine the residential patterns of both Woolwich and Sheerness in the middle years of the nineteenth century, socioeconomic, demographic and ethnic information were extracted from the census enumerators' schedules of 1861 in the case of Woolwich and 1871 for Sheerness.[1] Matrices were constructed in which the rows consisted of street blocks into which the towns were divided, whilst the

Table 5.1: Loading of the original variables on the first four principal components: Woolwich, 1861

Variable	Formulation		Loadings on components 1	2	3	4
1	*	Irish born	0.578	0.268	0.429	0.054
2	*	Scottish born	0.152	0.326	−0.401	−0.207
3	*	Welsh born	−0.212	−0.043	0.009	−0.472
4	*	Foreign born	0.364	0.382	0.005	−0.180
5	*	Lodgers	−0.089	0.369	0.095	0.616
6	*	Servants	−0.432	0.649	−0.158	0.262
7	*	Age over 60 years	−0.481	0.230	0.299	−0.316
8	*	Age 0–14 years	0.680	−0.460	−0.265	0.085
9	*	Female head of household	−0.193	0.273	0.234	−0.465
10	o	Social class I and II	−0.506	0.550	−0.259	−0.049
11	o	Social class IV and V	0.248	0.120	0.624	−0.182
12	+	Population density	0.776	0.347	−0.275	0.012
13	+	Multiple occupancy	0.787	0.325	−0.285	−0.017
14	+	Male–female ratio	0.221	−0.228	0.043	0.456
15	o	Dockyard employees	−0.249	−0.624	−0.484	0.000
16	o	Tertiary personnel	−0.157	0.429	0.042	0.443
17	o	Labourers	0.299	−0.182	0.794	0.130
18	o	Military and naval personnel	0.425	0.336	−0.247	−0.367

* As a percentage of population in each street block.
o As a percentage of economically active persons in each street block.
\+ As a ratio of all persons in each street block.

Table 5.2: Summary of results of principal components with eigenvalues greater than one, for Woolwich, 1861

	Component					
	1	2	3	4	5	6
Eigenvalue	3.31	2.54	2.14	1.66	1.27	1.13
Percentage explanation	18.40	14.08	11.87	9.25	7.04	6.28
Cumulative explanation	18.40	32.48	44.35	53.60	60.64	66.92

columns comprised eighteen variables taken from the census schedules reflecting the population characteristics of each street. Table 5.1 shows the variables selected and their loadings on the components derived from the subsequent principal components analysis. Location quotient plots were used to complement a principal components analysis of the matrices to produce a relatively detailed picture of the socio-spatial structure of Woolwich and Sheerness at this time. Subsequently, a discriminant classification algorithm was applied to the results of the component analysis.

The first four components of the principal component analysis of Woolwich accounted for some 53 per cent of the total variance explained (Table 5.2). The first component accounted for some 18 per cent of the total variance and, in loading heavily on population density and multiple occupancy, is clearly a measure of the intensity of housing use (Figure 5.5). The streets so delineated were sandwiched within the areas bounded by the Royal Marine barracks and the Royal Artillery barracks and consisted largely of back streets and courtyards. The area contained many families of low ranking military personnel, though, as the loading of military personnel on the component indicates, the male head of household was not always resident. The loading on the Irish variable is also related to the military presence, for many soldiers and their families were of Irish origin. These streets were marked by the absence of residents of high social class. In time, the demand for accommodation by married soldiers and their families led to such overcrowding in this part of Woolwich that government eventually constructed over 100 huts to the south west of Woolwich Common for their use (Rawlinson, 1851, p. 15).

The second and third components accounted for 16 per cent and 12 per cent of the total variance and are measures of high and low socioeconomic status, respectively. Streets characterised by high socioeconomic status were to be found in areas skirting the town to

Figure 5.5: High and low scores on component one: Woolwich

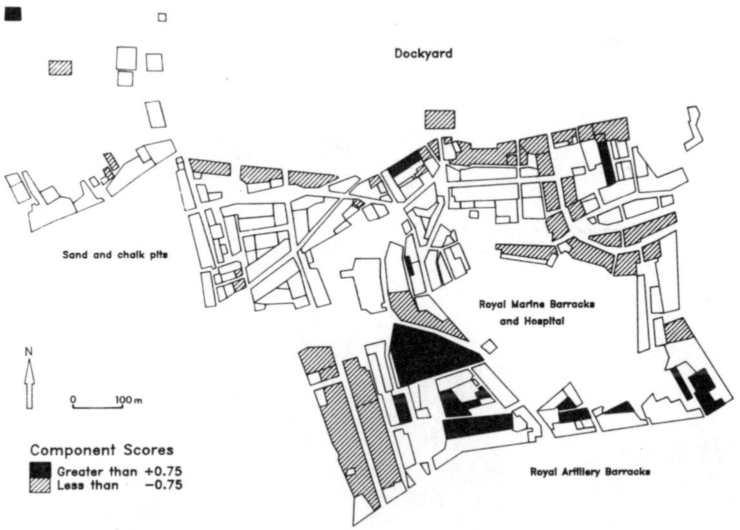

Figure 5.6: High and low scores on component two: Woolwich

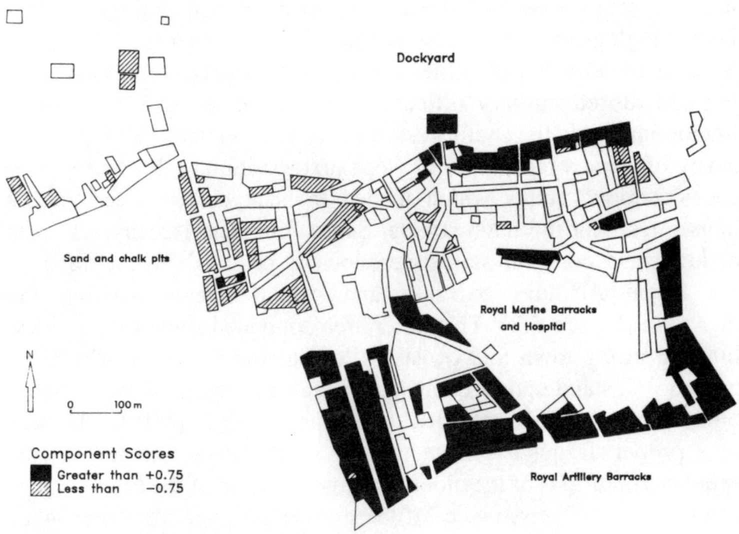

Figure 5.7: High and low scores on component three: Woolwich

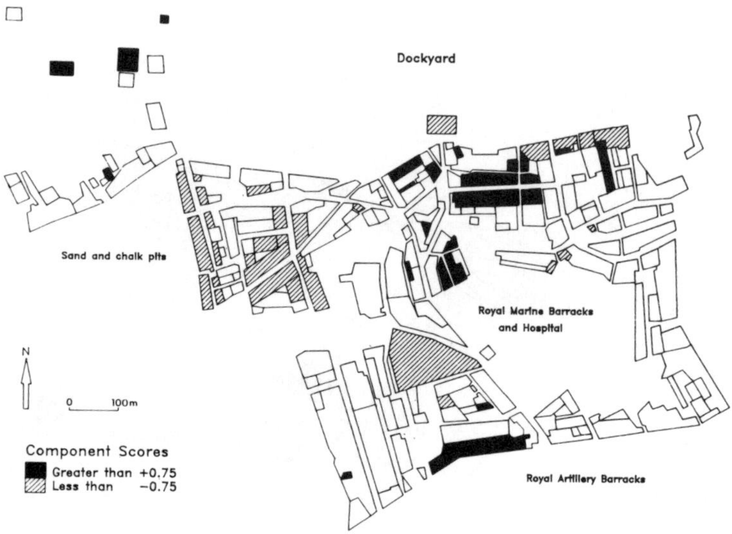

the south, south east and north east (see Figure 5.6). With the exception of the houses along the main Woolwich-to-London thoroughfare facing the dockyard to the north, these streets generally contained the most recently constructed housing in Woolwich and, by occupying the high ground, were also in the most healthy parts of the town. Vincent records that the elite of Woolwich largely comprised serving and retired military officers who, with their families, resided predominantly in the south west of the town (Vincent, 1890, p. 399). Many of these streets were in close juxtaposition with areas of low socioeconomic status which tended to back on to better quality houses fronting the main streets. Streets characterised by residents of low socioeconomic status were located primarily to the north of the Royal Artillery barracks and behind streets fronting the dockyard (Figure 5.7). This latter area contained some of the oldest housing in the town and consisted 'of narrow streets in which the houses . . . stand upon a damp and undrained subsoil; they are badly built, and are unduly crowded' (Rawlinson, 1851, p. 15). The lack of a proper drainage system throughout the town had led to 'the sanitary conditions of the older and lower portion of the town [being] made worse, in consequence of the surface drainage from the higher portions being passed into it' (Rawlinson, 1851, p. 15). In 1851, the

Figure 5.8: Location quotient of dockyard personnel: Woolwich

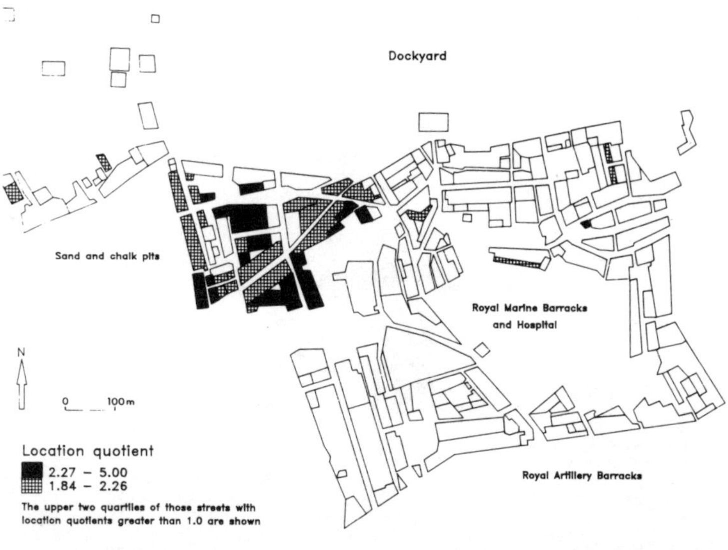

death rate in this area was double that of streets to the south of the town. Noticeably, dockyard workers loaded negatively on both component two and three, suggesting they were residentially differentiated from areas of both high and low social status. Indeed, a location quotient plot of dockyard workers shows that they occupied a very sharply defined neighbourhood to the north west of the town (Figure 5.8). Although not specifically identified in the principal component analysis, a discriminant classification analysis of the factor scores across all four components, highlights this very same area as being dominated by dockyard workers. This pattern bears marked similarity with the clustering of dockyard employees in New Brompton at Chatham and Marine Town in Sheerness (Figures 5.9 and 5.10).

Component four is predominantly a measure of male lodgers in the town who located in the thoroughfare fronting the naval dockyards (Figure 5.11). This street contained the oldest houses in the town and, because of their location and size, they had been adapted as lodging houses, public houses and shops. Subsequent components added little to the further interpretation of social patterns in the town.

Before discussing the implications of these patterns, it is possible

Figure 5.9: Location quotient of dockyard personnel: Gillingham

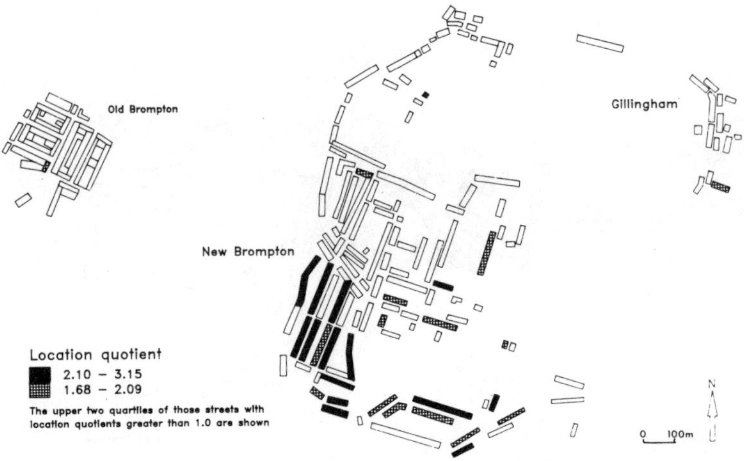

Figure 5.10: Location quotient of dockyard personnel: Sheerness

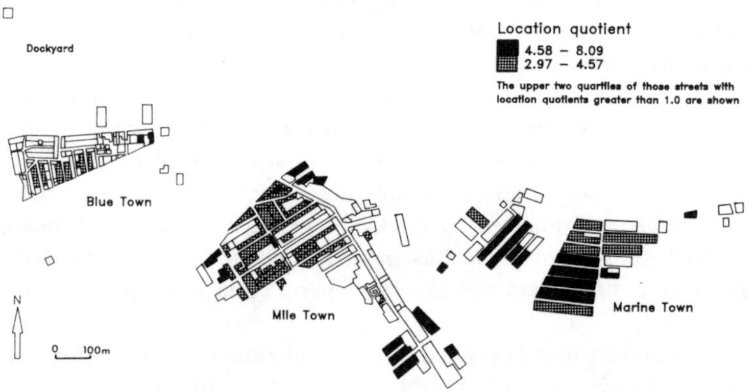

Figure 5.11: High and low scores on component four: Woolwich

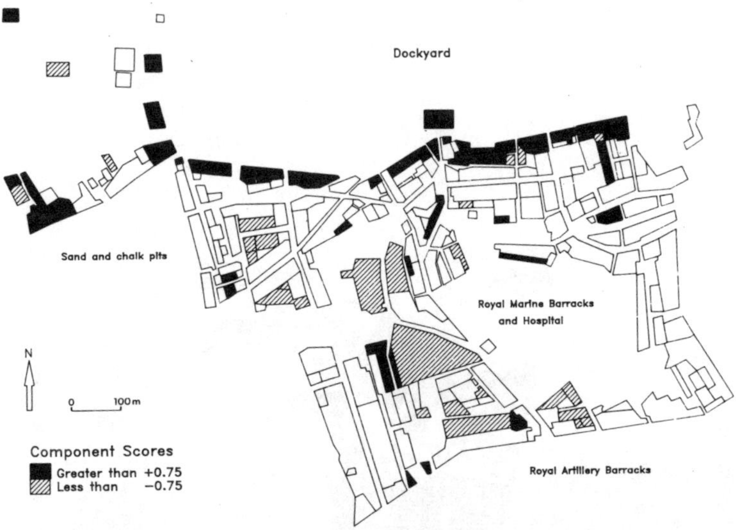

to obtain an overall view of residential patterns in Woolwich by classifying streets by means of a discriminant classification procedure (Cassetti, 1964; see also King, 1969). This procedure creates an optimal classification of streets according to similarities in their factor score loadings across the four components by maximising inter-class variation whilst minimising intra-class variation. The resulting map portrays a generalised picture of residential patterns in Woolwich in 1861 (Figure 5.12).

On the basis of inter-class and intra-class variation, a classification involving nine groups was found to be the most effective (Table 5.3). The patterns generated by this analysis naturally reflect many of those previously identified by the component score plots and location quotient plots. Thus, streets in groups one, two and seven were primarily characterised by the presence of residents of low socioeconomic status, though they differ from each other slightly in the extent to which lodgers were present. These streets clustered in that area of Woolwich known to be of low housing and environmental quality to the north of the Royal Marine barracks. As seen earlier, the streets between the Royal Marine and Royal Artillery barracks, identified by group four and group eight, were

Figure 5.12: Component scores classified into residential types: Woolwich

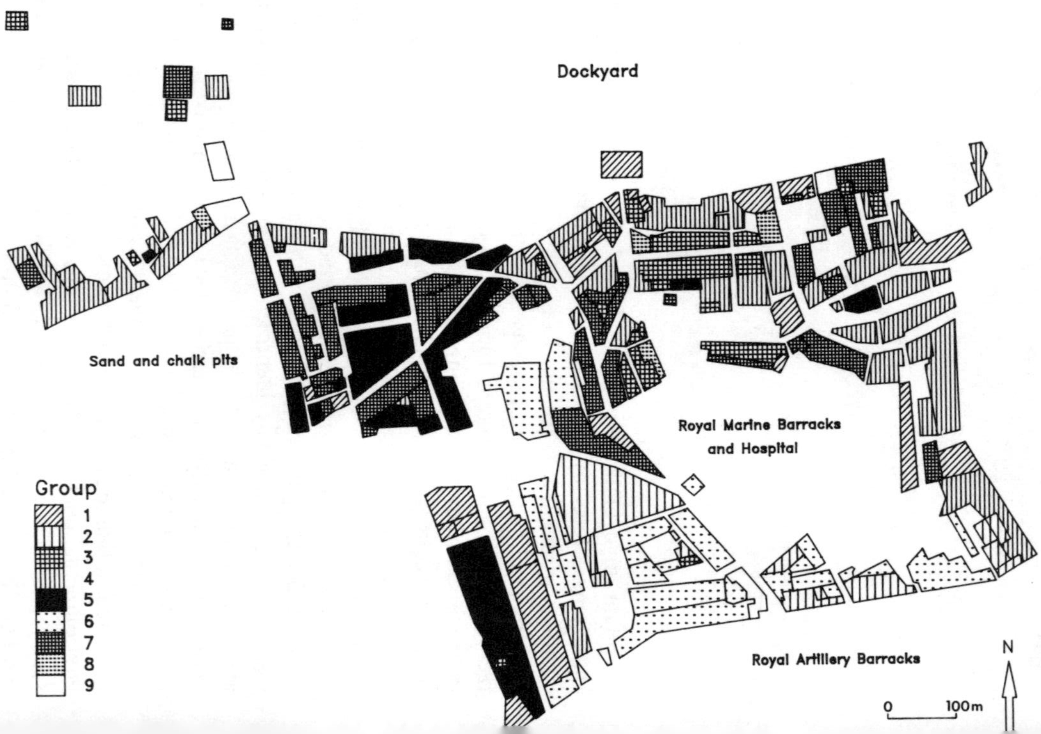

Table 5.3: Loadings of groups one to ten on original four principal components, for Woolwich, 1861

	Component			
Group	1	2	3	4
1	1.01	-0.02	1.29	1.91
2	-1.13	0.74	2.56	-2.39
3	0.04	-0.76	-0.41	0.08
4	0.58	0.69	-0.25	-0.62
5	-0.56	-0.93	-0.87	-0.68
6	-0.39	0.26	-0.09	0.78
7	0.04	-0.58	1.32	0.15
8	2.92	1.15	-0.65	-0.94
9	-1.52	1.90	-0.44	0.42

characterised by high population density, multiple occupancy and by residents of low socioeconomic status. To the west of this group and to the east and north east of the town, the streets delimited by group nine contained residents of high social class. Finally, streets identified by group six were noted for their lower population density and multiple occupancy rates.

Importantly, discriminant analysis has identified a cluster of streets in group three and group five in the north west of the town dominated by dockyard artisans. Such a pattern corresponds closely to the location quotient plot of dockyard workers referred to earlier (Figure 5.8). This area was also marked by the absence of residents of high and low social class. Streets in group five differ from those of group three only by slightly lower rates of multiple occupancy, population density and lodgers. It would appear that this was a neighbourhood in which streets delineated by group five formed a core cluster of dockyard artisans surrounded by streets of group three which differed only according to the extent of lodgers and multiple occupancy.

A number of relatively homogeneous residential areas can thus be discerned in Woolwich in 1861. Perhaps the most interesting aspect of the socio-spatial structure of Woolwich at this time was the residential segregation of dockyard artisans in a sharply defined enclave to the north west of the town. In the principal component analysis of both Woolwich and of Sheerness it is noticeable that skilled dockyard workers segregated residentially from the extremes of high and low socioeconomic groups. If this were accompanied by similar component loadings for tertiary personnel and those in local trades, then this group could perhaps be accepted as representing a group of middling socioeconomic status falling somewhere between the two extremes. That this does not occur suggests that dockyard workers segregated as an occupational group rather than strictly on the basis of social class. Studies of Sheerness and Chatham show that those of high and low socioeconomic status were often residentially closely juxtaposed in the dockyard town and that it was dockyard personnel who tended to segregate most within the community. Part reason for this may be due to the construction of lower quality housing in the gardens of high quality housing, as occurred extensively in Old Brompton adjacent to Chatham dockyard but, partly, this pattern of clustering may be attributed to the existence of a dockyard artisan elite. This aspect is discussed later in this chapter.

THE SOCIAL GEOGRAPHY OF THE FORTIFIED DOCKYARD TOWN: SHEERNESS

The yard at Sheerness was established as an outport to the yards of Chatham, Deptford and Woolwich. Its strategic position at the approaches to the up-river yards and its exposed situation had led to the yard being heavily fortified from the earliest years of its existence and it is representative of those yards which underwent extensive fortification programmes. Sheerness does differ, however, from other dockyard locations in the extent to which government was involved in the large scale provision of civilian accommodation. This involvement was forced on the authorities by the difficulties experienced in attracting workmen to this remote and inhospitable site and the associated lack of private investment in housing (Harris, 1984). The earliest accommodation provided by the authorities for workmen and their families was on board hulks sunk as breakwaters in the harbour. In the course of the next century these hulks attained the status of permanent 'streets' in the face of the housing shortage at Sheerness. Additionally, lodgings for workmen were also provided in the 'Great Alleys', barrack-like buildings in the adjacent fort.

Not until the second half of the eighteenth century was private housing constructed on a triangular stretch of land adjacent to the fort. It was surrounded on all sides by government-owned land. The development of Blue Town was central to the withdrawal of government-sponsored accommodation in Sheerness and, by 1820, all such provision had been withdrawn. It was unusual for the authorities to allow construction of private housing so close to the defences and, by the 1790s, the Board of Ordnance had accepted that the landward defences of Sheerness Fort were obsolete because of the presence of Blue Town. In line with defence schemes at other dockyard locations, a second outer system of bastion-trace fortifications was constructed on Ordnance land encircling the settlement. Encroachments on this land were fiercely resisted and the urban limits of Blue Town were firmly fixed.

During the boom years of the Napoleonic Wars, increases in the military and civilian population of Sheerness (shown in Figure 5.1) resulted in Blue Town expanding to the maximum size possible within the constraints of government land. It was the sheer inability of Blue Town to accommodate a rapidly increasing population which ultimately triggered the movement of inhabitants eastward beyond the encircling fortifications and glacis to establish Mile Town (see Figure 5.14). This colonising movement was further stimulated by government proposals in 1815 to compulsorily purchase and demolish the whole of Blue Town as part of the dockyard expansion scheme (Harris, 1984). The development of Mile Town, however, was not the end of the colonising process in Sheerness. Government concern over the proximity of the colony to the new bastion defences prompted the Board of Ordnance in 1827 to purchase all land, with the exception of that on which Mile Town stood, within 600 yards of the defences. This purchase enclosed Mile Town within a girdle of government-owned land and curtailed any further expansion of the settlement. This event subsequently led to a second colonising movement to the north east beyond the recently purchased government land to establish Marine Town. Nor did the process finish there, for the presence of Mile Town and Marine Town in front of the fortifications prompted construction of a further ramparted moat in 1862 to the east of Marine Town. With the sea to the north and Mile Town to the south, this defensive structure effectively prevented any expansion of Marine Town.

Government was instrumental, therefore, in determining the morphological development of the fortified dockyard town and considerably influenced its socio-spatial structure. Sheerness, in common with the other dockyard towns, contained a substantial body of military and naval personnel and, during the middle years of the nineteenth century, the military component in Sheerness comprised between 10 and 15 per cent of the total population. Additionally, military personnel amounting to 3.6 per cent of Sheerness residents lived in private accommodation. With their dependants, the military presence in Sheerness was substantial.

Besides the military, some 500 convicts were also stationed by government at Sheerness between 1812 and 1827 on board hulks moored in the harbour. The use of convict labour was a common practice in all the dockyards and especially those undergoing dock excavation or extension schemes. The presence of the convicts and their guards in the dockyard town, as with the military, gave a considerable boost to the local economy of the town. Indeed, when the convicts were removed to Woolwich following a petition for their removal by Sheerness residents, it was recorded that, 'it is supposed they will gain petition for their recall, thinking, perhaps the nuisance is preferable to the loss of trade' (Turmine, 1843, p. 32).

The proportion of females to males, 50.6 per cent of the population to 49.4 per cent, was similar to that found in Woolwich. The enumeration of many female heads of household recorded as 'wife of seaman' or 'wife of soldier' emphasises the extensive presence of wives of military personnel who were absent on active service. As a result, females dominated the age range 15 to 30 of the civilian population. A corresponding excess of males between the ages of 40 and 60 indicates the return of military personnel in later years to take up residence in the town following retirement from the armed forces. This was a common practice to which there are numerous references in the census enumerators' schedules.

Male employment in Sheerness was dominated by the dockyard. At least 38 per cent of the civilian male workforce were employed directly in the yard and this figure excludes the large number of labourers and artisans whose place of work was not designated in the schedules. Close scrutiny of the employment details in the schedules does suggest that as much as half of the male workforce could have been employed in the yard. Alternative male employment in Sheerness, other than in the tertiary sector and local trades, was non-existent. Necessarily, the fortunes of the service sector were heavily reliant upon the employment afforded by the dockyard and the purchasing power of naval and military personnel stationed in the town. Very few employment opportunities existed to utilise the pool of female labour. Only 16.4 per cent of all females were recorded as employed and they were in domestic service, the dressmaking trade, or other menial jobs. Sheerness was, without doubt, a single industry town heavily dependent upon the dockyard, the military, and government defence expenditure for its well-being.

In 1871, less than half the population of Sheerness was native born (Figure 5.13) and, in accordance with other dockyard towns, the migration field of Sheerness was dominated by neighbouring

Figure 5.13: Birthplace of Sheerness residents, 1871

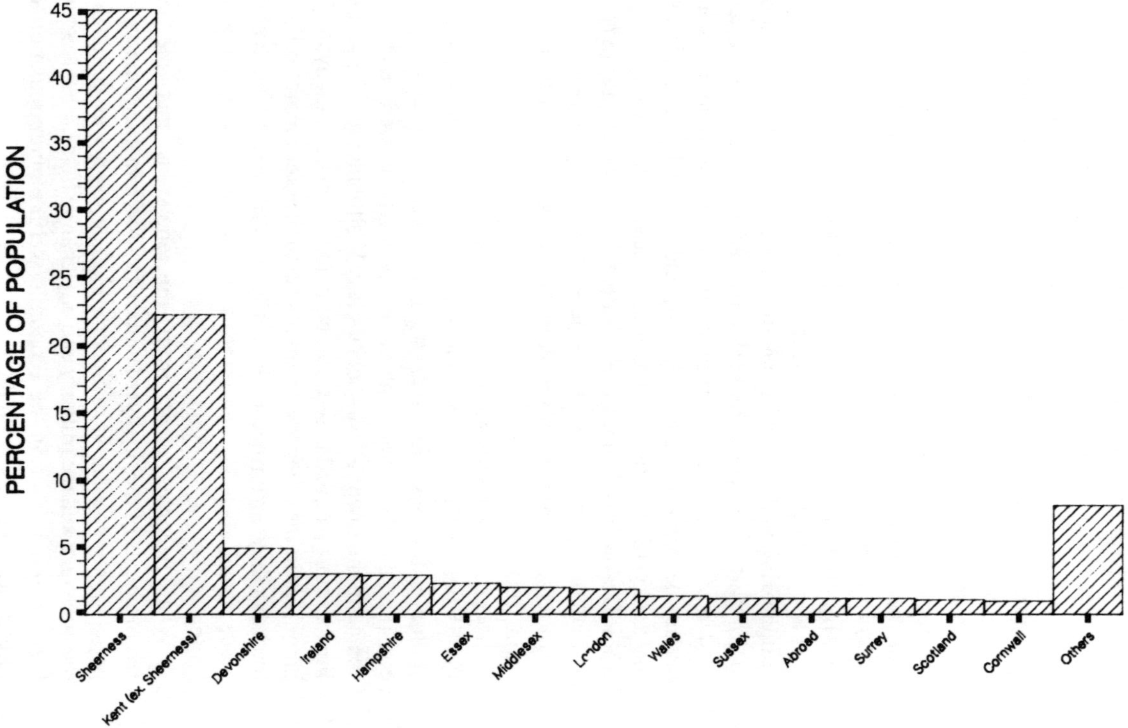

counties and the dockyard counties of Hampshire, Devonshire and Pembrokeshire. Dockyard towns were dominant in the migration network of Sheerness. An examination of the birthplace of children born to migrating parents shows that many migrants arrived in Sheerness by first being drawn into a migration network consisting predominantly of dockyard towns, and then circulating within it before entering Sheerness (Harris, 1982b). The dockyard towns, it seems, acted as a system of labour markets which 'captured' labour from outside and then retained it within the system. The role of information feedback mechanisms and linkages between these nodes contributed over a period of time to the formation of a migratory sub-system based on the dockyard-urban system. Such patterns reflect the specialist demands for labour by the dockyard authorities and the existence of a dockyard-urban system under the central control of government.

Migration into Sheerness was, therefore, spatially selective. It was also demographically selective, for migrants formed the major childbearing sector of the population and, importantly, provided the major part of the workforce (Harris, 1982b). There was certainly a tendency for migration from particular counties to be selective toward certain occupational groups and especially so in the case of the dockyard counties. For example, just under half the migrants from Devon and Hampshire resident in Sheerness in 1871 were skilled dockyard craftsmen, whereas less than 3 per cent were labourers. The situation was almost reversed in the case of migrants from Ireland.

Sheerness was a town dominated by persons of social class III and IV (55 per cent and 15 per cent, respectively), the skilled and semi-skilled categories. In contrast, social classes I and II, which constituted only 8 per cent of the population, were under-represented in the town, as was social class V although to a lesser extent. Furthermore, a good case could be made for placing many dockyard labourers in the category of semi-skilled workers more in line with the tasks they performed in the yards and this would effectively have made social class V even smaller and social class IV reciprocally larger.

What becomes clear from the above is that the labour requirements of the dockyard authorities had a marked impact on the population composition of Sheerness. The town was dominated by the dockyard and the military and any change in these basic activities had a major impact on the economic welfare and population structure of the town as a whole.

SOCIO-SPATIAL STRUCTURE IN 1871

The socio-spatial structure of Sheerness was greatly influenced by the employment base and the morphological development of the town. The process of colonisation imposed upon the township by the restrictions of the fortifications and government ownership of land, resulted in newer houses being constructed at an increasing distance from the dockyard. The resultant social patterns relate closely to the various stages of urban development in Sheerness. As in the case of Woolwich, a matrix of the population characteristics of each street block in Sheerness, based upon the census schedules of 1871, was subjected to principal component analysis (Tables 5.4 and 5.5).

As in the case of Woolwich, the analysis produced two components of contrasting socioeconomic status. The first component accounted for 15 per cent of the variance and reflects high socioeconomic status. Dockyard employees and labourers loaded negatively on this component. The component scores indicate that three distinct areas of Sheerness were characterised by residents of high socioeconomic status: in that area of Blue Town consisting of High Street and West Street; the Broad Street area of Mile Town; and parts of the more recently constructed Marine Town, particularly those fronting the sea (Figure 5.14). The location quotient plot of social classes I and II bears close resemblance to this pattern with the notable exception of High Street and West Street in Blue Town which were marked more by the presence of servants servicing hotel accommodation than by persons of high socioeconomic status.

Component two accounted for nearly 14 per cent of the total variance and is a measure of low socioeconomic status. Once again, dockyard employees loaded negatively on this component. They, it seems, were residentially differentiated from those of both high or low socioeconomic status. Streets characterised by residents of low socioeconomic status were concentrated in the older settlement of Blue Town and especially in the central and south eastern sections of the town (Figure 5.15). In Mile Town, such clusters occurred in the back streets, alleys and courtways of the town but were much less extensive than in Blue Town. Marine Town was practically devoid of labourers and those of low socioeconomic status.

The third component, amounting to 11 per cent of total variance, is a measure of high population density, a youthful population, the presence of Scottish born and of military personnel. The resultant component score patterns are complex and care must be taken not

Table 5.4: Loading of the original variables on the first five principal components: Sheerness, 1871

Variable	Formulation		Loadings on components 1	2	3	4	5
1	*	Irish born	0.074	0.531	0.907	−0.238	0.390
2	*	Scottish born	0.185	0.096	0.542	−0.194	−0.102
3	*	Welsh born	−0.153	−0.256	0.020	0.002	0.235
4	*	Foreign born	0.484	0.225	−0.138	−0.134	0.385
5	*	Lodgers	0.241	0.254	−0.264	0.331	0.529
6	*	Servants	0.648	0.016	0.381	0.289	−0.149
7	*	Age over 60 years	0.168	−0.123	−0.577	−0.085	−0.031
8	*	Age 0–14 years	−0.571	0.044	0.506	−0.093	−0.077
9	*	Female head of household	0.149	0.456	−0.375	−0.450	0.128
10	o	Social class I and II	0.772	−0.004	−0.005	−0.152	−0.217
11	o	Social class IV and V	−0.214	0.840	0.029	0.143	−0.218
12	+	Population density	−0.081	0.148	0.680	0.324	0.435
13	+	Multiple occupancy	−0.146	0.225	0.184	−0.321	0.496
14	+	Male–female ratio	−0.540	0.221	−0.114	0.227	−0.018
15	o	Dockyard employees	−0.442	−0.728	−0.008	−0.292	0.218
16	o	Tertiary personnel	0.256	−0.141	−0.077	0.693	0.099
17	o	Labourers	−0.470	0.630	−0.250	0.125	−0.295
18	o	Military and naval personnel	0.352	0.165	0.424	−0.334	−0.276

* As a percentage of population in each street block.
o As a percentage of economically active persons in each street block.
\+ As a ratio of all persons in each street block.

Table 5.5: Summary of results of principal components with eigenvalues greater than one, for Sheerness, 1871

	Component 1	2	3	4	5	6	7
Eigenvalue	2.72	2.50	2.02	1.52	1.44	1.35	1.17
Percentage explanation	15.10	13.80	11.26	8.44	8.00	7.48	6.52
Cumulative explanation	15.10	29.00	40.36	48.70	56.70	64.28	70.70

Figure 5.14: High and low scores on component one: Sheerness

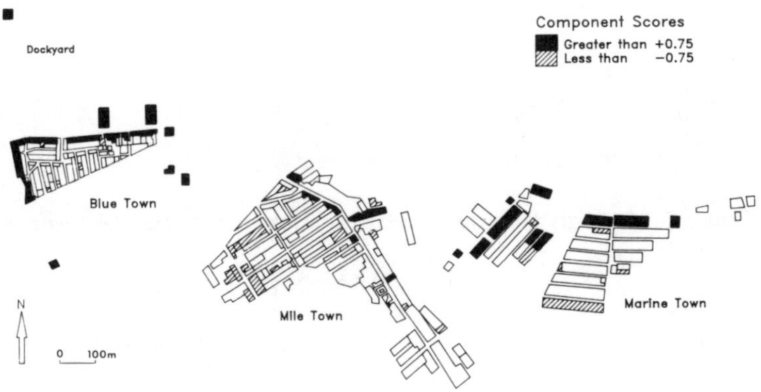

to confuse population density with overcrowding. For this reason, little emphasis is placed on patterns of population density. Military personnel appear to have dispersed throughout the town.

The fourth component is clearly related to tertiary activities which clustered in the known trading areas in Mile Town and in the traditional tertiary areas of High Street and West Street in Blue Town (Figure 5.16). This sector appears to have been quite extensive in 1871 and supported by workers resident in streets behind the main frontages. During the twentieth century, the tertiary sector in Blue Town was to wane dramatically in favour of the more central sector in Mile Town. The fifth component is an indication of the intensity of housing use in which the number of lodgers, multiple

Figure 5.15: High and low scores on component two: Sheerness

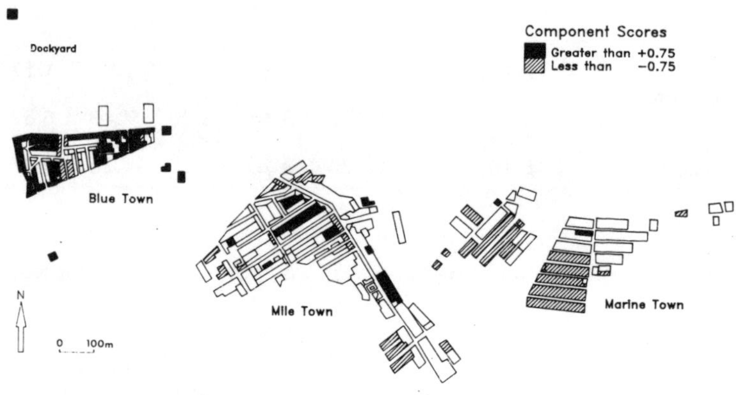

Figure 5.16: High and low scores on component four: Sheerness

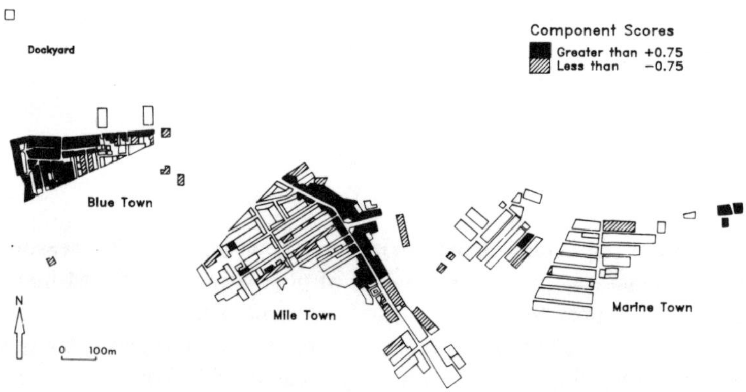

Figure 5.17: High and low scores on component five: Sheerness

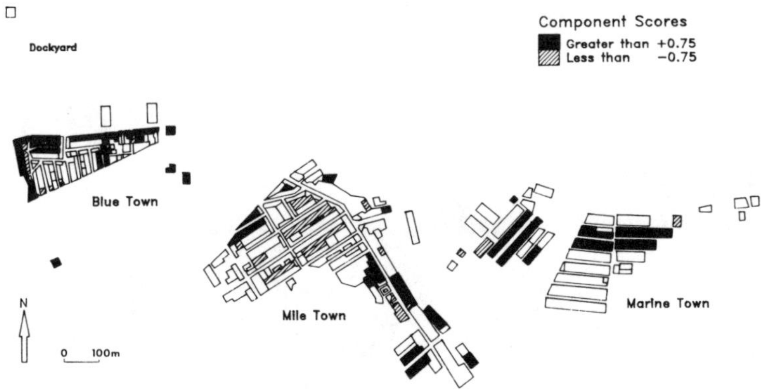

occupancy and population density are important elements (Figure 5.17). The lodging house area in Blue Town fronting the dockyard bears considerable similarity with that identified in Woolwich.

A discriminant classification analysis, as detailed earlier in this chapter, involving the classification of component scores across all five components, resulted in an optimal classification of streets into ten groups (Figure 5.18 and Table 5.6). As in the Woolwich analysis, the social patterns generated by such a classification mirrors those discussed earlier but they do add considerably to the delineation of relatively homogeneous social areas. Thus, streets identified by group one which clustered in those parts of Marine Town fronting the sea and in Blue Town, represent areas of high socioeconomic status in which dockyard personnel, labourers and tertiary workers were notably absent. Streets in group ten similarly contained residents of high socioeconomic status in conjunction with tertiary and military personnel and a high population density. These latter streets contained the known hotels and military quarters in Sheerness. The tertiary sector proper, devoid of the lodging and hotel component of group ten, is indicated by group three and consisted primarily of Broad Street in Mile Town.

Streets identified by group two, which occur only in Mile Town, represent areas of low socioeconomic status and low population density in which tertiary personnel were notably absent. Streets in

Figure 5.18: Component scores classified into residential types: Sheerness

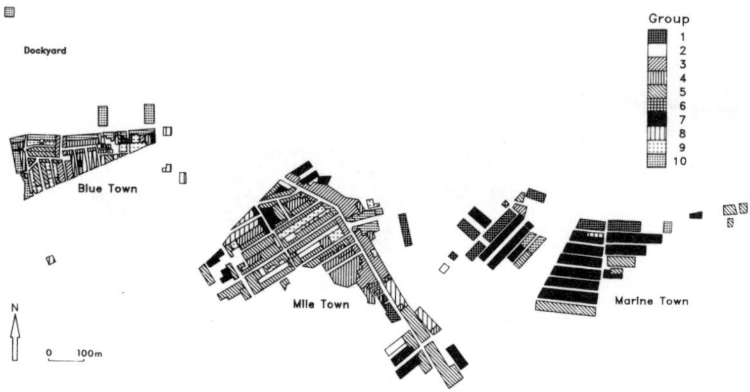

Table 5.6: Loadings of groups one to ten on original five principal components, for Sheerness

Group	Component 1	Component 2	Component 3	Component 4	Component 5
1	1.19	−0.10	0.18	−1.02	−0.81
2	0.05	−0.91	−1.48	−0.92	−0.21
3	0.61	−0.87	−0.69	1.18	0.08
4	−0.69	0.54	0.30	0.20	−0.72
5	−0.28	−0.23	−0.01	0.32	0.03
6	1.88	1.73	−2.32	−1.24	1.86
7	−0.62	−1.01	0.37	−0.57	0.41
8	−0.42	1.19	0.91	−0.80	1.25
9	−0.64	1.30	−0.93	0.44	−0.65
10	1.60	0.03	0.94	1.28	0.11

group four, located in the back streets of Blue Town and Mile Town, were also characterised by residents of low socioeconomic status and the absence of lodgers. Group eight comprised a composite of Irish migrants, residents of low socioeconomic status, low ranking military personnel, multiple occupancy and high population density. Dockyard personnel were notably absent from these areas which were primarily located in Blue Town and parts of Mile Town. Streets in group nine also contained residents of low socioeconomic status and an absence of dockyard workers and were to be found in Blue Town and in the alleys and courtways of Mile Town. Residents of low socioeconomic status were almost completely absent from Marine Town. Possibly as a result of very small street populations, no dominant component exists for group six.

Streets identified by group five and group seven dovetail closely together and correspond with the location quotient plot of dockyard personnel in Sheerness (see Figure 5.10). The former were characterised by the absence of residents of high or low socioeconomic status and the presence of both tertiary and some lower grade dockyard workers. This group dominated most of central Mile Town and several streets to the east of Mile Town and in Marine Town. Importantly, streets in group seven were similarly characterised by the absence of residents of high or low socioeconomic status and tertiary workers but were dominated by skilled dockyard artisans. As was found in Woolwich, these streets formed a distinct neighbourhood cluster in Marine Town and in peripheral parts of Mile Town. Dockyard artisans were almost completely absent from Blue Town.

A distinct socioeconomic gradient can be discerned in the social geography of Sheerness at this time in which residents of low socioeconomic status were prominent in Blue Town in the west and those of high socioeconomic status resided in Marine Town toward the east. This pattern had been greatly influenced by the morphological development of the town and, in this, government played a major role. There is little doubt that, as the colonising movement proceeded during the first half of the nineteenth century, the older congested residential areas in Blue Town were vacated by skilled dockyard artisans and those of high socioeconomic status who removed to more recently constructed and better quality housing, initially in Mile Town and subsequently to Marine Town. Indeed, the earliest inhabitants of Mile Town are recorded as having been dockyard artificers and clerks (Public Record Office, ADM 7/3189). The housing in Blue Town, with the exception of the hotel section in High Street and West Street, had subsequently filtered down to the poorer classes. Without analysis of the intervening years, between the first movement out of Blue Town in the 1820s and the patterns discerned in 1871, it is difficult to comment on the specific nature of the intra-urban movement which generated these patterns. It is possible that some residential movement out of Blue

Town may have, at a later date, been direct to Marine Town, but it is much more likely there was a staging process in which the initial decanting of residents out of Blue Town to Mile Town was then followed by a later duplicate movement out of Mile Town to Marine Town. Whatever the precise mechanics of the process, the colonising process in the fortified dockyard town facilitated the evacuation of skilled dockyard personnel from the older parts of the town to relocate and cluster in the colonies. This pattern is very similar to the residential segregation of dockyard artisans in the dockyard colony of New Brompton as well as that discerned in Woolwich (Harris, 1982a, pp. 216–28). The residential segregation of skilled dockyard workers to form an artisan elite is a distinct feature of the dockyard town and is considered in the following section.

A DOCKYARD ARTISAN ELITE

The residential clustering of dockyard artisans during the nineteenth century stemmed from occupational and workplace affiliations in the yards. The naval dockyards were the first craftbased organisations to become an industry involving a high degree of labour specialisation (Nef, 1934; and Coleman, 1953). Strict occupational demarcation existed in the dockyard in which employment comprised 'established' or permanent skilled employees, and 'hired' or temporary workers (Waters, 1977). The aristocrats of the dockyard workforce were the established shipwrights who made up between one-third to one-half of the workforce (MacLeod, 1925a and 1925b). At the other extreme, labourers largely fell into the category of temporary workers. The status of skilled 'established' craftsmen was maintained by a lengthy and restricted apprenticeship system.

During the nineteenth century, this high level of labour specialisation led to the development of an artisan ideology which was reflected in the residential segregation of the dockyard elite (Crossick, 1978). Crossick contends that the workplace and its relationship were central to this process of stratification within the working class at this time and that this led to the development of an artisan elite.

> The . . . artisan elite was separated from lower strata by a complex of social, economic and cultural characteristics, and to some extent divided internally amongst precisely demarcated crafts. This aristocracy of labour, and the skilled workers who

> shared its aspirations if not its achievements, was defined by more than income alone. Social status, opportunity and behaviour reinforced the elitist potential offered by a stable and relatively adequate income. These artisans were conscious of their superiority over other sections of the working class, especially their labourers and the 'dishonourable' sections of their own trades, and they held an ambiguous position at the very time when they were the only organised section of the working class, organised within trade unions and, with those white collar and petit-bourgeois groups with which they were seen by contemporaries to merge, dominating the benefit societies, building societies, co-operatives and working men's clubs . . . Their superiority rested partly on earnings and job security . . . and the type of work done (Crossick, 1978, pp. 60–1).

The strict demarcation in the dockyard workforce according to occupational status spilled over into the residential structure of the town. The permanency of employment as well as the level of wages must have played an important part in this process, for fluctuations in employment in the yards predominantly revolved around the laying-off and taking-on of unskilled 'hired' personnel. The residential areas of these workers were characterised by a highly transient population. This was in distinct contrast to the more highly paid, skilled, established workers who resided in better quality housing in distinct residential neighbourhoods. Furthermore, the artisan elite was itself comprised of a hierarchy based on occupational status and, as at New Brompton, this did result in the residential clustering of dockyard artisans based upon specific occupational trades (see Harris, 1982a, pp. 216–28).

The process by which this clustering occurred in fortified dockyard towns was greatly facilitated by nineteenth-century colonisation. Construction of housing in the colonies at that time permitted dockyard artisans to relocate and cluster amongst their peers in socially acceptable areas. The colonising process, however, was not a prerequisite for this segregation, as the formation of the dockyard artisan neighbourhood in Woolwich demonstrates. Here, the clustering took place in an area constructed in the decade following the establishment of the Steam Factory in the 1830s. The formation of similar neighbourhoods in the fortified dockyard town, as at Chatham and Sheerness, took place over a longer period, but was considerably facilitated by the development of new housing estates during the colonising process. It was thus the development of new housing estates during the nineteenth century which was important in the formation of artisan elite neighbourhoods.

CONCLUSION

The role of government in the genesis and development of the dockyard-urban system was fundamental. In many respects the central control exerted over the multisite dockyard organisation was an early precursor of more recent trends in industrial organisation which have become such important economic components of the contemporary spatial system (see, for instance, Goddard, 1977 and 1978). The development and well-being of the dependent townships was inextricably linked to defence funding, for very few alternative sources of employment existed in the dockyard towns. The stationing of military and naval personnel in the towns and the presence of other defence-related employment nearby, only served to emphasise the dependence of the communities on the decisions and funding of government.

The social composition of the dockyard towns clearly reflected their narrow employment base and the specialist labour requirements of the dockyards. Changes in defence policy affecting the operational use of the dockyards necessarily impinged upon population structure. Residential patterns in the towns were greatly influenced by government ownership of land and by the impact of fortifications on the morphological development of the towns. Furthermore, the residential segregation of the dockyard elite during the nineteenth century was the spatial expression of an artisan ideology based on workplace affiliations generated within the dockyards.

The dockyard towns possess many of the features of single function towns, although the long involvement of government with the dockyard-urban system can scarcely have an equal in this country. What the preceding discussion has demonstrated is that government involvement in urban and regional development via the allocation of defence-related funding is not a recent phenomenon.

NOTE

1. The choice of the 1861 census for Woolwich was enforced by the devastation caused by the closure of the dockyard in 1869. The sample sizes amounted to 8,570 individuals for Woolwich and 5,960 for Sheerness.

REFERENCES

Briggs, J.H. (1897) *Naval Administration 1827–92*, Sampson Low, London.
Cassetti, E. (1964) *Classificatory and Regional Analysis by Discriminant Iterations*, Technical Report no. 12, Computer Applications in the Earth Sciences, Department of Geography, Northwestern University.
Coleman, D.C. (1953) 'Naval Dockyards under the Later Stuarts', *Economic History Review*, 6, 134–55.
Crossick, G. (1978) *An Artisan Elite in Victorian Society: Kentish London 1840–1880*, Croom Helm, London.
Defoe, D. (1948) *A Tour through England and Wales*, Everyman, I, 97, reprint.
Goddard, J.B. (1977) 'Urban Geography: City and Regional Systems', *Progress in Human Geography*, 1, 296–303.
Goddard, J.B. (1978) 'Urban and Regional Systems', *Progress in Human Geography*, 2, 309–31.
Harris, T.M. (1982a) 'Government and the Development of a Specialised Urban System: the Case of the Royal Naval Dockyard Towns in Great Britain', unpublished PhD, University of Hull.
Harris, T.M. (1982b) *Sibling Time-Paths: an Examination of Nineteenth Century Migration to a Dockyard Town*, Occasional Paper no. 6, Portsmouth Polytechnic.
Harris, T.M. (1984) 'Government and Urban Development in Kent: the Case of the Royal Naval Dockyard Town of Sheerness', *Archaeologia Cantiana*, CI, 245–76.
HMSO (1869) *Parliamentary Papers* XXXVIII, 491, 495.
Herbert, D.T. and Smith, D.M. (eds) (1979) *Social Problems and the City. Geographical Perspectives*, Oxford University Press.
King, L.J. (1969) *Statistical Analysis in Geography*, Englewood Cliffs, 204–15.
Lyon, H. (1977) 'The Relations between the Admiralty and Private Industry in the Development of Warships', in Ranft, B. (ed) *Technical Change and British Naval Policy 1860–1939*, Hodder and Stoughton, London.
MacLeod, N. (1925a) 'The Shipwrights of the Royal Dockyards', *Mariner's Mirror*, 11, 276–90.
MacLeod, N. (1925b) 'The Shipwright Officers of the Royal Dockyards', *Mariner's Mirror*, 11, 355–69.
Naish, G.P.B. (1958) 'Ships and Shipbuilding', in Singer, C. (ed.) *A History of Technology 1500–1750*.
Nef, J.U. (1934) 'The Progress of Technology and the Growth of Large Scale Industry in Great Britain', *Economic History Review*, V, 3–24.
Pahl, R.E. (1977) 'Managers, Technical Experts and the State: Forms of Mediation, Manipulation and Dominance in Urban and Regional Development', in Harloe, M. (ed.) *Captive Cities*, 49–60.
Pollard, S. and Robertson, P. (1979) *The British Shipbuilding Industry 1870–1914*, Harvard University Press.
Ravenstein, A. (1885) 'The Laws of Migration', *Journal of the Statistical Society*, 48, 176.

Rawlinson, R. (1851) *Report to the General Board of Health on a Preliminary Inquiry into the Sewerage, Drainage and Supply of Water and the Sanitary Conditions of the Inhabitants of the Parish of Woolwich in the County of Kent*.

Riley, R.C. (1976) 'The Industries of Portsmouth in the Nineteenth Century', *Portsmouth Papers*, no. 25, Portsmouth City Council.

Sandler, S. (1967) 'The Emergence of the Modern British Capital Ship 1863–70', *Bulletin of the Institute of Historical Research*, XL, 118–20.

Smailes, A.E. (1943) 'Ill-balanced Communities: a Problem in Planning', in Gutkind, E.A. (ed.) *Creative Demobilisation*, Kegan Paul, Trench and Trubner, London.

Turmine, H.T.A. (1843) *Rambles in the Island of Sheppey*, Sheerness.

Vincent, W.T. (1890) *The Records of the Woolwich District*, J.S. Virtue, London.

Waters, M. (1977) 'Craft Consciousness in a Government Enterprise: Medway Dockyardmen 1860–1906', *Oral History*, 5, 1.

Williams, P. (1982) 'Restructuring Urban Managerialism: Towards a Political Economy of Urban Allocation', *Environment and Planning*, 14, 95–105.

6

The Evolution of a Naval Shipbuilding Firm in a Small Economy: Vickers at Barrow-in-Furness

Keith Grime

Barrow-in-Furness is located at the southern extremity of the Furness peninsula in Cumbria (Figure 6.1) and has today (1981 census) a population of 61,734. This total excludes the town of Dalton-in-Furness and the village of Askam-in-Furness which were added to Barrow in 1974. This adjustment has been made to ensure comparability with earlier census data. The town is dominated both economically and physically by the works of Vickers Shipbuilding and Engineering Ltd (VSEL).

VSEL is the biggest and most profitable warship building group in the United Kingdom and in 1984 made a trading profit of £17.7 million on a turnover of £259.9 million. The site covers some 187 acres and, in January 1986, 12,646 employees were on the payroll. In a recent debate on the future of VSEL — the company is currently being privatised — Dr Rodney Leach, the company's Chief Executive and Managing Director described Barrow as 'the British company town' *par excellence*. Few would venture to disagree.

Barrow is, perhaps, most famous for the production of submarines, the first of which was built exactly one hundred years ago but, since the yard was established in 1871, many cruisers, battleships and frigates in addition to liners and cargo vessels have also been built. VSEL not only build ships but also manufacture marine engines and, importantly, in the context of this book, naval and land armaments. In the past twenty-one years VSEL has built only one commercial vessel, but order books have been kept full with contracts for both the British Admiralty and foreign governments. VSEL is the only builder of nuclear submarines in the United Kingdom and three are currently being constructed, together with

Figure 6.1: The Furness peninsula — places mentioned in the text

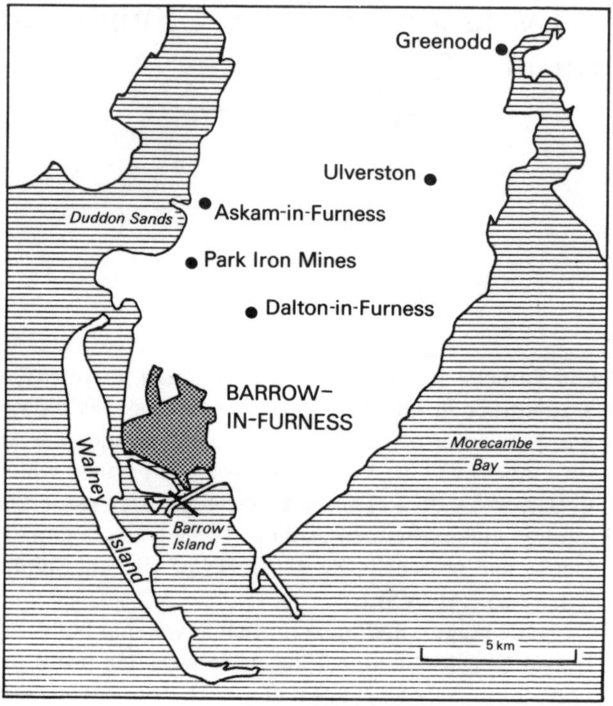

the first of a new class of conventional submarines. The most important project for the immediate future, however, is the contract for the production of four Trident missile-carrying nuclear submarines. Surrounded in controversy and likely to be scrapped if the Conservatives lose the next General Election, it throws into sharp focus the dilemma of being involved in defence contracts. Contracts are subject not only to the belligerence of nations but also to conflicting political ideologies. However, rising above the town is the physical symbol of the current project: a 25,000 square metre construction shed costing £230 million (see Plate 6.1).

This chapter is divided into three clearly defined sections and throughout an attempt is made to place the role of the shipyard and engineering works in the overall context of the town's development and economic structure. The first section, after briefly referring to

Plate 6.1: The new construction hall at Vickers Shipbuilding and Engineering Company Limited, Barrow-in-Furness, in relation to the town centre

the earliest recorded reference to warship building, explains how Barrow developed from the opening of the Furness Railway in 1846 to the establishment of the Barrow Iron Shipbuilding Company in 1871. This early development is considered to be very important for it demonstrates how the creation of the shipyard was the logical outcome of a variety of industrial projects which were highly interdependent. The second section covers the period from 1871 to the end of the Great War (1919) and indicates how by 1911, through a series of takeovers, the Iron Shipbuilding Company became Vickers Ltd. The reasons why Vickers built a model village, Vickerstown, are also given. The third and last section takes the story from 1919 through the Second World War and on into the nuclear age, culminating with an assessment of the importance of VSEL to the present structure of the economy. Not always has it been possible to isolate exactly how many jobs have been directly related to defence contracts, but for various years, particularly from 1933 to 1966, it has been possible to discover the value of sales which gives a reasonable proxy for employment. Another problem has been that often the data provided by the shipbuilding yard on the one hand and the engineers on the other, have proved to be incompatible. For example, the engineers provided much greater financial detail from 1956 to 1985 with respect to sales from different contracts than the shipbuilders who provided only employment totals. However, without the co-operation of VSEL it would have been impossible to write this section and I acknowledge the assistance given.

THE ORIGINS OF THE BARROW IRON SHIPBUILDING COMPANY

Although it was short-lived, early shipbuilding in Furness was in fact concerned with warship construction. Barnes (1968) reports that in 1667 Samuel Pepys 'caused a survey to be made of the harbour of Piel to ascertain its suitability for building Men-o-War. As a result a contract was granted to Sir Thomas Strickland to build a Third-Rate Warship at ''Pill of Fowdry'' using wood from the ''Forest of Myerscough'' across Morecombe Bay, the dimensions to be 122 feet keel, 38 feet breadth, making 937 tons at an approximate cost of £7,600'. An entry in a manuscript in the Public Record Office dated 1 April 1668 infers that a start was actually made, but the ship was never completed — a treaty of peace with Holland

Figure 6.2: Barrow-in-Furness, 1851

Crown copyright reserved

putting an end to naval building.

A small shipbuilding industry flourished in Ulverston and Greenodd in the eighteenth century and indeed the first Barrow shipbuilders gained their experience in Ulverston. William Ashburner, for example, who hailed from Ulverston, built his first ship, a schooner of 94 tons, in Barrow in 1852, and his success led to the opening of a repair yard by Joseph Rawlinson. This concern was sold in 1868 to James Fisher, the founder of a local shipping firm who expanded the business to repair his own ships and build new ones. In 1871 the Iron Shipbuilding Company was formed by James Ramsden, amongst others, and in 1877 the company received its first orders for naval vessels. The shipyard must not be viewed in isolation, rather it must be considered in the context of the way in which Barrow as a whole developed after 1846. Already it has been mentioned that this was the year which saw the advent of the railway (Figure 6.2), an event which irrevocably laid the foundations for the phenomenal developments which took place in the next twenty years. Simply to catalogue the events is insufficient; it is necessary to examine the personalities involved and trace the intricate linkages which bound most of the projects together, and which ultimately gave rise to VSEL.

Undoubtedly the Furness Railway, originally intended to facilitate the export of iron ore and slate, was hugely influential in the growth of mid-nineteenth-century Barrow. The railway was almost entirely financed by shareholders giving London addresses (Marshall, 1958), and indeed it is Pollard's (1952) view that Barrow's principal industrial enterprises were controlled by outside interests because of the comparative backwardness of the district. Whether we should agree with Barnes (1968) that, in the age of railway building, men of wide vision, fearless planning and competent execution were assembling the skeleton of Britain's industrial expansion, is open to question, but certainly in the case of Barrow, it is possible to demonstrate that the planning was dominated by a desire to provide a series of linked enterprises in which the directors of the railway company were always heavily involved.

It is easy, but rather unsatisfactory, to interpret the history of Barrow by focusing on the dominant personalities whose stone statues stand on roundabouts, reminding everyone of the time when they collectively decided the direction in which the embryonic town should develop. Men like James Ramsden, Henry Schneider, Lord Cavendish (originally the Earl of Burlington and later the seventh Duke of Devonshire), and the Duke of Buccleuch are immortalised in stone. If they failed with a statue they certainly have been remembered by a street, a dock or even a tenement block!

James Ramsden is, perhaps, the individual who most influenced the development of Barrow. He was appointed Locomotive Superintendent of the Furness Railway in January 1846 and, although only twenty-three, he fulfilled the duties of general superintendent from the outset. Later he became General Manager, the first mayor of the town when it became a county borough in 1867, a founder of the shipyard in 1871, and was knighted in 1872.

When Ramsden arrived in Barrow the population, according to the Mannex directory of 1846, was 300 and by the 1851 census it had only increased to 448. Even this small increase caused problems for the railway and, according to Pollard (1952), from its inception it was compelled to take on wider social responsibilities, of which the most important was the provision of dwellings for its staff. Before the line actually opened it had been decided to erect ten small cottages to be built 'as cheaply as could be, the price, if possible not to exceed £100 each'.

The first local building programme showed features which were subsequently to become familiar on a much larger scale, namely the use of the company's capital for purposes other than those of the railway itself. Trescatheric (1985) in a well-researched book on the development of Barrow, comments that the building of the ten houses by the railway set a pattern which Barrow followed, with few exceptions, for the next seventy years — company housing built as cheaply as could be, to alleviate surges in demand for workers' housing. Ramsden himself was instrumental in founding the Barrow Building Society in 1848, although few houses were constructed as a result. In 1848–50 a second block of cottages was built by the railway company, but it was not until 1854 that it was able to secure enough land to think in terms of major expansion. A master plan (Figure 6.3) was drawn up, signed by Ramsden in 1856, which envisaged houses for working men in close proximity to the proposed new workplaces.

The plan clearly shows the original nucleus of Barrow and the position of the railway works in relation to it, but its main feature consisted of the proposal to reserve land for engineers, iron founders, and shipbuilders on the shore of Barrow Channel which separates the mainland from Barrow Island on which the shipyard was later to be located. The four squares indicated the type of civic development envisaged, but only Market Square was completed. The streets to the north (Cornwallis, Duncan and St Vincent) were

Figure 6.3: The Ramsden plan for Barrow, 1856

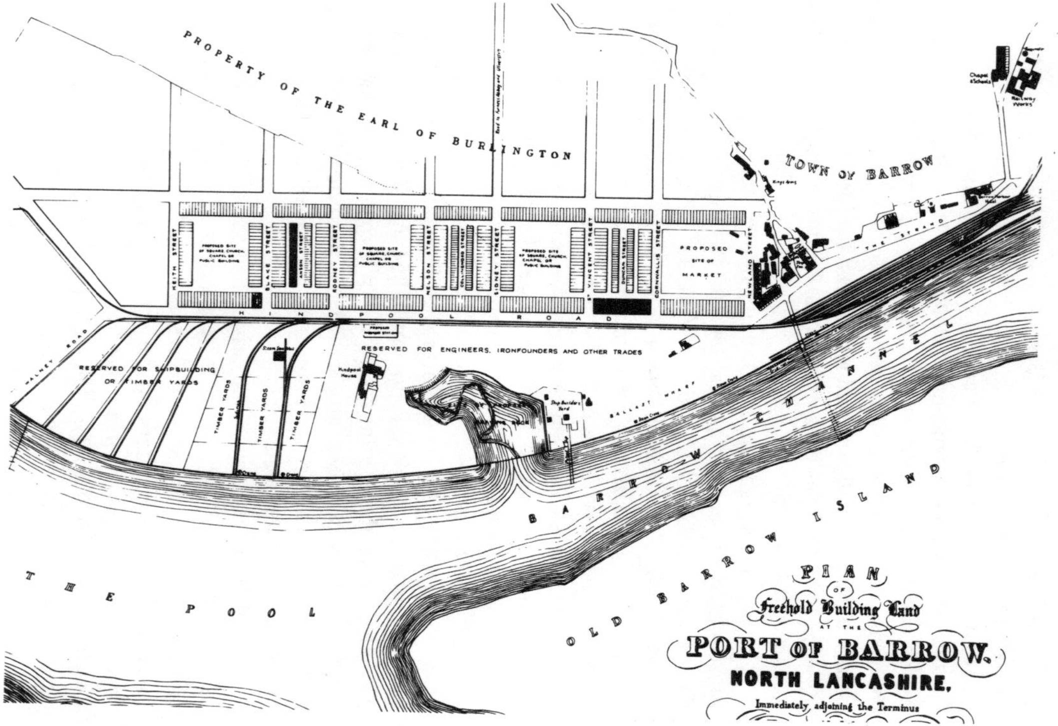

Figure 6.4: Barrow-in-Furness, 1873

actually built and, along with Keith and Sidney which were added later, remain to the present day. Hindpool Road which defined the area on the west, and Duke Street on the east, have been important morphological influences, but the rest of the planned squares and residential streets were never built in the anticipated form. Instead, by the mid 1870s, one had become a cricket ground and on the site of the other two flax and jute mills had been constructed (Figure 6.4). Ramsden is almost unique among industrialist/planners, observe the Bells (1969), in that he gave little attention to housing or to social services, but was concerned with such grandiose notions as avenues and squares. By and large, Barrow left the houses to private speculators, and the railway company concentrated on the provision of a suitably imposing framework, a view which tends to be at variance with Trescatheric's, quoted earlier.

Several very important industrial enterprises were founded after 1856 on land owned by the Furness Railway and in accordance with the Ramsden Plan. The most important by far occurred in 1859 when Schneider and Hannay established their iron works on the Hindpool estate. This was a logical outcome of Schneider's earlier activities because in 1851 he had discovered extensive deposits of iron at Park, and spent the next six years exporting the ore. However, in 1857 when the Furness Railway not only reached Lancaster, but also was linked through the lines of other companies to County Durham, he realised that coking coal could be easily imported. The logical outcome was to smelt the ore at Barrow, and the Furness Railway was closely associated with the project from its inception. It provided the site, the land for workers' dwellings, the roads and sewers, laid a special line of rails to the works, carried its pig iron and coke, and the royalties of the mines worked by Schneider and Hannay belonged to the leading shareholders of the Railway (Pollard, 1952). Even greater involvement followed when, in 1865, the Barrow Haematite Steel Company, planned by Ramsden to be financed by the same shareholders, was jointly promoted with Schneider and Hannay who added their mines and ironworks in return for a permanent seat on the board of directors. The promoters of the Steel Company now included virtually all the capitalists who were to be responsible for the development of Barrow in the next ten years.

In 1863 an Act of Parliament was obtained which vested Barrow Harbour in the Furness Railway Company, empowering it to build docks. Some £137,000 was to be raised as capital and the Dukes of Buccleuch and Devonshire invested heavily. The full system of

Table 6.1: Male and female employment, principal industrial sectors, Barrow-in-Furness, 1871–1911

	1871[a]	1891	1901	1911
Iron and steel	812	2,425	1,765	1,485
Shipbuilding	84	2,362	3,536	4,297
Ironfounding	—	—	304	502
Blacksmiths	190[b]	479	531	456
Erectors, fitters, turners, boilermakers, engineers	318	1,863	4,862	5,019
Hemp	—	1,457	564	520
Iron mining	—	375	223	—
Total industrial employment	4,115	16,798	20,228	20,124

a. Workers aged 20 and above.
b. 'Others in metals'.

Source: Census Reports.

docks was not completed until about 1879, but Gladstone opened the Devonshire Dock in 1867, the Buccleuch was ready by 1873, and the Ramsden Dock was commissioned in 1879. The Cavendish was completed by the end of the 1870s, but never brought into use, and its fate is a symbol of the collapse of the grandiose plans for a Barrow harbour rivalling Liverpool (Barnes, 1968).

The inaugural meeting of the Barrow Iron Shipbuilding Company took place in the private home of James Ramsden in January 1871, and it was agreed that there would be an initial capital outlay of £92,000. The Duke of Devonshire was in attendance and the project, in a sense, marked the culmination of financial interdependence amongst the industrial projects in Barrow, not all of which have been recorded here.

At the time of the formation of the company, Barrow had a male labour force of 6,170, and a total population of 18,774. The 1871 census recorded 4,050 males in industrial occupations, with 812 in iron and steel, 318 described as engine and machine makers and 84 as shipbuilders (Table 6.1). Almost half of the industrial male labour force were, however, listed as general labourers. The physical extent of the town in the mid 1870s is shown in Figure 6.4. The proximity of the housing to the workplaces is clearly seen as well as an indication of the rather haphazard infilling of houses around the 'grand design' proposed in Ramsden's plan of 1856. However, the town was poised for take-off, and during the next twenty years the industrial workforce quadrupled, while the total population

Figure 6.5: Barrow-in-Furness, 1895

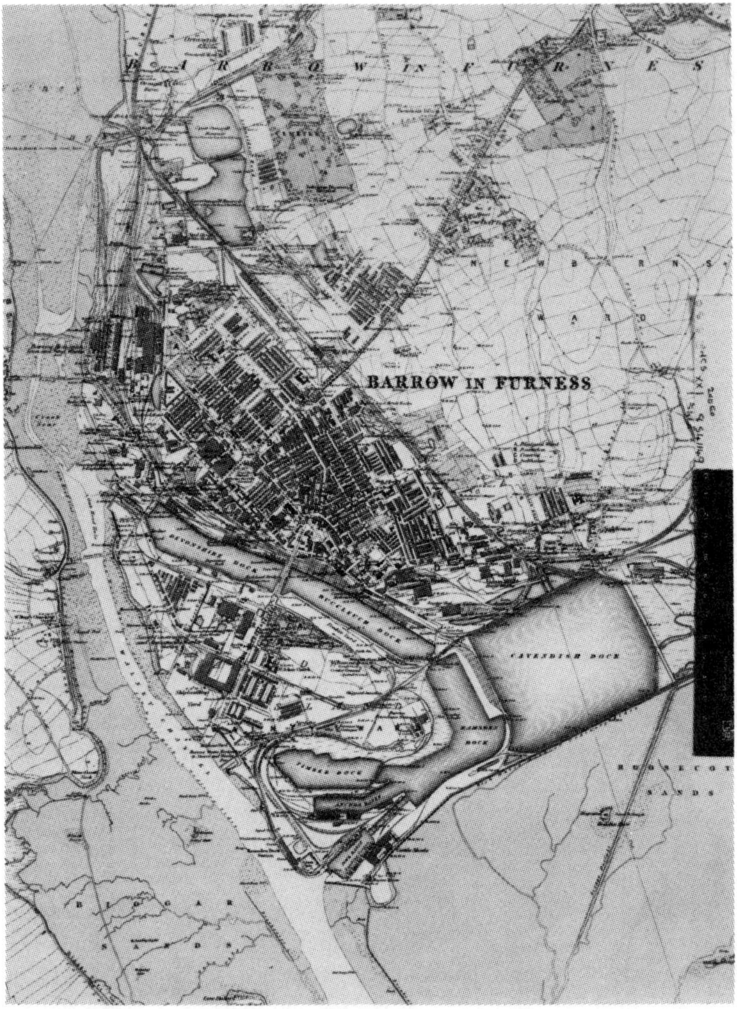

almost trebled, reaching 51,172 by 1891, expanding the town considerably as shown in Figure 6.5.

THE GENESIS AND DEVELOPMENT OF VICKERS, 1871–1911

The first warships, two small gunboats for the British Admiralty, were launched in 1877 and during the next eleven years ten more warships were completed, but most of the early work concentrated on merchant shipping. The development of the Barrow enterprise was strongly influenced by a Swedish engineer, Thorsten Nordenfelt, who came on the scene in the mid 1880s and linked the shipbuilding yard to the production of armaments.

Nordenfelt had patented a hand-powered machine gun in 1879 and manufactured armaments in Sweden. A British company, the Nordenfelt Guns and Ammunition Company Limited, was formed in 1886 and a site at Erith in Kent was bought in 1887. Nordenfelt himself was not only an engineer but also an inventor, and in a separate initiative the Barrow Shipbuilding Company built two submarines for him (neither of which were successful initially) in 1886. In 1887 it was agreed that the Barrow Company could use Nordenfelt's overseas agents, and in 1888, after Nordenfelt himself had joined the Board, the name of the company was changed to the Naval Construction and Armaments Company Limited.

The complicated story which has been fully described by Scott (1962) does not end here, because also in 1888 the Nordenfelt Company amalgamated with the Maxim Gun Company, which had been established in Britain in 1884 (Maxim was an American and inventor of a machine gun). The first chairman of Maxim was Albert Vickers, whose family owned extensive steel mills in Sheffield and who were looking for ways to diversify their portfolio. In 1897 all these interests came together when Vickers purchased the Naval Construction and Armaments Company for £425,000, and achieved an ambition to supply ships complete with engines, guns and machinery. In the same year, Vickers also purchased Maxim Nordenfelt for £1,353,000. The new company was named Vickers Son and Maxim.

Vickers Son and Maxim inherited a workforce of some 5,500 at Barrow and were located in a town which had grown to over 50,000. An indication of the contemporary industrial occupation structure of the town can be seen from the 1891 census (Table 6.1). There were 2,355 males actually engaged in building ships, which was slightly fewer than the 2,421 employed in the other major industrial enterprise — iron and steel. Without doubt the figure of 2,355 is an underestimate of those employed by Vickers Son and Maxim because, in addition to shipbuilders they must have had on the payroll a substantial proportion of the 479 blacksmiths, the 985 fitters and turners, the 581 boilermakers and some of the 1,480 general labourers. Female industrial employment was dominated by the hemp industry where 1,200 of the 2,693 classified as industrial workers were located.

By 1901 the total males in employment had risen to 22,120, of whom 3,536 were in shipbuilding, but again we must add a proportion of both the 2,392 erectors, fitters and turners and the 2,253 in engineering which included boilermakers. Undoubtedly a large number of the 531 blacksmiths would also be employed in the shipyard. Females in the labour force had declined largely because of the difficulties being experienced by the hemp industry (see Table 6.1).

The 1911 census indicates a small rise in total male employment to 22,363 and a rather larger percentage increase in female employment to 4,866. The number of males in shipbuilding rose to 4,297 but again we must add some of the 1,608 erectors, fitters and turners and a proportion of the 758 boilermakers. The number employed in iron and steel fell by almost 1,000 in the intercensal period, and although some of the variation is undoubtedly caused by changes in industrial classification, it nevertheless is clear that by 1911 the shipyard had established itself as the principal employer in the town (see Table 6.1). Between 1890 and 1896 ten warships, including the 14,200 ton cruiser HMS *Powerful*, were launched — all of them for the Royal Navy, and, after the amalgamation in 1897, orders continued to be placed by the Admiralty.

In 1899 an event occurred which proved to have a lasting impact on the future of the company. Yet again the company was influenced by an American inventor. In 1878 J.D. Holland had built his first submarine, but it took 20 years before his designs were accepted by the United States government. However, Isaac Rice bought Holland's patents in 1899 and signed an agreement which granted to Vickers a licence to manufacture Holland submarines. (Incidentally, there appears to have been no follow-up to the original Nordenfelt designs.) The first boat, launched in 1901, was built exactly to Holland's design and it was followed in quick succession by four more. Vickers developed their own submarines and thirteen 'A' class boats were built between 1902 and 1905 and eleven 'B' class in the period 1904–6. Output continued at a phenomenal pace and between 1906 and the end of the Great War in 1918 112 submarines were built, including two for the Australian Navy. Britain entered the war in 1914 with 75 submarines and all except the small Chatham contribution of twelve had been built in Barrow.

Although Barrow was building almost all Britain's submarines, the Royal Navy and foreign governments placed important contracts with the yard. Russia, Japan, Mexico, Peru, Brazil, India, China and Canada all had warships built in Barrow between 1900 and 1914.

The rapid development of the company after 1897 led to a substantial increase in the labour force, much of which moved to Barrow from other parts of the United Kingdom. This influx of population created a demand for housing which the local builders found difficult to satisfy. The new company decided to solve the problem themselves and pioneered a model village. Perhaps inevitably, it was named Vickerstown and followed in the tradition established by the Cadburys at Bournville, Lord Leverhulme at Port Sunlight and Rowntree at New Earswick, although there was not too much 'garden' in the 'village' of Vickerstown.

In 1898 a group of local businessmen announced their intention of developing speculative housing and a seaside resort on Walney Island, which faced the shipyard and was at that time linked to Barrow Island by a ferry. Vickers, meanwhile, were actively considering their own proposals, but in 1899 they decided to purchase the Isle of Walney Estate Company. Trescatheric (1985) believes that it had always been the intention of the local syndicate to attract Vickers into a profitable partnership. He reports that the *Barrow News* announced in the summer of 1899 that enough land had been purchased for a workers' estate, park and playing fields on the eastern side of the island, and that the houses would be of 'modern style' and a model plan similar to those built by the Sunlight Soap Company at Port Sunlight. The original plan was for 1,000 houses to be built in two estates north and south of a proposed valley park. The present-day layout of the development can be seen in Figure 6.6.

The first tenants moved into Vickerstown in November 1900 and by 1904 the original estate was completed: it consisted of approximately 950 houses. Tenants were specially selected: 'A man must prove himself a reliable worker before he can be recommended by his foreman as a tenant and, recognising that a man's home life directly influences his workmanship, the condition of the household

Figure 6.6: Barrow-in-Furness, 1973

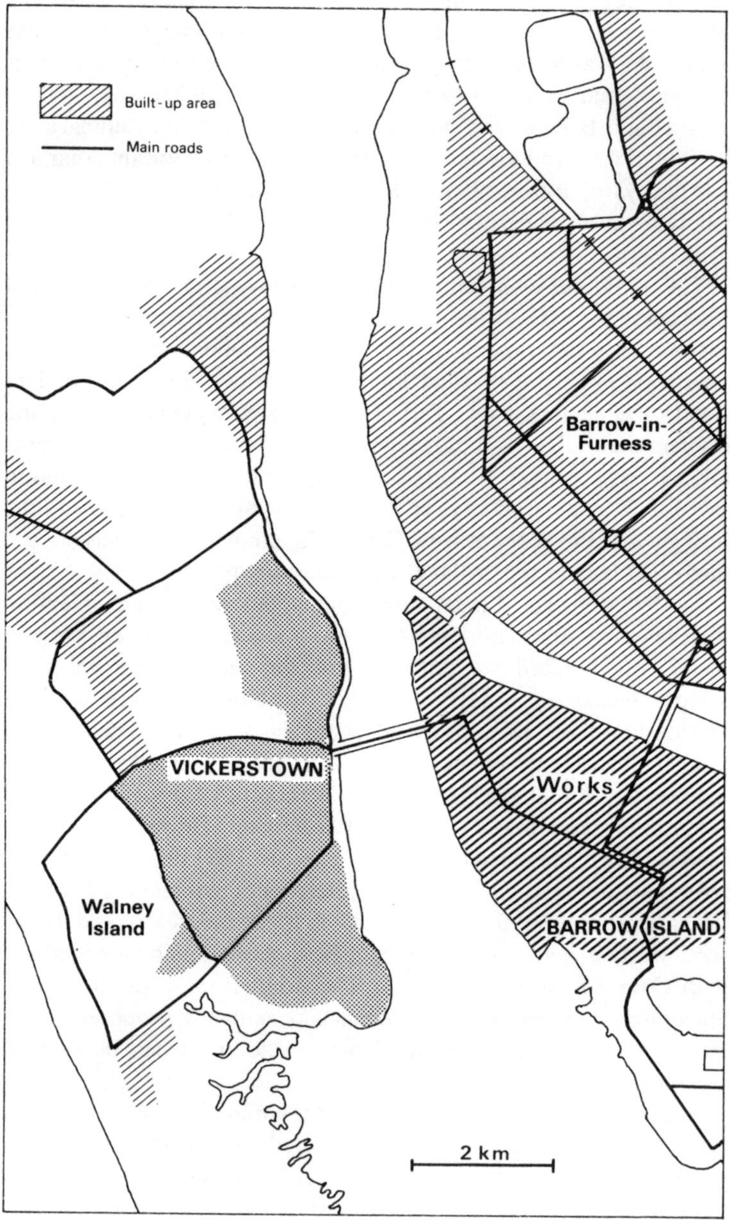

must be maintained satisfactorily to ensure continuance of occupancy. Apart altogether from the financial advantages, residence in Vickerstown thus confers a cherished distinction' (Vickers, 1902). It is clear that the scheme was based on the paternalism pioneered in Port Sunlight, but, because it was built out of sheer necessity, many of the garden city notions which were a feature of Port Sunlight were ignored. It was more an industrial village, but still superior to the existing housing and probably better than speculative builders would have provided.

As rearmament gathered pace so the Vickers labour force increased and by 1913 it had reached 15,600 and, in the summer of 1914 stood at 17,000. Such massive increases caused, once again, severe housing problems and the company entered into a partnership with the town council to purchase twelve acres of land on Barrow Island from the Furness Railway, and on it built one hundred houses. As Trescatheric reports, it was also decided to extend the Vickerstown development and in 1913 a further hundred houses were constructed. In spite of this action he suggests that Vickers commitment to Vickerstown was on the wane.

It is also probably true that, as a private company and in the extraordinary conditions created by the war, Vickers felt that it was not their responsibility to provide accommodation from their own resources. Instead a public utility scheme, called the Walney Housing Company, was established to finance the building of workers' accommodation and a number of houses were built in partnership with the Ministry of Munitions. The houses built in the war were basic and had no architectural distinction. The declining interest of Vickers may be judged from the fact that houses built by the Walney Housing Company were offered for sale although the vast majority of both the new dwellings and those in the original scheme remained in the hands of the company until the 1930s.

BARROW: A SHIPBUILDING ECONOMY

During the war, in 1917, the workforce at Vickers reached an estimated 31,000 made up of shipbuilders, engineers and munition workers. By July 1918 the payroll had fallen to 23,195 and by the time of the 1921 census (Table 6.2) which for the first time classified jobs by industry, it had been reduced to 16,064 of which 347 were women. The dominance of the Vickers Company in Barrow was now absolute. Amongst males the total of 15,717 represented 75 per

Table 6.2: Male and female employment, principal industrial sectors, Barrow-in-Furness, 1921–31

	1921	1931
Iron and steel	2,852	1,570
Shipbuilding	16,064	10,150
Other engineering	559	374
Hemp	279	3
Iron mining	160	14
Paper	465	526
Total industrial employment	22,832	14,232

Source: Census Reports.

cent of all industrial employment and 56 per cent of total employment. In contrast the iron and steel industry although important employed only 2,852, of whom 35 were women. Economic disaster came swiftly. By the summer of 1921 employment was down to 12,244, and in January 1923 only 3,769 were left in the yard. Around 44 per cent of males of working age were unemployed.

The intricate problems which faced the Vickers Company in general and the Barrow division in particular in the period from 1919 onwards are described in detail by Scott (1962). He reports that in 1919 the general manager Sir James McKechnie told the Board of Vickers that Barrow was practically assured of work for ten years, at a profit of not less than 10 per cent. This completely over-optimistic view was based on plans to build railway locomotives instead of armaments, and merchant ships in place of warships. Steam railway locomotives were never built at Barrow but there was some limited success in obtaining orders for merchant ships; for example, the *Orama* was launched in 1924 for the Orient line and the *Carinthia* for Cunard in 1925.

During the 1920s little Admiralty work was forthcoming, largely as a result of the Washington Treaty of 1922 which severely restricted the manufacture of armaments and warships. However, after the merger with Armstrongs in 1927, but not because of it, a limited number of cruisers, destroyers and submarines were built. In 1931 the census (Table 6.2) showed that since 1921 there had been a drop of 7,997 in total male employment in Barrow — almost all in the industrial sector which decreased by 7,880. Shipbuilding and marine engineering accounted for 5,896 of this reduction. In spite of the fall, the 9,821 men employed at the shipyard still represented 74.5

Table 6.3: Vickers Armstrongs Limited: Barrow works — engineering and shipbuilding division combined sales by product, 1933–50 (£000)

Year	Total productive wage	Land and air armaments	Naval armaments	Shipbuilding	General engineering	Others	Total
1933	598	347	615	1,995	164	25	3,145
1934	855	136	847	1,586	138	47	2,755
1935	966	94	917	3,513	385	54	4,964
1936	1,718	262	1,119	2,175	292	124	3,973
1937	1,672	204	1,314	3,438	621	152	5,728
1938	1,623	297	1,581	3,290	382	213	5,762
1939	1,769	543	2,497	2,860	245	322	6,466
1940	2,638	620	1,507	6,733	288	787	9,935
1941	3,090	166	3,527	7,140	362	854	12,049
1942	N/A	672	4,110	9,611	343	1,386	16,121
1943	N/A	143	2,819	6,090	475	970	10,497
1944	N/A	196	2,718	5,737	622	1,478	10,752
1945	N/A	486	1,279	5,889	479	1,672	9,804
1946	N/A	223	4,314	3,062	395	56	8,015
1947	N/A	1,029	1,638	5,545	475	38	8,712
1948	N/A	846	1,655	6,126	959	52	9,638
1949	N/A	803	1,539	7,414	2,481	86	12,323
1950	N/A	570	580	8,890	3,363	142	13,544

Source: VSEL.

per cent of all male industrial workers. During the decade iron mining and the manufacture of hemp had ceased and 1,000 jobs had been lost in iron and steel. Only the paper industry maintained its labour force intact.

In 1933 the total wage bill at Vickers was £598,355 which increased to over £3,000,000 by 1941. An estimate of the relative importance of defence contracts can be made by considering the value of sales (Table 6.3). In 1933 the sale price of all armaments — land, air and naval — was £961,780; by 1936 it had risen to £1,382,088; and at the outbreak of war in 1939 it stood at £3,039,353. Unfortunately the data for shipbuilding in the 1930s are not subdivided between commercial and warships, but the total value of sales gradually rose from slightly under £2,000,000 in 1933 to £2,860,325 in 1939. These figures should be treated with a little caution because payments are irregular and can be misleading but the general upward trend is clear. What is also known is that, although seven passenger liners of over 20,000 tons were built in the period 1930 to 1937, little warship work was undertaken. However, in the second half of the decade orders from both the British Admiralty and foreign governments gradually increased and four warships for Argentina, three for Portugal, two for Estonia and one for Brazil were built between 1934 and 1937.

The Barrow yard specialised in warship construction during the Second World War when 99 submarines were built for the Royal Navy. Receipts from the sales of ships reached a peak of £9.6 million in 1942 (Table 6.3) in which year armaments valued at over £4 million were also sold. The peak year for the sale of armaments was, surprisingly, 1946 but this probably is explained by the government being late in making payments.

The immediate post-war years saw considerable structural change in both the shipbuilding and engineering divisions, but the trauma of unemployment experienced in the 1920s was not repeated. Revenue from land, sea and naval armaments (Table 6.3) fell to just over £1 million by 1950, but additional sales of general engineering products compensated for this decline. Receipts from shipbuilding steadily increased and by 1950 amounted to £8.9 million almost all being derived from merchant rather than naval orders, although the data do not allow a precise breakdown to be calculated.

For the period 1951 to 1954 a clear picture of the contribution made by merchant and warship building is possible (Table 6.4). The total sales increased rapidly but, because of the erratic timing of payments it is impossible to regard any year as typical. However,

Table 6.4: Vickers Armstrongs Limited: Barrow works, engineering and shipbuilding division combined sales by product, 1951–4 (£000)

	Land, air and naval armaments	Warships	Merchant ships	Engineering	Other	Total sales
1951	1,011	312	6,760	1,578	1	9,662
1952	621	2,343	5,035	2,841	–	10,840
1953	2,024	2,391	2,622	3,177	–	10,214
1954	3,164	1,987	10,498	3,531	–	19,180
Total	6,820	7,033	24,915	11,127	1	49,896
Average 1951–4	1,705	1,758	6,229	2,782	–	12,474

Source: VSEL.

Table 6.5: Vickers Armstrongs Limited, shipbuilding division sales of commercial and warships, 1956–66 (£000)

	Commercial	Warships	Total
1956	7,719	4,486	12,205
1957	4,375	3,461	7,836
1958	5,472	3,341	8,813
1959	283	13,507	13,790
1960	12,285	7,836	20,121
1961	3,319	1,052	4,371
1962	6,805	14,801	21,606
1963	276	6,275	6,551
1964	4,677	376	5,049
1965	5,843	22,627	28,471
1966	1,458	26,200	27,658
Total 1956–66	52,510	103,962	156,472
Yearly average	4,774	9,451	14,225

Source: VSEL (shipbuilding).

on average, it can be seen that armaments and warships played a relatively minor role, contributing only 27.8 per cent towards total receipts. Almost half the revenue was derived from the construction of merchant ships which consisted mainly of oil tankers, although two large liners for the P&O Line, the *Oronsay* and the *Orsova*, were launched in 1950 and 1953 respectively.

From 1956 to 1966 income from warship building accounted for exactly two-thirds of total receipts (Table 6.5), although it has to be admitted that a substantial proportion of this figure was received in the last two years of the period under review; 1959 and 1962 were also good years for payments on warships. This decade was the last in which commercial shipbuilding was undertaken in Barrow and it culminated (and terminated) with the launch of Britain's first 100,000 ton oil tanker in 1965. The decade also witnessed the start of nuclear submarine construction at Barrow, as the sales figures for the engineering division show.

Engineering work on nuclear submarines first started in 1958 and by the end of the decade the contribution to total sales was substantial (Table 6.6). Receipts for work done on merchant ships peaked in 1960 and then fell as did revenue derived from warships other than submarines. Gun mountings, too, steadily declined in importance but 'other engineering', including a large contract to build Sulzer diesel engines for British Rail, increased substantially.

The Sulzer contract was completed in 1967–8 and 'other engineering' has subsequently played a less significant role. After the large payments in 1965 and 1966, receipts from nuclear submarine work were surprisingly small throughout most of the 1970s, but since 1979 have become increasingly important, as have revenues from gun mountings, for both naval- and land-based deployment. So by 1984 gun mountings accounted for 38.8 per cent of all sales made by the engineering division, while nuclear submarines added a further 33 per cent. In total 90 per cent of all receipts were directly attributable to defence contracts.

Defence contracts now account for all the work undertaken in the shipyard and, although sales figures are not available, this has largely been the case for the past twenty years. Only one non-military vessel was built during this period — a cruise ship ordered by a Danish shipping line but eventually sold to the Soviet Union.

In 1946 total employment in the combined engineering and shipyard division was 14,500 (Figure 6.7), which probably was below the peak employment achieved during the war (figures for that period are not available). A sharp fall occurred in 1947, but since then total employment has remained remarkably constant, fluctuating between just over an estimated 11,000 in 1956 to 14,000 employed in 1977. This overall consistency belies many changes which have occurred in working practices and changing demands for different skills, but perhaps most significantly of all it belies the remarkable turnround in the contribution to total employment made by the two divisions of the company.

From 1947 to 1964 employment was dominated by the engineering division. Consistently engineering accounted for two-thirds of the total workforce. In the mid 1960s, however, a crossover point occurred and since that time the shipyard division has assumed greater importance, so that at the present time (1985) 67 per cent are employed in the shipbuilding division. Perhaps it is significant that the increasingly important contribution made by the shipbuilding side dates precisely from the time that Vickers became involved in nuclear submarine construction.

The significance of Vickers to Barrow can be placed firmly in perspective by considering the town's male employment structure at the time of each post-war census (Figure 6.8). These data relate only to males resident in the town itself and not to the total labour force employed by Vickers, some of whom live outside the administrative area. However, it is the importance of Vickers to Barrow which we

Table 6.6: Vickers Shipbuilding and Engineering Limited, Barrow works, sales by product, 1956–66 (£000)

	Gun mountings	Submarine parts	Nuclear submarines	Other warships	Merchant ships	Other engineering	Total
1956	2,543	103	–	1,838	3,052	1,949	9,485
1957	3,371	180	–	3,582	4,813	2,916	14,862
1958	1,623	222	4	2,051	4,349	3,973	12,222
1959	2,521	114	2,391	4,344	3,151	4,701	17,222
1960	3,608	84	7,450	3,629	5,089	5,966	25,826
1961	2,171	141	4,250	719	4,079	10,443	21,803
1962	4,535	329	5,441	2,550	2,790	6,291	21,936
1963	1,413	295	2,352	3,292	3,196	7,510	18,058
1964	652	–	2,107	10	895	10,184	13,848
1965	1,222	–	13,927	224	1,756	11,179	28,308
1966	1,293	–	12,780	1,747	1,790	10,352	27,962
1967	1,901	–	16,722	166	1,980	8,336	29,105
1968	1,896	–	9,567	214	487	7,080	19,244
1969	2,388	–	4,254	13	678	3,485	10,818

1970	3,085	—	5,675	—	472	2,873	12,105
1971	5,929	2,711	3,417	—	1,054	3,871	16,982
1972	4,535	264	2,786	3,127	100	1,430	12,242
1973	6,284	1,857	3,387	1,451	—	3,011	15,990
1974	7,447	1,379	3,798	4,126	116	1,762	18,628
1975	8,184	1,777	4,430	1,597	—	3,064	19,052
1976	6,828	3,069	4,797	1,822	43	5,448	22,007
1977[a]	12,770	3,400	4,736	1,436	34	5,676	28,052
1978[b]	14,196	2,541	6,046	2,820	49	2,956	28,608
1979	19,851	3,134	7,445	2,402	103	3,167	36,102
1980	34,163	3,070	9,331	2,747	140	3,106	52,557
1981	29,216	4,810	11,161	2,532	83	2,722	50,524
1982	27,160	4,442	13,275	3,583	219	3,997	52,676
1983	31,086	6,916	17,100	4,241	132	3,776	63,251
1984	21,586	6,755	18,362	3,134	73	5,655	55,565

a. Estimated from a 6 month figure.
b. Estimated from a 9 month figure.

Source: Accounts department VSEL (engineering division).

Figure 6.7: Barrow works: employment in shipbuilding and engineering, 1946–85

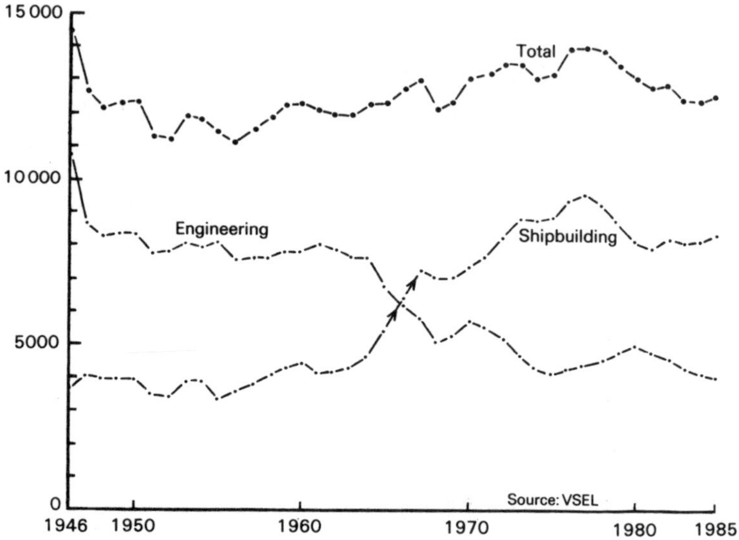

Source: VSEL

are attempting to measure, and the figures enable this to be calculated.

The first and most important point to note is that in 1951, 1961 and 1971 over 10,000 males living in Barrow worked at Vickers, which represented between 43.2 and 45.6 per cent of the total male labour force. No other manufacturing industry remotely challenged this pre-eminent position. Indeed if we consider only manufacturing employment then Vickers accounted for between 65.1 and 72.4 per cent of the total. Such dominance means that effectively Vickers *is* Barrow, and, in spite of government sponsored attempts to diversify the employment structure, especially after the closure of the iron and steel works, other manufacturing enterprises remain insignificant in comparison.

In 1981 the figures for employment are available on a different geographical base compared to earlier census years, but still serve to show how shipbuilding and marine engineering dominate the local economy. In the Barrow-in-Furness travel to work area which

Figure 6.8: Barrow-in-Furness: male employment by industry, 1951–71

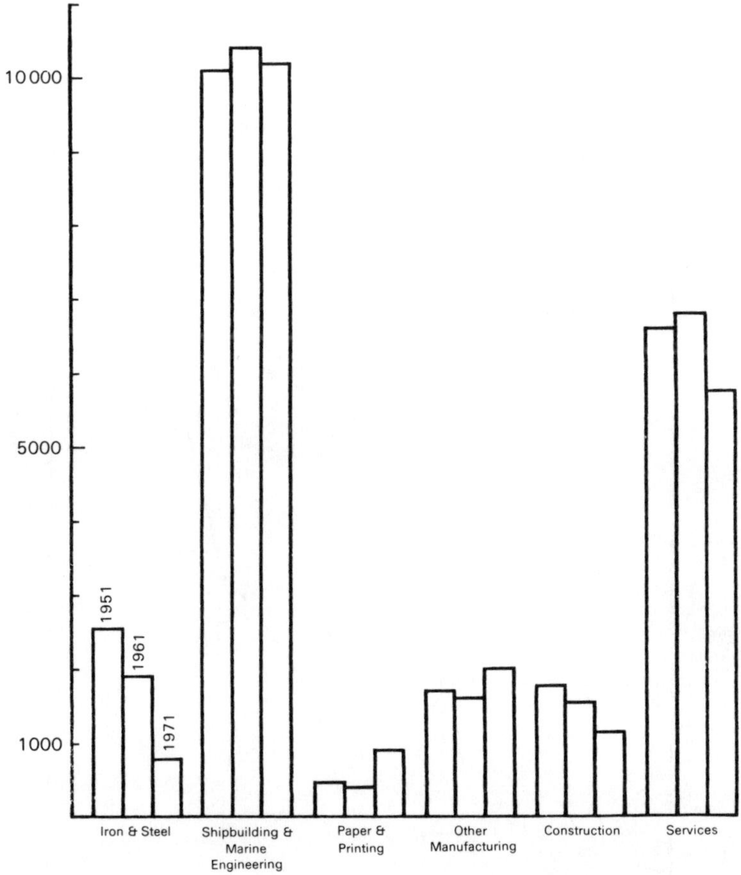

Source: Census of England and Wales, 1951, 1961, 1971

includes Dalton-in-Furness and Ulverston, the total male labour force was 26,063 of whom 11,277 worked at Vickers. This is 43.3 per cent of all male employment and 67.5 per cent of male manufacturing employment. There are only two other manufacturing industries in the whole of the Furness peninsula which employ people on a large scale: Glaxo Pharmaceuticals at Ulverston and Bowater Scott

Figure 6.9: Barrow works (engineering division): income from employment, 1963–84

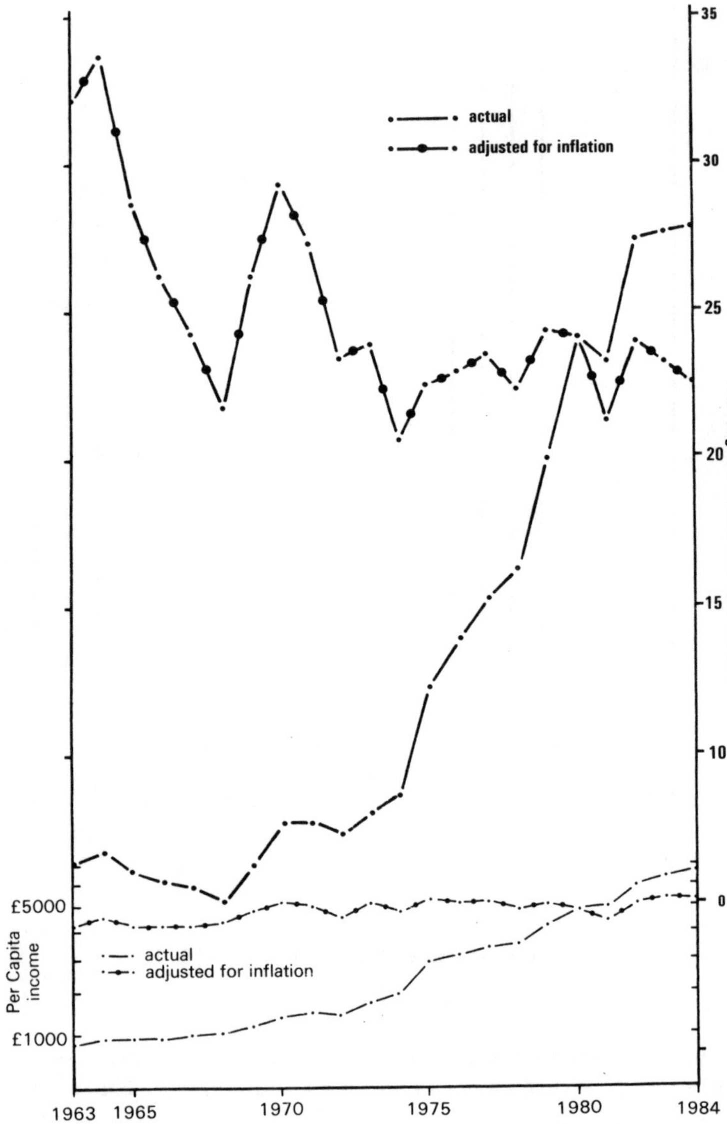

Source: VSEL

at Barrow (paper manufacturers). These two industries account respectively for 11.9 per cent and 8.1 per cent of the male manufacturing employment.

An indication of the spending power injected into the local economy can be seen from Figure 6.9, which shows income from employment for the engineering division of VSEL on an annual basis from 1963 to 1984. During this twenty-one year period the per capita income rose from £818 to £6,558, and the total wages bill increased from £6.2 to £25.7 million. Much of this increase is, of course, attributable to inflation, but the adjusted figures do show a rise in real income from £4,218 in 1963 to £5,349 in 1984 on a per capita basis and a fall in the total wages bill from £32.1 to £22.6 million during the same period. These changes are consistent with the decrease in employment which occurred during this time. (The adjusted figures were found by using the index *Income from Employment* (1980 = 100) which is to be found in Table 1.16 of the United Kingdom National Accounts (1985) produced by the Central Statistical Office and published by HMSO.)

Although figures have not been made available it is, perhaps, reasonable to assume that wage rates are similar in the shipyard division, and on this basis knowing the size of total employment we can multiply this figure by the per capita income known to exist among the engineers, and arrive at an estimated total bill for shipyard employees of £53.5 million in 1984. Adding the two totals produces a figure of £79.2 million which is the best estimate of the total gross earnings for the whole of the VSEL labour force.

The dominating presence of the shipyard since 1871, through all its changes of ownership, has permeated the social, economic and on occasions even the physical fabric of the town. Not always has Vickers at Barrow been synonymous with defence but, at the present time, the dominance is absolute and the political controversy surrounding the privatisation plans have focused the nation's attention on the town more sharply than ever before. Barrow *needs* Vickers, as it has done for over a century, but whether Britain needs Trident and the nuclear submarines to transport the missiles is a controversial political issue beyond the scope of this analysis.

ACKNOWLEDGEMENTS

I am grateful for the considerable assistance given by various members of the staff of Vickers Shipbuilding and Engineering

Company Limited, Barrow-in-Furness, and also to the company for permission to reproduce Plate 6.1. Bryn Trescatheric provided helpful information on Vickerstown, and Ron Smith of the Cumbria Library Service, Barrow-in-Furness, arranged for Figures 6.3 and 6.4 to be reproduced. Figures 6.2 and 6.5 were provided by the Map Division of the British Library. The research was supported by a grant from the Campus Venture and Enterprise Fund of the University of Salford. Finally, but very importantly, I am indebted to Marie Partington and Moira Armitt for typing from my manuscript.

REFERENCES

Barnes, F. (1968) *Barrow and District*, Barrow-in-Furness Corporation.

Bell, C. and Bell, R. (1969) *City Fathers*, Barrie and Rockliff, London.

Marshall, J.D. (1958) *Furness and the Industrial Revolution*, reprinted 1981 and published by Michael Moor, 41 Roper Street, Whitehaven, Cumbria.

Pollard, S. (1952) 'Town Planning in the Nineteenth Century: the Beginnings of Modern Barrow-in-Furness', *Transactions of the Lancashire and Cheshire Antiquarian Society*, 63, 87–116.

Scott, J.D. (1962) *Vickers: A History*, Weidenfeld and Nicholson, London.

Trescatheric, B. (1985) *How Barrow was Built*, Hougenai Press, Barrow-in-Furness.

Vickers (1902) *Official Vickerstown Souvenir*, Vickers Son and Maxim.

7

Married Quarters in England and Wales: A Census Analysis and Commentary

Kelvyn Jones

To know the origins of this study is to know its aims and limitations. In a social classification of Hampshire (Norris and Jones, 1986), clustering techniques were used to group 937 areas into 23 cluster types on the basis of over 70 census variables. On further analysis and mapping, two of the cluster types were found to be military married quarters (Bateman *et al.*, 1985). In the Hampshire context, these areas are not only socially and demographically distinctive but are also quite extensive. In this one county there were 37,000 persons serving in the armed forces in 1981, a figure which far exceeds the number of another socially distinctive group, 'born in the New Commonwealth', who currently live in the county. While this latter social group has attracted prodigious research effort over the last 20 years, military families have received comparatively little attention, and this is despite their considerable social problems, their marked geographical concentration and their number. In 1981 there were nearly 250,000 people usually resident in England and Wales who were members of the armed forces.

This present study represents an extensive design (Sayer, 1984) whereby census data are used to reveal the attributes and correlates of married quarters housing. The discussion is organised into three parts: firstly there is a consideration, albeit a brief one, of what can be called the social context of 'camp followers'. This is followed by a census analysis that allows the identification and location of military housing and shows the distinctiveness of such areas. Finally, there is a commentary that expands the census analysis to reveal the particular problems affecting military families and the local authority areas in which they are concentrated.

CAMP FOLLOWERS: THE SOCIAL CONTEXT

The recognition that servicemen had wives who might wish to accompany their husbands and to be accommodated in married quarters is of relatively recent origin. Before the Crimean War, women could only accompany their husbands as washerwomen. Five or six were allowed per company and the lucky few were drawn by lots from those who applied, the rest being left behind to fend for themselves. However, by the 1860s there was a general agitation for reform and the Army started building married quarters from that date. Nowadays, the number of Army dependants, totalling nearly 250,000 in the early 1970s according to Spencer (1976), considerably exceeds the number in the uniformed Army which was approximately 170,000 at the same date. The Navy was even slower to appreciate these needs, failing to provide any married quarters until after 1945, but within the next 30 years, 14,000 married quarters had been built or acquired as naval hirings (Seebohm, 1974). This can be seen not as an act of *noblesse oblige* by the Navy, but as a necessity if it was to recruit and keep the men of the ability that it increasingly required. In the past, marriage was actively discouraged. Earlier this century, official consent was not granted before the age of 30 for officers and 27 for other ranks. Indeed, until 1970, marriage allowances and married quarters were not officially available until the age of 21 for other ranks and 25 for officers. The age limit is now 18 years, and this has resulted, as we shall see, in young servicemen and young wives.

Service wives, unlike other 'incorporated wives' such as diplomats' wives (Callan and Ardener, 1984), are not integrated into their husbands' occupation on the premise of non-aggression. Arms are seen as a man's trade and it remains very much a closed world with women being effectively excluded. As Chappell (1983, p. 356) reports in her interviews with army wives in Aldershot:

> He never talks about what he does or what's going to happen next. None of them do, even about non-secret stuff. He'll talk to his mates, but if there are women in the room he just doesn't want to know.

According to MacMillan (1984) wives are regarded as a potential source of discord for the military hierarchy and, while they cannot commit a military offence, they are effectively restrained from complaining and campaigning by loyalty to their husbands and by the fear of potential damage to their husbands' careers. For example, Pickering (1977) was invited by the wives unofficially and in secret to discuss their problems; while the Soldiers', Sailors' and Airmen's Families Association (SSAFA) recognised in their submission to Seebohm's (1974) inquiry on Naval welfare that there was a major difference between the 'Old Navy' of long-servers and the 'New Navy' of recent recruits:

> the 'Old Navy' despises welfare as something only 'drips' would require, while the 'New Navy' is much more anxious about the welfare of their (*sic*) wives and family.

These changes are themselves reflected in the Seebohm inquiry and in its Army equivalent (Spencer, 1976), both of which produced far-reaching recommendations concerning the nature and extent of welfare and social support for service families. But despite these changes there remains some unease about the role of married women and their potential demands. For example, in 1978, at a time of a relative decline in military pay, a group of wives in Church Crookham in Hampshire launched a campaign related to better communications and problems of paying rent. At that time, wives were being sent home from Germany to their parents for being in rent arrears. They became known as the 'revolting wives of Church Crookham' and while a committee was appointed to examine their problems, it contained no women and never met (MacMillan, 1984).

While the wives are not integrated into the services, they marry on the basis that the forces come first, and that its requirements must override their thoughts and considerations. Indeed, fiancées are asked to sign an acceptance of their intended husband's terms of service and the intending husband must still ask the permission of his officer to marry. Pickering (1977) in his conversations with army wives found resentment here: for example, one complained that, 'when you get married, no one explains Queen and country are coming into bed with you'; and another stated that, 'if we follow the rules we have even got to ask permission to become an Avon Lady'.

Overall, it is perhaps fair to say that service families and dependants have been given greater attention since the Second World War and particularly so in the last 15 years. The forces are increasingly realising that they are making particular demands on the uniformed men, both in peace and war, and that their families are expected to cope with considerable difficulties that are often different in degree and in kind from those experienced by civilian families. As

MacMillan (1984, p. 90) writes, 'Military wives are camp followers, never settling, never accumulating possessions, not belonging to any social group but their own'.

SPATIAL DISTRIBUTION OF MILITARY HOUSING

It is possible to study the national distribution of the military by examining the 1981 population census (Rhind, 1983). The census asked the occupation of each adult in the country and one in ten of the replies was assigned to one of 17 socioeconomic groups (SEGs). If the respondents stated that they were in the armed forces they were counted in the specific category, SEG 16; data were collected on ranks but this has not been made available and no distinction is made between the three forces in the census. Using the computer package SASPAC (Rhind, 1982) it is possible to derive counts and percentages for those persons in the ten per cent sample who were identified as belonging to SEG 16.

Figure 7.1 shows the distribution of the number of heads of households who are classified as SEG 16. The data are at the scale of the district, and only those districts with over 1,000 such heads are shown. There are 31 districts with numbers in excess of this figure and they are quite clearly concentrated in the south and east of the country in what constitutes 'lowland' Britain; indeed one-third of these districts are in the one southern county of Hampshire. Four districts have in excess of 3,000 military 'heads' and they are, in ascending order of size, Portsmouth, Huntingdon, Gosport and Plymouth, three of which reflect the scale and concentration of housing associated with the Navy.

These absolute numbers to some extent hide the relative importance of the military in some areas; for some districts the numbers employed directly in the armed services can form a substantial part of total employment. For example, in the Gosport district in Hampshire over 30 per cent of the active male labour force are in the forces. When the figures take account of those employed in providing local ancillary services, military expenditure may dominate the local economy, and this is an area that, curiously, has gone unresearched by those examining the impact of defence expenditure. Indeed, in the Hampshire context (Bateman *et al.*, 1985), it was possible to find a distinctive type of civilian housing that was associated with people servicing the military.

Of course, the census permits a much finer spatial scale of

Figure 7.1: Districts in England and Wales with more than 1,000 residents employed in the armed forces

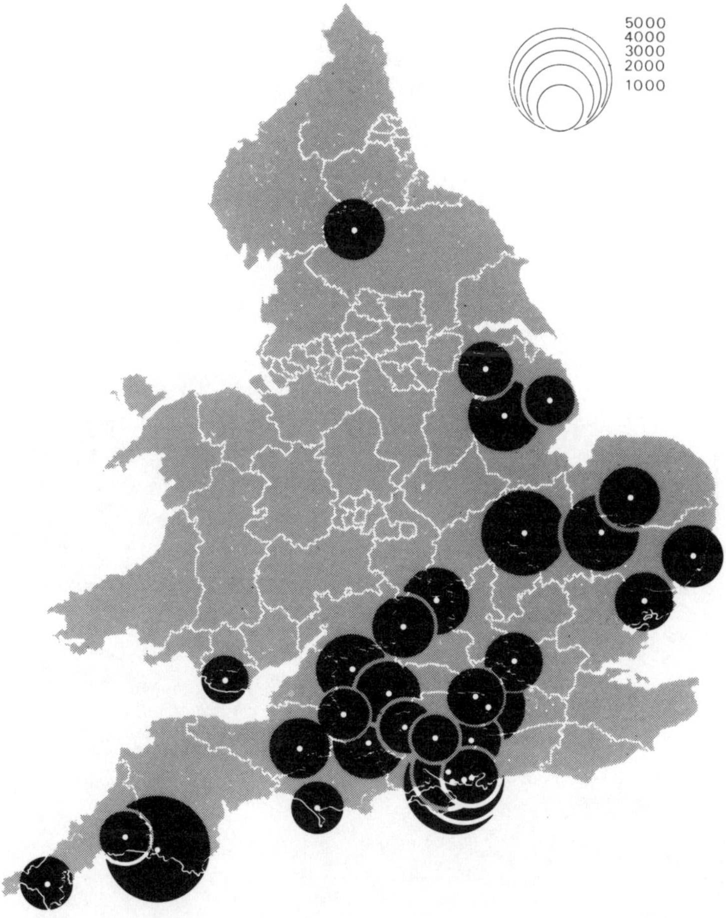

resolution than the district, and some 5,000 'counts' on demographic, social and economic information are available for over 110,000 enumeration districts (EDs). Each of these EDs is supposed to be reasonably socially homogeneous and they contain roughly 150 persons in a rural area and 500 persons in an urban area. The census also allows us to distinguish between three major types of military accommodation. Firstly, we can recognise areas of concentrations of service personnel who are not in private households but are living

Figure 7.2: Enumeration districts with married quarters

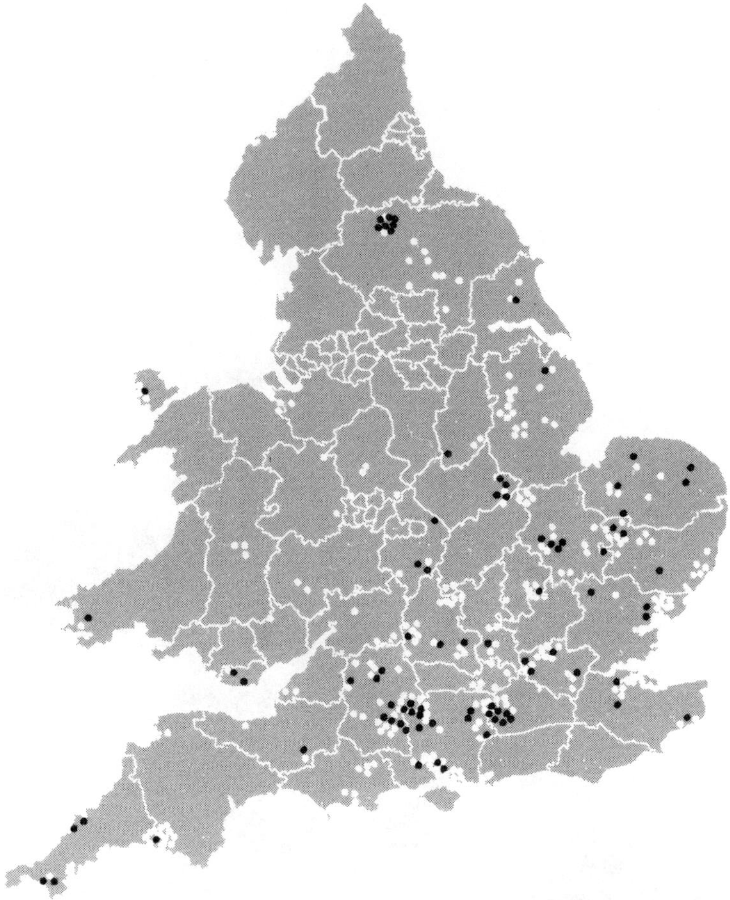

in communal establishments. These are likely to be young and single men living in barracks and they are usually of sufficient size to be distinguished as 'special' EDs. If this is the case, only limited census data are made available and such areas will not be considered here. The military households living in private accommodation can be subdivided so that our second major type is 'owner occupiers', and the final type is 'rented by virtue of employment'. Owner occupiers are those who are buying or who have bought their own house, and these can be expected to be of higher rank, less mobile and generally older than those who rent. For the army, Spencer (1976, p. 123) found that only 3 per cent of 'junior other ranks' were owner occupiers, but this rose to over 56 per cent for senior officers. The households that rent by virtue of employment are identifiable from the census and they represent the major group for subsequent analysis — military married quarters.

It is important to realise that census data are not available for individual households and therefore we have to select EDs with high concentrations of the military. Figure 7.2 shows the distribution of all EDs in which a majority (i.e. over 50 per cent) of the private households have a head who is employed by the military. This information was obtained by the SELECT IF option in SASPAC. This distribution confirms the concentration in lowland Britain and it is possible to discern the major groupings of the Navy at Plymouth (Devon), Portsmouth and Gosport (both Hampshire), and of the Army at Aldershot (Hampshire), Bulford-Tidworth (Wiltshire), Colchester (Essex) and Catterick (North Yorkshire). A more detailed examination will reveal that there are very few such EDs in metropolitan areas and on the whole, concentrations tend to be located in relatively small towns, in rural areas or on the fringes of larger cities.

Also shown by a black dot in Figure 7.2 are those EDs with over three-quarters of the private households having armed services heads of households as well as three-quarters of the private households renting by virtue of employment. These then are the married quarters as identified by the census, and in the analysis that follows, the data for married quarters are derived from these 88 EDs. The high cut-off of 75 per cent was chosen to minimise the risk of the ecological fallacy (Robinson, 1950) and to ensure that these were indeed the military married quarters (in fact, the majority of them have rates of over 90 per cent for both variables). Although there are relatively few such EDs, they are again quite concentrated or in rural areas so that they are likely to have a greater impact than their mere numbers suggest.

CENSUS ANALYSIS

The methodology used to produce this census analysis is straightforward: SASPAC was used to derive a large number of counts and ratios for the 88 EDs previously identified as married quarters and these were compared with the national values for all EDs in England

Figure 7.3: Age-pyramids: England and Wales and married quarters

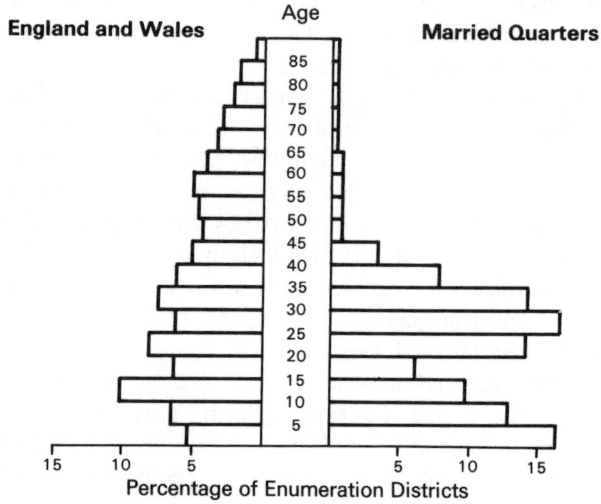

(a) MEN

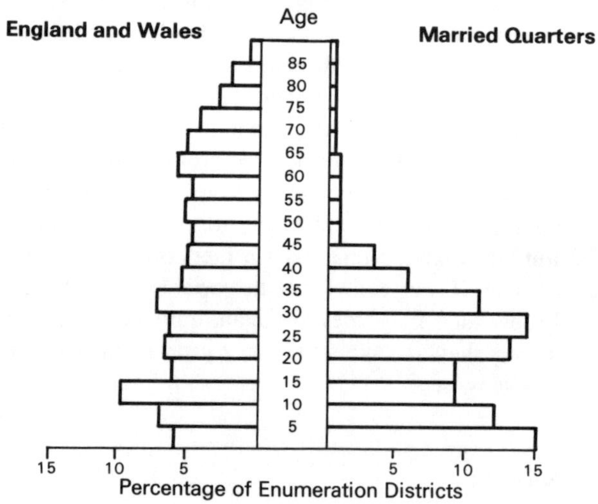

(b) WOMEN

and Wales. A selection of comparisons is shown in Figures 7.3 to 7.6; the national figures in Figures 7.3 and 7.4 are taken from the national census volumes, while the national distributions of Figures 7.5 and 7.6 are taken from Craig (1985). The discussion of these comparisons deals with demography, household composition, housing and household amenities and employment.

The demographic structure of married quarters (Figure 7.3) is a striking one and the exceptionally youthful population is highly reminiscent of underdeveloped countries. The majority of the population is under 30 and there are very few people over 44 years of age. The result is that any particular ED is likely to be fairly homogeneous in age structure and to consist of young parents and their young children. This pattern of course reflects the nature of service recruitment for it is possible to join at the age of 17½ and receive full pay; the career soldier or sailor normally serves 22 years and departs at the age of 40 (in the RAF, retirement is often at 55 years of age). The youthful age structure also reflects the relatively high fertility rate found in married quarters. Defining the fertility rate as the number of children aged 0–4 per hundred women aged 16–44, Figure 7.4b shows that the rates for all but a few married quarters are substantially higher than the national rate. Figure 7.4a shows the very high female teenage marriage rates, reflecting Spencer's (1976) finding that the average age at marriage of the wives of corporals and lower ranks was 20.1 years. The rate of lone parent families was, however, considerably below the national average and only 5 EDs out of the 88 had more than 5 per cent of families falling into this category. This is a result not of especially low levels of estrangement and divorce but of the housing policy of the services that expects 'headless' families to vacate married quarters quickly once the husband has left the wife and moved back into the mess or barracks.

The houses that comprise the married quarters are of a high standard in terms of amenities and the vast majority of houses have inside WC and a bath. In terms of overcrowding (over 1.5 persons per room) there appears to be little cause for concern for only 8 EDs had more than 5 per cent of the households living above this level. As Figure 7.4c shows, some of the EDs have a relatively high percentage of flats although this does not represent the majority of accommodation. In census terms, therefore, the military appear to be housed in good quality accommodation, but the reliance on this limited data may create a false impression. Chappell (1983, p. 356) described the drab nature of housing in Aldershot, 'the plank and

Figure 7.4: Comparisons of census variables for married quarters with rates for England and Wales

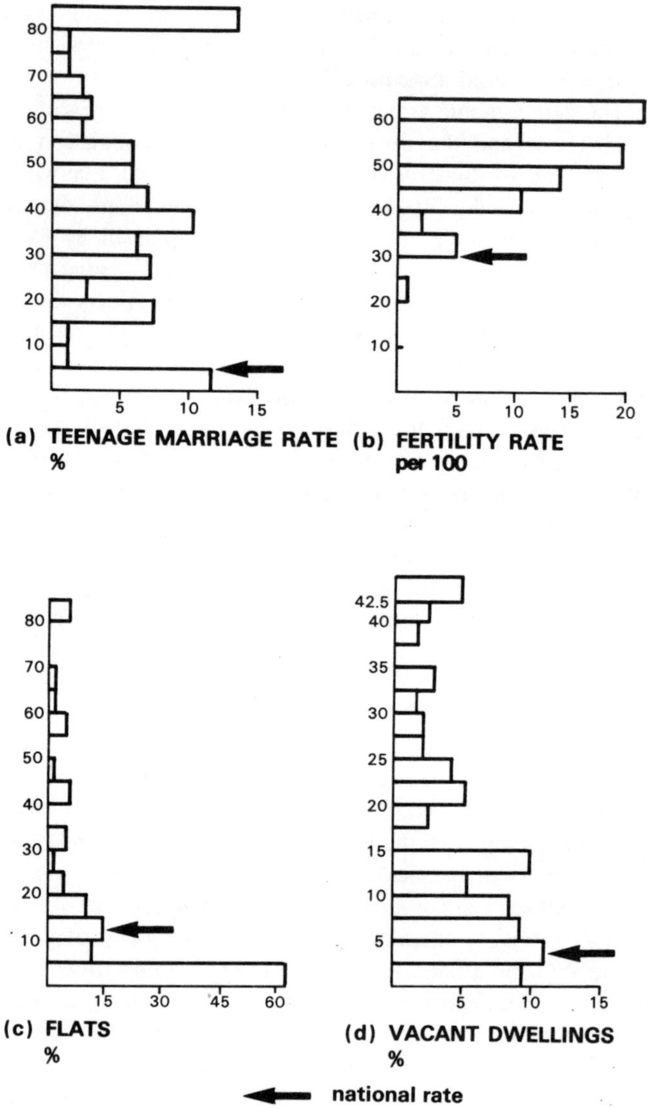

Figure 7.5: Comparisons of census variables for married quarters with distributions for England and Wales

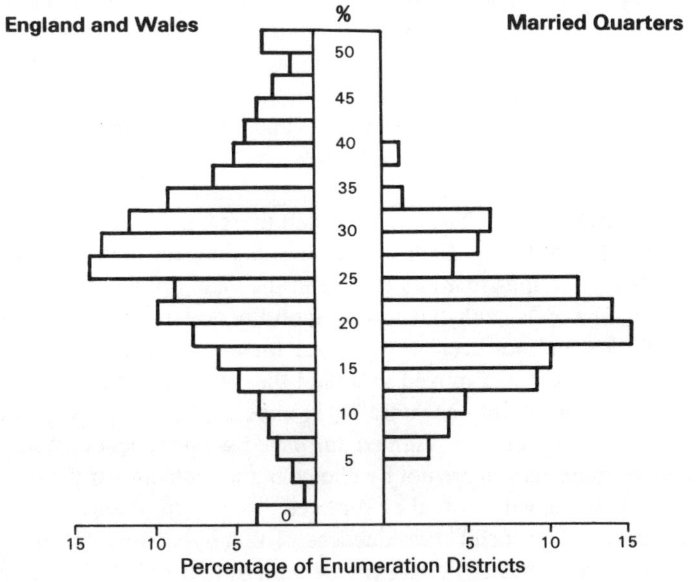

(a) FEMALE EMPLOYMENT FULLTIME

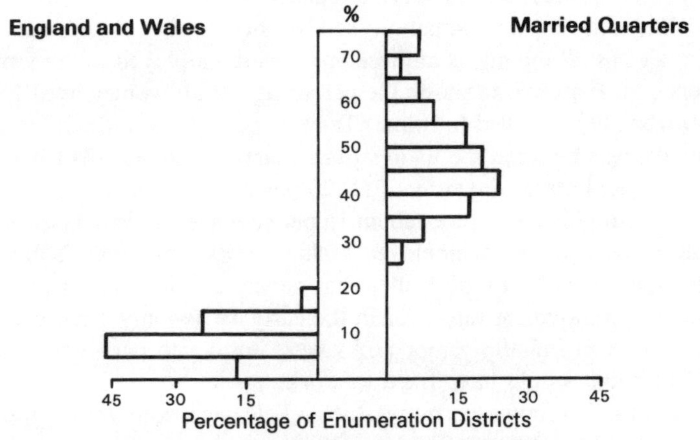

(b) MOVED WITHIN LAST YEAR

concrete units, suffer from patches of obvious damp and peeling, . . . they are officially classified as sub-standard', while Pickering (1977, p. 121) likened the married quarters he visited to, 'a dumping ground for families at the rough end of a council estate'. The service families themselves complained to the Seebohm and Spencer inquiries of the difficulty of getting repairs done (the Department of the Environment manages the estates) and of the identical decor and furniture, provided according to rank, that was often to be found throughout the estates.

One feature of the housing of which there can be no doubt is the high level of mobility. Figure 7.5b reveals the very high percentage of military families that had moved in the year prior to the census. Even in the EDs with the lowest mobility, over a quarter of the households had not been in residence for a year and in some EDs over 90 per cent had moved in within the last twelve months. Such rates of mobility are considerably in excess of the highest civilian rates (those for privately-rented furnished accommodation) and as many of these moves are not by choice but an outcome of the operational requirements of the services, social problems can be anticipated. The social consequences of this hyper-mobility will be discussed later, but one effect can be seen in Figure 7.4d in the very high rates of unused dwellings that are to be found in married quarters. Such vacant dwellings reflect not only a high turnover but also that some accommodation in particular areas is now surplus to requirements. Indeed, the amount of service housing stock is currently being reduced and, as in the case of the Rowner naval estate in Gosport, houses are now being sold off to the public and local authorities, and to service tenants.

The employment situation needs only to be considered for females as all the males in these areas were employed in the armed services. Figure 7.5a shows the percentage of all women aged 15 to 60 who are employed full-time. There appears to be little difference on average between the national and married quarters distribution. In a typical married quarters ED, 20 per cent of women aged 16 to 60 are employed full-time, about 15 per cent are employed part-time and 6 per cent are unemployed seeking work. In comparison with the Spencer (1976) report, there has been a considerable rise in the female employment rates, for in the early 1970s only 4 per cent of the wives of infantry junior ranks were employed part-time, while 74 per cent would have liked to work.

Figure 7.6 shows car ownership and clearly a substantial proportion of service households are without cars and, in comparison to

Figure 7.6: Car ownership: England and Wales and married quarters

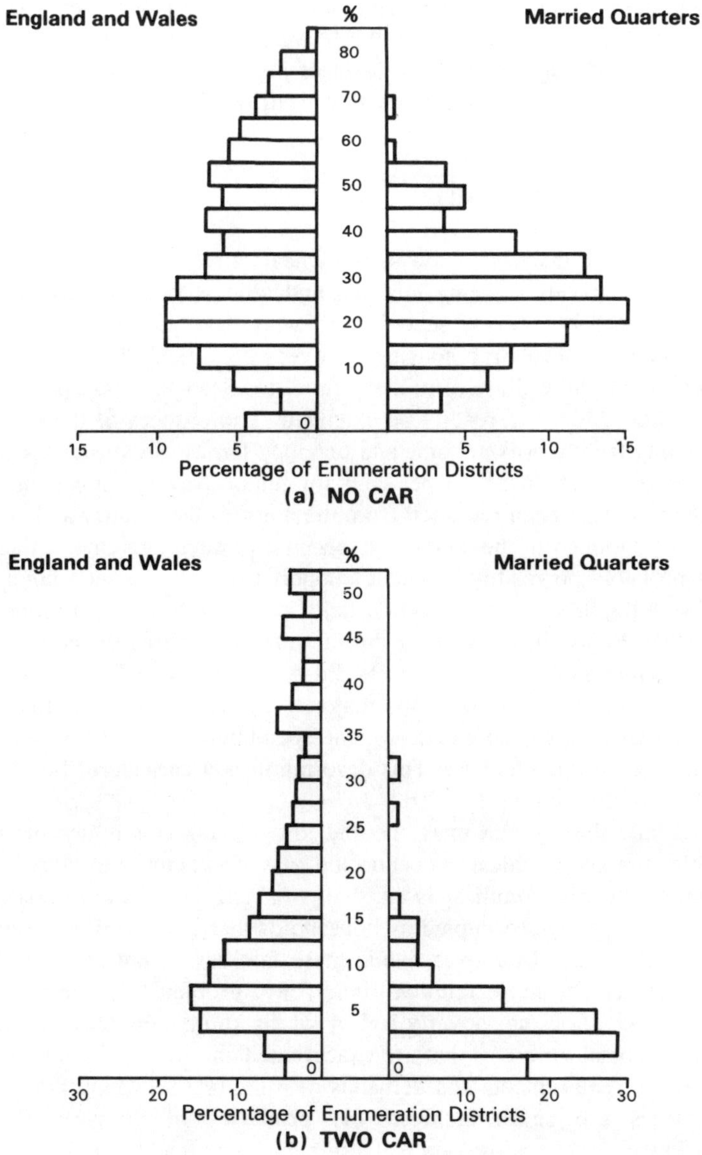

national figures, very few service households have two or more cars. Their lack of car ownership is comparable to the national figure but this conceals the point that the rates are well below those commonly found in rural and suburban locations where most married quarters are located. Moreover, as shown in the Spencer inquiry, although over 40 per cent of junior ranks have cars, only 19 per cent of the wives were able to drive.

SOCIAL COMMENTARY

The census analysis of the stereotypical family living in married quarters reveals a young husband and wife with young children, some probably of pre-school age, who have moved into their adequate if rather drab housing very recently. Using the two major reports on the welfare of military families (Seebohm and Spencer), the description can readily be extended. The chances of the father coming from a broken home and unhappy family circumstances are relatively high (over 40 per cent for junior Naval ratings), he is likely to have been recruited from the north of the country and now to be stationed in the south and, because of such movement, there is probably no readily available support from an extended family. The wife, like her husband, usually has few formal educational qualifications. In the case of the infantry, two-thirds of the junior and senior ranks and their wives did not possess one CSE between them. Furthermore, while the majority of the wives would like to work, many are unable to do so, and spend much of their time looking after young children. This description is a caricature, but it is not grossly unfaithful.

While their age at marriage and low social status is unremarkable, the geographical concentration of such young, and therefore 'inexperienced' families, is unusual. Married quarters are substantial housing areas occupied by households that effectively represent an *under*-class. Moreover, while these families do not particularly experience the more familiar 'inner city' problems of unemployment, poor housing, poverty and racial discrimination, they do face major social problems that are exacerbated and even caused by the specific requirements and demands of military life. Many military families are suffering from the processes of discrimination, turbulence, separation, and isolation which can lead to more severe social difficulties for a minority.

Discrimination

It appears to many of the military families that there is a major divide between armed and civilian life and that the ordinary civilian does not appreciate the problems that are associated with living in married quarters. Some of the respondents in Nicholson's (1980, p. 10) survey said that:

> Civilians do not understand Naval slang and jargon or the continual moving and the fact that we have to put up with it . . . I don't try to explain life in the Navy to my civilian friends.

For many, the divide is more than a lack of appreciation and nearly 50 per cent of single and married junior ranks in Spencer's (1976) survey reported civilian hostility in public bars and cafes. While the men complained of this hostility in relation to their social life, many women felt that they had experienced discrimination in terms of employment by being service wives, while recognising that potential employers found the transitory nature of forces life a drawback to employment. One wife told Seebohm (1974, p. 42): 'As soon as they discovered my husband was in the Navy . . . the whole tone of the interview changed. They weren't very friendly.'

Turbulence

This is the term given by the services to describe the problems associated with frequent moves. There were many complaints to the Seebohm and Spencer committees that the families did not know how long they were likely to remain and where they were likely to be posted. Such unpredictability appeared not only to relate to 'emergencies' (such as the recently announced transfer of additional troops to Northern Ireland), but sudden and unexpected postings seem to be the routine. The three services differ in the extent of mobility, with the Army experiencing the most and the RAF the least. The Army is, of course, the service with the greatest geographical spread, with over 150 towns in the United Kingdom having 20 or more married quarters and there remains a substantial overseas presence; indeed, about a third of the Army at any one time is stationed in Germany as the British Army on the Rhine. The mobility of the RAF is much less for there are fewer bases, and while officers are generally posted every two years, many airmen stay for seven or more years in the same station. Moreover, the turbulence for the RAF is least because future flying plans appear to have a greater certainty than Naval and Army operations.

A high level of transfer entails not only the physical and emotional ordeal of moving, which can be acute when there are young children, the mother is pregnant and the father has already been posted, but also an understandable concern over the possibility of temporary homelessness. Some areas have an excess of married quarters while others have a shortage and there are again differences between the three services. Spencer in his study of the Army found that at the end of a posting the husband frequently gets a leave of about six weeks and the majority of families cannot stay in their current quarters, for they are wanted by the new arrivals, nor can they move directly to their new camp, which has not yet been vacated. The result is a double move with the family going to stay with their parents and relatives until the new camp is ready. Spencer found that 10 per cent of the junior ranks of the infantry were accommodated with their relatives at the time of his survey. Moreover, the camps may not have sufficient quarters for all who desire them and there is a waiting list based on a points system. This operates in such a way that it favours senior soldiers while the youngest families tend to be offered less popular accommodation, often located away from the main camp, and experience a wait of up to six months before being allocated a quarter. Similar problems were also found by Seebohm for Naval families and he notes that one area had a thirteen month waiting list. In recent years the situation has improved for Naval families and they are now allowed to occupy married quarters when the husband is required to go to sea and they are given two months' notice to leave after the husband is drafted from one shore base to another. The Navy has pursued a long-term policy to build married quarters in sufficient numbers to permit those who want to remain in service housing the opportunity to do so — the so-called 'roof-to-roof' policy. The RAF has relatively more married quarters in appropriate locations, and there is consequently less turbulence.

Separation

The physical separation of the husband from the rest of the family remains a major problem for Naval families and is likely to remain so as long as there are no married quarters aboard ship. Many Naval families experience in effect, a part-time father and husband. The Navy attempts a balance of 50 per cent of the career afloat and 50 per cent ashore. While this balance is achieved throughout an individual service, sea liability for officers and ratings is greatest in their early twenties. Consequently, those who are recently married and those with young families are more likely to experience separation. Indeed, in the Seebohm survey, 50 per cent of families are separated within the first two months of marriage and a similar percentage had to deal with periods of separation of six months or over in the first year of marriage. A particular problem that he noted was that a quarter of Naval husbands were absent at the time of the birth of their children. Nicholson (1980, p. 28) found in her Eastney (Portsmouth) survey that 13 per cent of families had spent half their married life separated, and over 50 per cent had been separated for over a quarter. Given such levels, it is perhaps not surprising that separation was mentioned five times more frequently than any other disadvantage of Naval life by Seebohm's survey of Naval wives; he found that 12 per cent of them detested it, 30 per cent actively disliked it, and another 21 per cent disliked but accepted it. Seebohm recommended that separation should not exceed six months (the maximum period of separation of nine months was only introduced in 1972) and should be followed by a leave of at least fourteen days.

In the past the Army tended to move as a family with long tours of duty overseas but, with the shrinking of the British sphere of influence, there has been an increase in shorter (under six months), more frequent and unaccompanied foreign tours and more frequent training courses in other parts of Britain away from home base. The result has been an increase in separation, but not to the extent of that experienced in the Navy. The Spencer survey found that the average number of weeks of separation for infantry corporals and lower ranks was 15 weeks in the last twelve months; and about 30 per cent of UK-based infantry experienced periods of separation of over six months in the last twelve months. For particular units, the problem can be even more severe and Chappell (1983) in her discussion with the wives of 'Two Para' in Bruneval Barracks, Aldershot, found wives that had only seen their husbands for six weeks in the past year as they had been on tours of duty to Belize, the Falklands, and Northern Ireland, each lasting about four months. In some ways this separation can have a greater effect on Army than on Naval estates, for in the latter the husbands are likely to be attached to a variety of different ships and shore duties and not all will be away at any one time. An Army estate, however, may represent a particular regiment and their absence may make the estate into a temporary one-sex society for the wives that remain. The RAF again offers a marked contrast with the other two services, separation is only frequent for aircrews and then it usually involves a matter of days rather than months.

Isolation

While the RAF wives are unlikely to suffer turbulence on the scale of the Army wives nor separation at the level of the Navy, all three services can be expected to experience 'isolation' to some degree. The term in this context refers to what Smith (1977) has called 'place deprivation' that is poor accessibility to goods and services because of geographical location. Many married quarters are located in rural areas or at least at some distance from major population centres. The problems for families in these camps are often made worse by the lack and high cost of public transport, low levels of car ownership and ability to drive, and the fact that as most recruits are from urban areas they expect good access to services. Spencer found that a relatively high percentage of army families were not 'within easy reach' of a variety of amenities, particularly playgroups and schools (see Table 7.1). In a study of the large Naval estate at Rowner in Gosport, there were complaints of poor public transport, the high prices and lack of choice in local shops and that competitive shopping was too far away (Oglesby, 1974, pp. 7–8). This survey was done in 1964 but similar research twenty years later (*Naval News*, March, 1984) revealed that there was still some concern over lack of facilities and over 90 per cent of the respondents put a dispensing chemist as their first priority.

Another aspect of isolation is the lack of nearby relatives and

Table 7.1: Percentage of families not within easy reach of amenities

Amenity	UK-based infantry Junior rank	 Senior rank
Shops	19	15
Doctor	18	16
Transport	26	18
Playgroup	52	45
Schools	36	18

Source: Spencer (1976).

especially parents. In a survey of 29 families resident in Gaydon army base, the majority had no local relatives and more than half the wives saw their parents less frequently than once every two months (May, 1977), while in the Spencer survey, more than half of the wives defined themselves as not within easy reach of close relatives. Even for the Navy, which has tended in the past to recruit more heavily from the home ports, the majority do not live close to a network of relations; Nicholson (1980) in her study of Eastney found that 80 per cent of her sample had no close relatives living nearby.

SOCIAL PROBLEMS

While discrimination, turbulence, separation and isolation will probably affect the majority of service families at some time in their lives, for a minority these processes can develop and combine to produce more severe social problems and here we will briefly discuss loneliness, children's problems, and estrangement and divorce. These problems can reach high levels in certain camps at times of high stress. Lerwill (1975) reports that one particular garrison of 4,000 families generated over 900 formal referrals to local authority social services in an eleven-month period, over and above those problems dealt with within the service by regimental officers and padres. Indeed, such a relatively high need was one of the major reasons for both Spencer and Seebohm recommending the setting up of family and personal services specifically for military families. The scale of the response to these recommendations may be gauged from the fact that the Chief Commandant of the Housing and Welfare Services in the Aldershot garrison now controls four housing commandants, seven playgroups, a day nursery, and three social workers. It must, however, be stressed that there is still heavy reliance on volunteers, particularly wives of officers, to provide social support.

Loneliness

The uncertainty and impermanence of service life may lead to feelings of rootlessness and difficulties in making and keeping friends. Thus, while Nicholson (1980, p. 48) found that the average number of friends was relatively high (at 7.6) for the Eastney married quarters in Portsmouth in comparison to the civilian population, there was a noticeable lack of 'close' friends and there were some women who were 'desperately isolated and lonely'. If the wife lacks extended family support, as well as close friends and confidants, then separation can be the final straw. In the Spencer survey nearly 80 per cent of young wives said that they felt lonely and isolated when their husbands were away. Crossley (1974, p. 32), a community worker operating within a Naval estate found that: 'reactions in extreme cases are almost as desperate as those of widowhood, and separation is no easier to bear on the second, third or subsequent occasions.' Lis (1974) notes that elevated levels of psychiatric morbidity have been found among wives at a Naval air station in comparison to civilians, and that: 'Naval wives in Portsmouth attempted suicide by poisoning at an alarming rate especially in the early years of marriage.'

Children

Lerwill (1975) surmises that, because of the lack of a 'roof-to-roof' policy and the high level of mobility, a child of Army parents could lose up to a complete year of schooling, for most authorities are unwilling to take a pupil for less than half a term. Indeed, Plowden (1967, p. 59) in her report categorises service children as a 'seriously deprived' group (along with gypsies) and states that, 'evidence exists of serious backwardness among them and of high turnover of pupils and teachers'. Other commentators have been more optimistic, believing that there would be no lasting effect on educational attainment providing that the children were of average or above average ability. Firth (1974), for example, found that turbulence led to little special difficulty except in cumulative skills like arithmetic for the handicapped and children of below average ability.

American research on service families has identified what has been called 'the military family syndrome' (Lagrane, 1978) in which children become disruptive because of the high mobility and impermanence of their parents' life, the problem being made worse by a rigid autocratic discipline imposed by the father. In Britain, Spencer's survey found that 20 per cent of the wives of young soldiers and 40 per cent of the wives of older soldiers were concerned about their children's behavioural problems. Matthews (1974) found that in relation to control groups, the children of Navy families had an increased incidence of attention-seeking, stealing, aggressiveness and destructiveness. Finally, and most worryingly, May (1977) and SSRIU (1975) report high levels of suspected non-accidental injury ('baby-battering') amongst military families.

Divorce

Until recently divorce was viewed as an offence against the accepted code and according to MacMillan (1984) it meant that an officer would have to resign or at least be transferred to another regiment. Nowadays there is less stigma attached to divorce and the problem is aggravated by the ease which the husband can move from married quarters into the mess or barracks. The result has been an increase in what are called 'headless' families who are therefore 'irregularly' occupying married quarters; Chappell (1983) found that at any one time there were about 80 such abandoned families in the Aldershot district. The wife is usually given a month's notice to quit the quarters and if this is not done there is eventually a Court Order for possession and eviction, which is not only meant to remove the family but also to enhance their case for re-housing by the local authority. In districts with a large military presence, irregular tenants with young families are a major problem for social services, particularly where suitable accommodation is limited, and represent a substantial cost for the local authority if they have to be found emergency privately rented accommodation (SSRIU, 1975, 1976).

CONCLUSIONS

It has been stressed in recruiting drives that it is a 'man's life' in the forces. Undoubtedly, there are many benefits of service life and Weigall (1975) lists security of employment, 'unrivalled opportunity for a man to better himself', a reasonable wage, good facilities for sport and recreation, opportunity for travel, availability of good quality housing, and access to a comprehensive welfare organisation. At the same time, however, the forces impose considerable social stress on the men they employ and their wives and families. While similar stresses may be experienced by young civilian families, it is the cumulative nature of enforced geographical mobility, turbulence, separation, and isolation, coupled with youthful inexperience and lack of family support, that may lead to a difficult life for many and severe problems for a minority.

Moreover, because the forces have built sizeable, segregated estates, there may be an unusual and marked geographical concentration of social problems in areas and local authorities that normally would not expect to experience such a concentration. Indeed, a number of commentators have likened these estates to inner city areas, with for example the Association of Directors of Social Services in their evidence to Spencer (1976, p. 54) finding that: 'a community, although it is geographically placed in a rural setting, is presenting numerically and in complexity social problems more akin to a densely-populated urban area.' Others have gone further and likened married quarters to ghettoes. According to a Portsmouth doctor (reported in Oglesby, 1974, p. 4-4): 'I think that it is the first time in history that an authority has . . . produced ghettoes — and they have gone even better than ordinary ghettoes — these are single-sex colonies without even the stabilising influence of normal family life.'

REFERENCES

Bateman, M., Jones, K. and Moon, G. (1985) *A Social Atlas of Hampshire*, Dept of Geography, Portsmouth Polytechnic.

Callan, H. and Ardener, S. (1984) *The Incorporated Wife*, London, Croom Helm.

Chappell, H. (1983) 'Married to the Army', *New Society*, 1 December, 354–7.

Craig, J. (1985) *Statistical Summaries of Between-Area Differences for Some 1981 Census Variables*, OPCS, Occasional Paper no. 32.

Crossley, W.P. (1974) 'Special Problems of Service Families', *Proceedings of the Triservice Multidisciplinary Conference*, 2, 29–35.

Firth, J.V. (1974) 'Occupational Mobility, Turbulence and Children's Attainment', *RAF Quarterly*, XIV (2).

Lagrane, D.M. (1978) 'The Military Family Syndrome', *American Journal of Psychiatry*, 135, 1040–3.

Lerwill, I. (1975) 'The Lifestyle of the Serviceman and his Family Problems', *Proceedings of the Triservice Multidisciplinary Conference*, 3, 3–14.

Lis, N. (1974) 'Social Support of the Naval Family', in Oglesby, A.J. (ed.) *The Effects of Geographical Mobility on the Naval Rating's Family Unit*, Defence Fellowship, University of Southampton.

MacMillan, M. (1984) 'Camp Followers: A Note on Wives of the Armed Services', in Callan, H. and Ardener, S. (eds), *The Incorporated Wife*, London, Croom Helm.

Matthews, P.C. (1974) 'Emotional Difficulties Encountered in Naval Families', in Seebohm (Lord) *Report of the Naval Welfare Committee*, London, HMSO.

May, J. (1977) 'Army Enlists Social Services', *Health and Social Service Journal*, 24 June, 964.
Nicholson, P.J. (1980) *Goodbye Sailor: the Importance of Friendship in Family Mobility and Separation*, Inverness, Northpress.
Norris, P. and Jones, K. (1986) 'Planning Applications of Areal Classification: Some Examples from Hampshire', *Journal of Economic and Social Measurement*, 1, forthcoming.
Oglesby, A.J. (1974) *The Effects of Geographical Mobility on the Naval Rating's Family Unit*, Defence Fellowship, University of Southampton.
Pickering, P. (1977) 'Camp Followers', *New Society*, 4 August, 221–3.
Plowden (Lady) (1967) *Children and Their Primary Schools*, London, HMSO.
Rhind, D. (1982) 'Academics and the 1981 Population Census', *Area*, 14, 104–7.
Rhind, D. (1983) *A Census User's Handbook*, London, Methuen.
Robinson, W.S. (1950) 'Ecological Correlation and the Behaviour of Individuals', *Sociological Review*, 15, 351–7.
SSRIU (1975) *Problems of Re-Housing Ex-Service Families in Gosport*, Dept of Social Studies, Portsmouth Polytechnic.
SSRIU (1976) *Problems of Re-Housing Ex-Service Families in Rushmoor (Hampshire)*, Dept of Social Studies, Portsmouth Polytechnic.
Sayer, A. (1984) *Method in Social Science*, London, Hutchinson.
Seebohm (Lord) (1974) *Report of the Naval Welfare Committee*, London, HMSO.
Smith, D.M. (1977) *Human Geography: A Welfare Approach*, London, Arnold.
Spencer, J.C. (1976) *Report of The Army Welfare Inquiry Committee*, London, HMSO.
Weigall, S.H.D. (1975) 'The Lifestyle of the Serviceman and his Family: Benefits', *Proceedings of the Triservice Multidisciplinary Conference*, 3, 15–21.

8

British Overseas Military Expenditure and the Balance of Payments

Michael Asteris

Since the end of the Second World War, the United Kingdom has maintained substantial military forces and installations overseas. This external presence has represented a cost to the balance of payments as a consequence of two foreign exchange leakages: first, government spending in overseas economies to provide and maintain a military capability; and secondly, expenditure by servicemen and their dependants on local goods and services. Both of these outflows constitute deficit items in the invisibles section of the balance of payments. The significance of this spending becomes apparent when it is borne in mind that since the beginning of the nineteenth century Britain has sought to offset a tendency towards deficit in her visible trade by earning a surplus on her invisible trading accounts. The magnitude of the invisible surplus is determined by two variables, (a) the size of net private currency earnings from service trades and overseas investments, and (b) the magnitude of the currency outflow on government account; under which heading the cost of maintaining British forces outside the United Kingdom is included.

During the post-war period, government activities abroad have claimed a significant proportion of net private invisible earnings. Indeed, the proportion has rarely been less than 25 per cent and sometimes has exceeded 60 per cent. Moreover, defence expenditure abroad has often accounted for more than half of the total government deficit on the current account balance of payments. Official spending overseas is, of course, the foreign exchange flow most amenable to direct state manipulation. For this reason, successive administrations, when attempting to improve Britain's external payments positions, have, sooner or later, tended to be attracted to reductions in foreign military payments.

In the light of this fact, the purpose of this chapter is twofold: to discuss the role of balance of payments considerations in the contraction of Britain's military horizons during the past four decades; and to suggest that, as North Sea oil output declines, foreign exchange issues may again prove of considerable importance in shaping defence policy.

THE AFTERMATH OF WAR, 1945–9

Disequilibrium in the balance of payments constituted the most urgent manifestation of the economic difficulties facing the United Kingdom in 1945. Exports had shrunk to less than one-third of their pre-war volume, net income from overseas investments in 1945 was expected to be less than half that received in 1939, while huge sterling debts had accumulated largely because of wartime overseas defence expenditure (HMSO, 1946a). Substantial balance of payments deficits were therefore anticipated for several years. Consequently, a delegation was sent to Washington in February 1945 to seek aid from the USA. The American response was to grant the UK a line of credit totalling $3,750 million which could be drawn on at any time prior to the end of December 1951.[1]

The critical economic position of Great Britain pointed to the need to minimise the size of her armed forces. Unfortunately, the unsettled conditions during the aftermath of war generated military commitments which placed severe constraints upon such a course of action. Pre-war defence responsibilities had been supplemented by new commitments in Western Europe, the Eastern Mediterranean and South East Asia. Immediately after the war, Britain was engaged in a struggle to maintain order in the Indian subcontinent, Palestine and Greece while providing forces for the occupation of large parts of Germany, Austria and Venezia Giulia (HMSO, 1946b). Furthermore, troops were required for the liquidation of the Japanese occupation of South East Asia. As a result, in mid 1946 the armed forces still numbered almost two million, more than a quarter of whom were stationed outside Europe. The burden of supporting such a sizeable military establishment was reflected in defence expenditure during 1946 equal to approximately one-fifth of the gross national product (GNP).

For some 18 months after the defeat of Japan, the government shrank from the disagreeable task of deliberately abandoning selected overseas commitments. Nevertheless, the Chancellor of the Exchequer, Hugh Dalton, was convinced that Britain's weak

Table 8.1: United Kingdom: Current account of the Balance of Payments, 1938 and 1946 (£ million at current prices)

	1938	1946
Visible trade	−302	−176
Invisible trade	+232	−172
of which (a) Government (net)	−16	−363
(b) Other	+248	+191
Current balance	−70	−348

Sources: Bank for International Settlements, *The Sterling Area*, Basle, 1953, p. 8; and Treasury, *United Kingdom Balance of Payments 1946–1950*, London, HMSO (1950) Cmd 8065, 7.

economic position precluded a continuance of existing spending patterns. As early as February 1946 he had cautioned the Cabinet in the following manner:

> I must solemnly warn my colleagues that, unless we can reduce our overseas military expenditure drastically and rapidly, and avoid further overseas commitments, we have no alternative but to cut our rations and reduce employment through restrictions in the import of machinery and raw materials.
>
> There is no way round this arithmetic and all our overseas policy must be conditioned by it. (PRO, 1946a)

The need to reduce external defence spending was highlighted by the balance of payments outcome for 1946. As is evident from Table 8.1, the current account exhibited a marked deterioration compared with 1938. The figures in this tabulation show that the substantial deficit of 1946 was a direct consequence of changes in the pattern of invisible items.

The regression of £404 million in the invisibles position was, in large measure, the consequence of a huge rise in government spending outside the United Kingdom. Military outlays of £374 million constituted by far the most substantial item of government payments, though £123 million was devoted to overseas relief and rehabilitation. The result of the high level of British spending overseas was that the North American loan was being used up much too quickly — corrective action could not be postponed for much longer.

By the start of 1947 British resolve to maintain existing commitments had waned. Two factors were primarily responsible for the change of heart, one political and the other economic. To begin with, the United States was adopting a less accommodating policy towards the Soviet Union than twelve months earlier, which indicated that the UK might be able to count on greater American support in the Middle East.[2] Secondly, in the early months of 1947 the rapid post-war recovery of the UK was temporarily arrested by a shortage of fuel which brought the reality of Britain's precarious economic position into sharp focus.

Between late January and early March, Britain suffered a succession of blizzards, which severely disrupted the mining and distribution of coal. Since the majority of factories and power stations held only small stocks of fuel, the adverse effect on economic activity was immediate. The crisis resulted in a temporary rise in the unemployment level to over two million within a fortnight. The cost, in terms of lost exports alone, was later estimated at £200 million (Hansard, 1947a, quoted in Dow, 1968, p. 22). In the midst of the grim domestic economic situation it was announced that the UK was to shed direct responsibility for three particularly onerous responsibilities — India, Palestine and Greece.

A major factor in the decision to quit India sooner rather than later was the awareness that the attempt to remain in control in the face of rising disorder would have required sending reinforcements of five divisions to the subcontinent.[3] A substantial portion of the forces stationed in Germany, Southern Europe and the Middle East would therefore have to be redeployed. Clearly, the opportunity cost of maintaining the Raj would have been immense when measured in terms of Britain's position nearer home. Yet, departure from India was a mixed blessing in that henceforth the manpower of the Indian Army would no longer be available to support British strategy east of Suez.

Palestine was, in early 1947, a heavy responsibility because of the bitter conflict between Arab and Jew, with Britain cast in the unenviable role of mediator. Maintaining British rule in such circumstances had already cost £82 million during the previous two years and was currently requiring the presence of 84,000 troops (Hansard, 1947b). Both the government and people of the United Kingdom were rapidly becoming weary of the expense and effort involved in attempting to solve the Palestine question solely under British auspices. The problem was therefore referred to the United Nations. Following the vote for partition by the General Assembly in November 1947, Britain announced that the Mandate would terminate on 15 May 1948.[4]

British troops had been stationed in Greece since 1944, but responsibility for preventing the emergence of a Communist regime rested mainly with the 100,000 strong Greek Army. The maintenance of this force required £15 million a year expenditure in sterling, a sum which was met largely from UK sources (PRO, 1946b). In aggregate, British involvement in Greece between 1944 and March 1947 had cost the Exchequer £87 million in direct expenditure (Hansard, 1947b). Economic constraints were thus very much to the fore in the decision to terminate large-scale military aid to South East Europe. Throughout 1946 Britain had sought to reduce the scale of her presence in Greece and had gone so far as to withdraw 15,000 troops in the latter part of the year. Then, on 21 February 1947, two terse notes from the British government to the State Department informed the USA that, in view of her own situation, Britain could not render further assistance to either Greece or Turkey.

In the light of the British disclosures, the Truman administration made rapid preparations for American intervention in the Eastern Mediterranean. On 12 March the President addressed a joint session of Congress. The speech began by outlining the situation in Greece and Turkey and then placed the crisis in the wider context of an ideological confrontation between the United States and the Soviet Union. The President then came to the heart of his address which, almost immediately, became known as the Truman Doctrine:

> I believe that it must be the policy of the United States to support free people who are resisting attempted subjugation by armed minorities or by outside pressures. I believe that we must assist free peoples to work out their own destinies in their own way. (Reprinted in Bernstein and Matusow, 1966, p. 255)

Congress was asked to provide authority for $400 million to be shared between Greece and Turkey, and for permission to send civilians and military personnel to supervise reconstruction and training in the two countries. Both Houses of Congress approved the proposals: the United States had accepted the obligations which Britain was relinquishing. During the winter of 1947 'Pax Britannica' came to an end.

Whatever its implications for Britain's status as a great power, the reduction in external obligations had an impact on overseas government transactions which was little less than spectacular. The details of the transformation are shown in Table 8.2. From the

Table 8.2: United Kingdom: Overseas government transactions, 1946 to 1948 (£ million at current prices)

	1946	1947	1948
Payments:			
Military	374	209	113
Administrative, diplomatic, etc.	20	25	29
Relief and rehabilitation	213	118	31
Colonial grants	10	7	10
Total	527	359	183
Receipts:			
War disposals, settlements, etc. (net)	−164	−129	−96
Total government transactions (net)	363	230	87

Source: Treasury, *United Kingdom Balance of Payments 1946–1950*, London, HMSO (1950) Cmd 8065, 7.

figures presented, it is apparent that military expenditure overseas contracted by almost half between 1946 and 1947 and then almost halved again between 1947 and 1948. This steep rate of decline can be seen to have been reflected in net government transactions overseas which by 1948 were at less than a quarter of the 1946 level.[5]

By the close of the 1940s, military spending outside the UK was no longer of such magnitude as to threaten the viability of the economy. Moreover, manpower in the armed forces had declined to less than 800,000 while defence expenditure as a proportion of GNP amounted to 7 per cent, little more than a third of that in 1946. Nevertheless, both military expenditure and government payments abroad were still of quite disproportionate magnitude compared with pre-war.

THE OVERSEAS PRESENCE, 1950–64

While Britain's commitments in many parts of the world were progressively reduced, the military commitment to Germany was maintained. Immediately after the war, British forces were stationed in Germany as agents of one of the occupying powers but as the split between East and West grew wider they gradually assumed the role of protectors. This function increased in importance with the outbreak of the Korean War in June 1950 because fears of a sudden

Communist attack upon Western Europe were heightened. However, a major defence contribution from Germany was essential if Western security was to be substantially improved without undue economic sacrifice by the leading members of the Atlantic Alliance. On the other hand, a number of European countries were understandably reluctant to re-arm their former adversary. Britain played a leading part in obtaining their agreement to a revival of Germany's military establishment by accepting a long-term commitment to maintain four divisions and the Second Tactical Air Force on the Continent. The only qualifications to the obligation were that forces could be withdrawn in the 'event of an acute overseas emergency', or the placing of 'too great a strain on the external finances of the United Kingdom'.[6]

British forces in Germany thereby assumed a third role, that of underwriters for Germany's re-entry into the community of nations. At the time, the commitment to deploy troops on the Continent was not viewed as having considerable economic significance. Until twelve months after the ending of her occupation status, Germany continued to meet the cost of Allied forces on her soil but it was made clear by the Federal Republic that further budgetary support would be regarded as abhorrent. Reluctantly, the British accepted that they would have to shoulder the budgetary costs of the Continental commitment virtually unaided, but sought assistance with the foreign exchange costs in the light of an overall balance of payments deficit with Western Europe. For the next quarter of a century the economic aspects of troop stationing was dealt with by the periodic negotiation of 'offset' agreements.[7] In essence, these were based on the premise that if Germany contracted to purchase additional imports from Britain equal in value to the gross Deutschmark outlay incurred in troop stationing, then the foreign exchange consequences of defence spending in Germany could be neutralised. In the event, full restitution was never achieved but the offset mechanism was greatly prized by the British, particularly during periods of acute weakness in the external payments position.

The formal commitment to maintain a substantial garrison in the Federal Republic was undertaken at a time when the overall economic burden imposed by troop stationing was considered to be within acceptable limits. In particular, there was little concern with the balance of payments aspects of imperial obligations, because almost all the major garrisons were located within the Sterling Area. This state of affairs ensured that, as a consequence of close commercial and financial ties, a large portion of any military expenditure would be reflected in an increased demand for UK exports. In any case, even the gross balance of payments penalties of the imperial defence function were fairly small in the early part of the decade, averaging less than £90 million a year (see HMSO, 1959, p. 50).

During the 1950s a huge global presence appeared not merely sustainable, but also worthwhile since forces stationed overseas were felt to be protecting vital trade and investment interests. However, enthusiasm for the retention of imperial obligations foundered under the impact of growing third world nationalism and increasing costs.

Nationalist feeling was particularly intense in the case of Britain's main Middle East base, the Suez Canal Zone. This huge military complex was capable of supporting operations over a wide area. Unfortunately, by 1953, Egyptian hostility to the British presence was such that 50,000 troops were required to protect the 30,000 maintaining the base (*The Economist*, 26 September 1953, p. 839). The impracticality of operating the facilities efficiently was an important factor in Britain's decision to withdraw her forces from Egypt. The subsequent attempt, in 1956, to re-occupy the Canal Zone by force was indirectly responsible for the loss of base facilities in a number of other Middle East countries. As a result, by the end of the 1950s, rapid transit for British forces across the Middle East could no longer be guaranteed.

After the Suez crisis the UK revised the size and shape of her military establishment in an attempt to make it more cost effective. In the 1957 White Paper on defence it was made clear that a basic aim of future policy was to be the provision of well-equipped forces which made minimal demands upon manpower and other national resources (HMSO, 1957, p. 2). To this end, it was proposed to reduce forces overseas and to reinforce them at short notice, where and when necessary, with forces stationed in the United Kingdom.

In pursuance of the aims of the White Paper, the British Army of the Rhine was cut from 77,000 to 55,000 men. Similarly, forces in the Mediterranean were reduced in the certain knowledge that they could be reinforced from home. Further east, however, garrisons needed to be self-sufficient in the short term because of the emergence of a Middle East transport barrier. Facilities at Singapore were therefore complemented by the development of bases at Aden and in Kenya. Consequently, the rapid decline in the overall size of the armed forces after 1957 was not fully mirrored in the numbers deployed east of Suez.

Despite a reduction in the number of troops involved, the

budgetary and balance of payments costs of military obligations overseas rose sharply in the late 1950s and early 1960s.[8] This state of affairs was primarily a consequence of ending National Service. The pay and allowances of regular troops were far higher than those of conscripts. Furthermore, the substitution of volunteer for conscript forces produced a sharp rise in the proportion of married servicemen, thereby necessitating the construction of houses, schools, maternity departments and other welfare facilities at major stations overseas. Arguably, many of these building programmes were ill-conceived. Lavish facilities had been or were being provided in locations where future tenure was subject to considerable doubt.[9] In addition, a high proportion of the works programme was being devoted to projects which were secondary to the prime function of overseas bases.[10]

Even while expenditure of doubtful long-run military utility was being incurred in many parts of the world, Britain's external payments position was deteriorating. The relevance of rising defence spending to the balance of payments problem is apparent from Table 8.3, which presents the main components of the current account for the years 1957–64.

The figures in Table 8.3 demonstrate that the visible balance fluctuated markedly during the years shown, achieving a small surplus in 1958 and particularly large deficits in 1960 and 1964. In contrast, the invisibles balance showed a consistent surplus throughout the period. However, the surplus was tending to decline. It fell from a peak of £318 million in 1958 to less than half that figure in 1964. The declining balance was clearly not attributable to any weakening in net private invisible earnings, since the annual average surplus on this item showed an encouraging upward trend. Instead, the fall in the annual surplus could be attributed to the rapid rise in net government spending abroad, which increased from only £144 million in 1957 to £432 million in 1964. This rise, in turn, was mainly the consequence of an increase of some 450 per cent in overseas military expenditure during the period under consideration. Thus, during the early part of the 1960s, some scaling down of Britain's external military presence was becoming increasingly attractive because of the need to conserve foreign exchange. Not that the state of the balance of payments was the only problem associated with the deployment of forces outside the UK.

The intricacy, cost and obsolescence rate of weapons had all greatly increased during the post-war period. Until the early 1960s, however, it had been possible to minimise the consequences of this

Table 8.3: United Kingdom: Current account of the Balance of Payments, 1957 to 1964 (£ million)

	1957	1958	1959	1960	1961	1962	1963	1964
Visible balance	−29	+29	−118	−408	−153	−104	−43	−545
Government (net)								
Military	−61	−126	−129	−172	−198	−223	−236	−267
Other	−83	−93	−98	−110	−134	−136	−145	−165
Private invisibles (net)	+406	+537	+494	+432	+490	+590	+580	+575
Invisible balance	+262	+318	+267	+150	+158	+231	+199	+143
Current balance	+233	+347	+149	−258	+5	+127	+116	−402

Source: Central Statistical Office, *United Kingdom Balance of Payments*, London, HMSO (1967) 4.

trend by giving priority to the European role, in the provision of new equipment, while simultaneously maintaining other obligations largely with the material legacies of the Second World War and re-armament. Such a policy had proved feasible during the 1950s because the size of forces deployed could compensate for most equipment deficiencies, which in any case were not felt too greatly because the majority of potential foes were endowed with even less sophisticated military resources. However, during the 1960s, third world nations were increasingly in receipt of modern equipment which British forces would need to match at considerable cost, if they were to remain formidable. Hence, though little awareness of the fact was apparent at the beginning of the decade, Britain was faced with a choice, which could not be long delayed. Either, existing deployments could be maintained, thereby incurring a sharp increase in the proportion of resources devoted to defence, in order to re-equip the imperial forces, or alternatively a different level of trade-off between commitments and expenditure could be fashioned.

GEOGRAPHICAL CONTRACTION 1965–79

The Labour administration which entered office in October 1964 was determined to reduce the proportion of GNP devoted to defence from 7 per cent to only 6 per cent, motivated partly by the wish to expand various social programmes without a substantial rise in either taxation or overall public expenditure. At the same time, there was a desire to reduce overseas military spending in the light of the worsening balance of payments situation. In pursuance of substantial budgetary savings the Cabinet decided that in 1969–70 defence expenditure, at constant prices, would be pegged at £2,000 million instead of rising to £2,400 million, as had been contemplated by the previous government. The policy of 'cuts' commenced with the cancellation of a number of military procurement projects, including the TSR-2 which had been intended as a replacement for the Canberra bomber. However, such measures could not have a significant impact upon the foreign exchange costs of defence spending. Attention therefore began to focus on external obligations.

By the mid 1960s, forces overseas were deployed so as to undertake two prime functions, namely the support of NATO and the maintenance of a substantial military presence in the eastern hemisphere. This distribution of troops was reflected in the pattern of budgetary and foreign exchange expenditures outside the UK. Table 8.4 presents the breakdown of the £605 million budgetary spending directly attributable to forces stationed overseas in 1966–7. The figures include the pay and allowances of personnel in each area; the cost of facilities; and the costs of purchasing, operating and maintaining equipment, but exclude any apportionment of overhead costs incurred at home. Of the total spent abroad, approximately half can be seen to have been accounted for by east of Suez commitments while a further third was attributable to Germany. Table 8.5 which relates to actual outlays in foreign currency expended in support of troops abroad, shows a similar dominance of the statistics by the eastern hemisphere and Germany. Substantial expenditure reductions overseas would therefore have to come mainly from either or both of these areas.

Initially it appeared that the brunt of any cuts would be borne mainly by forces stationed in Germany.[11] In the event, economies were fashioned largely from the military presence on the perimeter of the Indian Ocean. This choice was the outcome of both political and economic considerations. To begin with, the UK was aware from past experience that any attempt to tamper with the Continental commitment was bound to elicit an adverse response from leading Allies. There was therefore understandable reluctance to adopt a course of action which would alienate the very nations upon whose goodwill Britain's eventual entry into the European Economic Community depended. Moreover, when faced with the distinct possibility that Britain might withdraw significant numbers of troops, Germany, though never eager to do so, accepted the need to cover a substantial part of the foreign currency cost of the Army of the Rhine through offset arrangements. Indeed, under the terms of

Table 8.4: Geographical attribution of overseas defence spending, 1966–7 (£ million)

Germany (excluding Berlin)	199
Berlin	4
Far East (excluding Hong Kong)	235
Hong Kong	16
Middle East	66
Mediterranean	67
Other overseas areas (including RAF staging posts)	18
Total	605

Source: *Statement on the Defence Estimates 1968*, London, HMSO, Cmd 3540, Annex H, Table 1.

Table 8.5: Foreign exchange expenditure, 1966–7 (£ million)

Local defence expenditure by area					Other HQ expenditure	Total
Germany	Far East	Middle East	Mediterranean	Other areas		
89	95	28	38	31	19	300

Source: *Statement on the Defence Estimates 1968*, London, HMSO, Cmd 3540, Table 3.

the various agreements negotiated during the second part of the 1960s, Germany could be regarded as covering more than two-thirds of the total foreign exchange costs of the Rhine Army. The pressure on Britain to cut forces in Germany for balance of payments reasons was thereby eased.

The case for giving priority to a west-of-Suez policy was reinforced by events in South East Asia. Enthusiasm for a major extra-European role began to wane as the cost of 'confrontation' with Indonesia in Borneo mounted. Between 1963 and 1966 service personnel in the Far East increased by some 50 per cent to 63,000. As is evident from Tables 8.4 and 8.5 during the mid 1960s the Far East constituted Britain's single most costly overseas defence obligation in terms of both budgetary and foreign currency expenditure. Some constraint upon future British commitments east of Suez was therefore becoming an increasingly attractive proposition for a government anxious to achieve substantial savings in defence costs.

The first moves, in a process which was to reduce drastically the British military presence east of Suez, were taken in February 1966, when it was decided that the existing carrier force should be phased out without replacement. In a sense, this resolution constituted little more than the abandonment of yet another projected military investment but, in practice, it implied an eventual curtailment of obligations. The gradual elimination of Britain's major strategic capability in the Indian Ocean was to be compensated for by placing tighter limits upon non-European military involvement. The new parameters were specified in the Statement on the Defence Estimates for 1966:

> First, Britain will not undertake major operations of war except in co-operation with allies. Secondly, we will not accept an obligation to provide another country with military assistance unless it is prepared to provide us with the facilities we need to make such assistance effective in time. Finally, there will be no attempt to maintain defence facilities in an independent country against its wishes. (HMSO, 1966, p. 7)

In keeping with the third of the new guidelines, the White Paper stated that the Aden base was to be evacuated as soon as South Arabia was granted its independence (HMSO, 1966, p. 8). The proposed withdrawal from Aden was of major consequence since Britain's defence strategy, in the eastern hemisphere had for a number of years rested heavily on the concept of two major bases. Henceforth, there would be only one relatively isolated concentration of British military power outside Western Europe now that the original global 'chain' of bases had been reduced to the point where the residual constituted little more than a series of staging posts. On the other hand, withdrawal from Aden would eliminate a large part of the £66 million annual defence expenditure incurred in the Middle East. The fact that a substantial portion of the reduction would constitute a foreign exchange component provided an added incentive. The process of reducing commitments so as to produce foreign exchange savings, in addition to budgetary relief, had thus begun. The White Paper also stated that defence cuts were to be made in the Mediterranean (where the proposals met with strong local resistance for economic reasons), but in the main remnant of the Imperial Commitment, namely Malaysia and Singapore, no changes in force levels were possible so long as the conflict with Indonesia continued (HMSO, 1966).

By August 1966, the agreement with Indonesia which ended

confrontation at last offered the opportunity to make a complete reassessment of the nature and scale of Britain's role east of Suez. A new defence review was therefore initiated within the previous £2,000 million ceiling. The results of the second defence review were contained in the White Paper of July 1967 (HMSO, 1967). This contained a statement of intent with respect to British commitments in South East Asia to the effect that, 'We plan to withdraw altogether from our bases in Singapore and Malaya in the middle of the 1970s' (HMSO, 1967, p. 3).[12] The Defence Secretary, Mr Denis Healey, explained the rationale and implications of this decision to the House of Commons on 27 July (Hansard, 1967). He pointed out that, as a result of the ending of confrontation, manpower in the Far East had been reduced by some 10,000 but during 1970–1 numbers working in and for the forces in Malaya and Singapore would have been reduced by a further 30,000. In Mr Healey's view this reduced deployment altered the entire cost-benefit equation of the fixed base strategy:

> Once our presence in the Far East is reduced by one-half, once our commitments particularly in SEATO are reduced, the sort of base facilities we maintain at present on the Asian mainland become very bad value for money indeed. (Hansard, 1967, col. 990)

This conclusion was based on the high fixed cost element involved in the provision of base facilities. Forces were needed to guard those who ensured the security and usability of large quantities of equipment; base personnel and their families required a host of facilities; moreover, to a considerable extent, both men and equipment had to be duplicated at home so as to permit duty rotation and to ensure efficient training. In the Defence Secretary's opinion, such lavish facilities could only be justified in the unlikely event of large-scale warfare.

By altering the size and composition of forces in the Far East and by eliminating 'wasteful' duplication, the Defence Secretary envisaged substantial savings in personnel by the mid 1970s. Service manpower would by then have fallen by 75,000 and civilians working for the forces by a further 80,000, of whom some 50,000 would be overseas employees. This reduction in manpower would facilitate large reductions in expenditure and foreign exchange outflows now that the last important remnant of the 'Imperial Garrison' concept was to be abandoned.

The pattern of defence spending at last appeared to have been clearly mapped out — but in little more than four months military expenditure was the subject of yet another searing reappraisal. In November of 1967, the government implicitly acknowledged the failure of its policies to correct the balance of payments by announcing a 14.3 per cent devaluation of sterling. As part of a post-devaluation package of public expenditure measures, defence spending was to be cut yet again. The withdrawal from the Far East was to be accelerated so as to complete the process by the end of 1971. This was, of course, merely a change of timing. The new element, however, was the decision to withdraw British forces from the Persian Gulf by the same date.

In aggregate, the defence policy changes of the mid 1960s constituted the most fundamental revision in military strategy of the entire post-war period. In 1964, Britain still clung to the remnants of its former global defence framework, within which non-European commitments were considered of equal importance to those of Europe. Little more than a decade later, the field of operations had been reduced to a European perspective. Yet this basic re-shaping of Britain's defence posture had never been intended by the incoming administration of 1964, it was simply the outcome of a series of particular short-run responses to a changing situation over a period of less than four years.

The policymakers of the mid 1960s tended to justify reductions in defence expenditure by attributing Britain's economic failures to the size of her military establishment. This identification of military spending as a crucial factor in explaining the inability of the British economy to perform as well as its major industrial counterparts rested on the acceptance of two unproven assertions. Firstly, that defence expenditure was at such a level that it represented an unacceptably high opportunity cost in terms of investment, growth and exports. Secondly, that the proportion of defence expenditure resulting in foreign exchange flows was a major cause of Britain's balance of payments problems.

These two arguments also provided much of the underpinning for the measures introduced by the incoming Labour administration of 1974. Labour's plans envisaged a reduction in military spending to only 4.5 per cent of GNP by 1983–4, an objective which was to be achieved by an even greater concentration of the defence effort upon the United Kingdom, the Eastern Atlantic and the central region of NATO (see HMSO, 1975, pp. 4 and 7). To this end, geographical contraction was to be taken a stage further in that Naval forces would no longer be permanently deployed in support of NATO in the Mediterranean and residual extra-European activities were to be further curtailed.

THE EXTERNAL PRESENCE: TRENDS AND PROSPECTS

The early 1980s constituted the end of an era in defence policy in the sense that the prime post-war method of controlling defence expenditure, through the progressive curtailment of commitments outside Europe, was all but exhausted. A depleted garrison in Hong Kong was the sole significant remnant of the former east of Suez presence. Elsewhere only tiny pockets of the former imperial garrisons survived: Cyprus-based forces were at a minimum operational level, while a mere token presence was maintained in Gibraltar, Belize and the Falkland Islands. In effect, Britain's defence horizons had shrunk to little more than Western Europe and the Eastern Atlantic. Nevertheless, by the start of 1981 the seemingly inexorable rise in the cost of the two major defence inputs, men and equipment, again required a realignment of defence expenditure and available resources. This situation had arisen despite a steady increase in the size of the defence budget in the wake of the NATO request to aim at an annual rise, in real terms, of some three per cent.

The outcome of the defence review of January–June 1981 was published in a White Paper entitled *The United Kingdom Defence Programme: The Way Forward* (HMSO, 1981). This document represented an attempt to restore balance in the defence budget, while minimising the adverse impact on military outputs. It proposed a number of cutbacks including a reduction in the size of the surface fleet and in the number of military personnel. Nonetheless, Britain's basic defence posture emerged unaltered. Had the state of the balance of payments still been a major cause of concern, then the scale of Britain's military presence in Germany might have become a focus of attention. In fact, as Table 8.6 makes clear, in the early 1980s the UK was basking in the warmth of a massive current account surplus generated largely as a result of swiftly rising oil output from the North Sea. The across-the-exchanges cost of British Forces Germany was not therefore a pressing issue at the time of the 1981 defence review.

Since then, continuing rises in the real cost of defence inputs and amendments to the military programme in the wake of the Falklands

Table 8.6: United Kingdom: Current account of the Balance of Payments, 1980–4 (£ million)

	Oil balance A	Non-oil balance B	Visible balance C(A + B)	Invisible balance D	Current account C + D
1980	+ 315	+ 1,046	+1,361	+1,739	+3,100
1981	+3,111	+ 249	+3,360	+3,168	+6,528
1982	+4,643	− 2,312	+2,331	+2,332	+4,663
1983	+6,976	− 7,811	− 835	+4,003	+3,168
1984	+7,136	−11,237	−4,101	+5,036	+ 935

Source: CSO, *Economic Trends*, no. 383, September 1985.

conflict have raised the claims on national resources imposed by security needs. This situation notwithstanding, in the 1984 Public Expenditure White Paper it was announced that 1985–6 would be the last year in which Britain would attempt to implement three per cent real growth in annual spending (HMSO, 1984, vol. 1, para. 9). Thus, in pursuance of the aspiration of restraining public expenditure, level funding appears to be the best that the military sector can expect during the remainder of this decade. Strong pressures on the defence budget therefore appear inevitable, despite recent attempts to mitigate them by means of improvements in the efficiency of defence provision. It seems clear that in an endeavour to meet commitments the initial response to a tightening of the budget constraint will be a resort to all-round economies in the defence programme rather than drastic surgery in a particular area.[13] However, the historical record suggests that, sooner or later, the government of the day will have to try and eliminate the root causes of a growing disparity between inadequate funding and escalating costs, rather than merely accommodate the problem by permitting an across-the-board dilution of force capabilities. At such a time, the economic case for pruning Britain's commitment in Central Europe may prove compelling.

Directly and indirectly, Britain's contribution of ground and tactical air forces in the European theatre probably absorbs almost two-fifths of the defence budget (suggested by Greenwood, 1984, p. 29). In large measure, this high ratio is a reflection of the fact that the Army of the Rhine is a labour-intensive contribution to NATO which, in terms of numbers, has remained substantially unchanged since the late 1950s. British Forces Germany is not expensive merely in budgetary terms for, as the estimates presented in Table

Table 8.7: Defence Balance of Payments: invisible payments, 1985–6[a] (£ million)

Local defence expenditure	1,164
Germany	920
Other NATO areas	80
Mediterranean	132
South Atlantic	8
Far East	–19
Other areas	42
Other military services[b]	251
Transfers/contributions to international defence organisations	44
Total debits	1,459

a. Estimates.
b. Including contributions to infrastructure projects (net) and payments for R & D levies.

Source: *Statement on the Defence Estimates 1985*, London, HMSO, Cmd 9430–11, Table 2.10.

8.7 emphasise, the Federal Republic of Germany accounts for almost two-thirds of Britain's defence-related invisible payments.

This currency drain is not viewed with apprehension at the present time because it is supported by the foreign exchange earnings of North Sea oil. However, as Table 8.6 emphasises, the growing surplus on trade in oil has been accompanied by a marked deterioration in non-oil trade. Indeed, since 1983 there has been a peacetime deficit in manufactured goods for the first time since the Industrial Revolution. This major structural change might not be considered a cause for concern were it not for the probability that oil output is at its peak and could begin to decline rapidly by the close of the decade. Increasing returns on overseas investments will be of insufficient value to compensate for the contraction in the oil export surplus. Consequently a fall in the real exchange rate (thereby increasing the Deutschmark cost of British Forces Germany) will be necessary in order to improve the competitive position of British industry in domestic and foreign markets. Nevertheless, the past performance of the manufacturing sector suggests that it will experience considerable difficulty in improving its relative performance, even with the aid of a declining exchange rate.

The decline in oil production thus seems likely to result in the return of external payments problems. The nation's dependence on a healthy invisibles balance therefore appears destined to increase during the next decade. In such circumstances, the record of the post-war years indicates that the Treasury will be reluctant to accept an erosion of the invisibles position as a result of rising military outlays in Germany. Balance of payments considerations a few years hence may thus highlight the Continental commitment as an attractive candidate for pruning should the cumulative pressures on the defence budget prove too great. Should this occur, and the precedents of the last few decades suggest that it will, national financial constraints will once again have succeeded in shaping military thinking, and in turn determining the nature and geographical distribution of the country's armed forces.

NOTES

1. A further $1,250m was subsequently put at Britain's disposal by Canada.

2. A clear manifestation of America's growing awareness of the strategic significance of the Eastern Mediterranean and the Middle East occurred in August 1946, when the Russians sought a revision of the Montreux Convention so as to permit joint Turkish–Soviet defence of the Dardanelles. The United States responded by despatching Naval units to the Eastern Mediterranean, thereby demonstrating a willingness to use force in order to prevent a further expansion of Soviet influence.

3. The military implications of providing the forces necessary to maintain imperial authority were explained to the Cabinet in a memorandum from the Defence Committee in June 1946. See PRO Cab. 129/10 CP (46) 68, India — Military Implications of Proposed Courses of Action, the Defence Committee, 12 June 1946.

4. For the official British view of the factors leading to the surrender of the Mandate, see Colonial and Foreign Office, *Palestine: Termination of the Mandate 15th May, 1948*, London, HMSO, 1948.

5. Largely as a result of the fall in government spending, the current account deficit was reduced from £348m in 1946 to only £80m in 1948. However, reduced public spending abroad could contribute little to easing the acute imbalance of trade with the Dollar Area because such expenditure was confined to areas where the Dollar outlay was of little consequence. Indeed, no economic instruments at the disposal of the United Kingdom could deal adequately with the Dollar shortage which was a world problem. The imbalance in regional trade flows was eventually eliminated with the help of the Marshall Plan.

6. See Protocol no. 11 on Forces of the Western European Union, Article 6, Paris, October 1954.

7. The offset arrangement ended on 31 March 1980 with the expiry of the agreement for the period 1977–80. See *Exchange of Notes between the Government of the United Kingdom of Great Britain and Northern Ireland and the Government of the Federal Republic of Germany for offsetting the*

Foreign Exchange Expenditure of British Forces in the Federal Republic of Germany, Cmd. 6970, London, HMSO, 1977 (Treaty Series no. 101).

8. The foreign exchange implications of maintaining forces within the Sterling Area also became of greater consequence when the pound was made fully convertible in 1958.

9. See, for example, the comments on building projects at Benghazi in House of Commons, Ninth Report from the Estimates Committee, Session 1963–4, *Military Expenditure Overseas*, p. xvi.

10. Perhaps the most striking example of this tendency was Cyprus, where, in 1962–3 some £2.5m was provided for married quarters and the completion of a hospital but only £311,000 for airfield works, at a time when the 'operational facilities at the airfield were less than could be desired'. House of Commons, Tenth Report from the Estimates Committee, Session 1962–3, *Military Expenditure Overseas*, pp. vii–viii.

11. This was certainly the impression to be gained from the 1965 Defence White Paper which stressed the importance of Britain's non-European military role, while adopting a highly critical attitude to the scale of continental commitment. See *Statement on the Defence Estimates 1965*, Cmd. 2592, London, HMSO, 1965, pp. 8 and 9.

12. See HMSO (1967) p. 3. The announcement was received with considerable gloom in Singapore. Britain's bases on the island employed directly more than 30,000 civilians, supporting probably 200,000 of a population of some two million. Moreover, local spending by troops and their dependants averaged more than £25m a year (see *The Economist*, 29 April 1967, p. 447). In the event, the economy of Singapore adapted remarkably swiftly and successfully to the termination of a major British presence on the island.

13. Salami-slicing rather than amputation in the face of severe financial pressure would undoubtedly be the preference of the Service Chiefs. See House of Commons, Third Report from the Defence Committee, Session 1984–5, *Defence Commitments and Resources*, vol. 11, para. 1366.

REFERENCES

Bernstein, B.J. and Matusow, A.J. (eds) (1966) *The Truman Administration, A Documentary History*, Congressional Record, Eighteenth Congress, first session, New York.

Dow, J.C.R. (1968) *The Management of the British Economy 1945–60*, Cambridge.

Greenwood, D. (1984) 'Managing the Defence Programme and Budget', *The Three Banks Review*, 142, June.

Hansard (1946) *House of Commons Debates*, 434, 6 March 1946, col. 651.

Hansard (1947a) *House of Commons Debates*, 441, 7 August 1947, col. 1662.

Hansard (1947b) *House of Commons Debates*, 443, 18 February 1947, col. 993.

Hansard (1967) *House of Commons Debates*, 750, 27 July 1967, cols. 385–991.

HMSO (1946a) *Statistical Material Presented During the Washington Negotiations*, Cmd. 6706, Appendix V, London.
HMSO (1946b) *Statement Relating to Defence 1946*, Cmd. 6743, 4–5, London.
HMSO (1957) *Defence: Outline of Future Policy*, Cmd. 124, London.
HMSO (1959) *United Kingdom Balance of Payments 1946–1957*, Treasury, London.
HMSO (1966) *Statement on the Defence Estimates 1966, Part 1: The Defence Review*, Cmd. 2901, London.
HMSO (1967) *Supplementary Statement on Defence Policy*, Cmd. 3357, London.
HMSO (1975) *Statement on the Defence Estimates 1975*, Cmd. 5976, London.
HMSO (1981) *The United Kingdom Defence Programme: the Way Forward*, Cmd. 8288, London.
HMSO (1984) *The Government's Expenditure Plans 1984–85 to 1986–87*, Cmd. 9143, London.
PRO (1946a) *Balance of Payments for 1946*, Memorandum by the Chancellor of the Exchequer, 8 February 1946, Cab. 129/7 CP (46) 53.
PRO (1946b) *Greece*, Memorandum by the Secretary of State for Foreign Affairs, 30 May 1946, Cab. 129/10 CP (46) 213.

9

Military Training in National Parks: A Question of Land Use Conflict and National Priorities

Mark Blacksell and Fiona Reynolds

There has never been a single, coherent policy towards land use in the United Kingdom and in so crowded a country, where the average population density is 227 persons per square kilometre, it may well be unreasonable and, certainly, unrealistic to suppose that categoric and immutable decisions about who should do what and where can be made. Nevertheless, in those instances where the government has pronounced how land should, or more frequently should *not*, be used, it has often proved hard in practice to adhere to the policy because of rival claims. A classic instance of such conflict is the demand for military training areas on land designated as National Parks in England and Wales.

BACKGROUND TO THE CONFLICT

Many of the most fundamental decisions about present day land use in the United Kingdom were taken in the hectic period of legislative activity immediately after the end of the Second World War. Effective land use planning, with the possibility of zoning, then became a reality and ten National Parks and a number of other protected landscapes were designated, mostly under the terms of the National Parks and Access to the Countryside Act 1949. Seven of the National Parks (Dartmoor, Exmoor, the Lake District, Northumberland, the North York Moors, the Peak District, and the Yorkshire Dales) are in England and three (Brecon Beacons, the Pembrokeshire Coast, and Snowdonia) in Wales. None has been designated in either Scotland or Northern Ireland.

All the National Parks are in the uplands of north and west Britain and much of the land they encompass is either open moorland, rough grazing or permanent pasture, where the intensity, though not the extent, of agricultural activity is relatively low. In many of these areas, notably Dartmoor, Northumberland and the Pembrokeshire Coast, military training has been an important activity since the nineteenth century and is well integrated into the local pattern of social and economic life. Even so, it was recognised from the outset that the use of National Park land for such purposes was a source of serious, potential conflict, which could only be resolved ultimately by government.

In his seminal report on the feasibility and desirability of establishing a system of National Parks in England and Wales, prepared at the behest of the Minister of Town and Country Planning, John Dower proposed that National Parks be defined in the following terms: 'A National Park may be defined, in application to Great Britain, as an extensive area of beautiful and relatively wild country in which, for the nation's benefit and by appropriate national decision and action, (a) the characteristic landscape beauty is strictly preserved, (b) access and facilities for public open-air enjoyment are amply provided, (c) wild life and buildings and places of architectural and historic interest are suitably protected, while (d) established farming use is effectively maintained' (Dower, 1945, p. 6). He recognised that such a definition would inevitably lead to conflict, referring specifically to military training: 'Considerable stretches are being used, more or less intensively, for large scale afforestation, quarrying and mining, *military ranges* [our emphasis] or other purposes which cannot be successfully combined with National Park requirements' (Dower, 1945, p. 7). Later in the report Dower expanded on the potential conflicts, again picking out 'military occupation, especially in permanent artillery, tank and bombing ranges' (Dower, 1945, p. 16) and suggested some important principles which might be adopted to help reduce them. 'It is not, of course, a question of prohibiting such uses of land anywhere and everywhere: most of them — although not in any unavoidable ugliness or wastefulness of form — are essential to the national economy, and suitable sites must be found for them. But it matters enormously *where* and *how*. In National Park areas the less of them the better. They must be made subject to a control no less effective than that which applies to ordinary building development; and, if continuance of uses and works already established must usually be accepted, any new exploitation — or major extension of an existing one — should be permitted only on clear proof that it is required in the national interest and that no satisfactory alternative site, not in a National Park area can be found. Such cases should be rare' (Dower, 1945, pp. 16–17).

In July 1945 the government set up a committee, chaired by Sir Arthur Hobhouse, to consider Dower's proposals and to recommend those areas to be selected first for designation as National Parks. When the committee reported in 1947 it had a number of clear and unequivocal comments to make on military training and service use, describing the conflicts in the following terms: 'The extensive demands of the Service Departments for training areas in the wild uncultivated land of England and Wales have most serious implications for National Parks, especially where land is required for training with live ammunition. From this land the public would be excluded on account of danger from firing and from unexploded missiles. Moreover, the problem is not confined to considerations of acreage alone, for many of the areas involved are of outstanding interest and beauty. *It would be no exaggeration to say that the appropriation of a number of particular areas now listed for acquisition by the Service Departments would take the heart out of the proposed National Park areas in which they are sited, and in certain cases render our proposals for the designation of individual National Parks entirely nugatory* [our emphasis]. Service Department occupation and use will also involve other subsidiary objections, such as the disturbance by gunfire of peace and harmony of far wider areas than those actually appropriated, the disfigurement of the landscape by camps and military buildings, serious detriment to agriculture, interference with wildlife, the inevitable defacement of the surface of the land and destruction of its vegetation by tracked vehicles, and the danger and annoyance occasioned on narrow roads by military traffic' (Hobhouse, 1947, p. 34). The report went on to make four crucial recommendations:

(i) the setting up of permanent machinery to review Service Department holdings in National Parks, so that military uses may be discontinued as soon as they are no longer essential for national security;
(ii) all new acquisitions of land for purposes of military training should be sent to the National Parks Commission for comment, so that their views may be given due weight;
(iii) any land being disposed of by the Service Departments should be notified to the Commission, so that it can itself

acquire land or property which might be of value for National Park purposes, or make recommendations about its disposal or reinstatement to the appropriate government department;

(iv) all low flying aircraft in or near to National Parks should be prohibited except for cases where it is essential for national defence or air communications.

In principle, successive governments accepted the recommendations of the Hobhouse Committee, but, in the first instance, the overwhelming priority was to ensure that National Parks were actually designated, rather than imposing too severe restrictions on what exactly took place within their boundaries. Thus, while there was some military training in all ten National Parks, in Dartmoor, Northumberland and the Pembrokeshire Coast it was, and still is, a major land use and an important source of conflict, which was bound to lead to friction and public disagreement over national priorities.

The problem initially facing the local authorities and special planning boards charged with managing the National Parks was not resisting further incursions by the military, but rather finding ways of curbing and reducing their already extensive activities. For more than 20 years successive governments resisted all attempts to challenge or formally review the scale of military activities, as recommended by the Hobhouse Committee, and it was not until 1971 that a Defence Lands Review Committee was set up under the chairmanship of Lord Nugent. One of the main tasks of this committee was to review all land holdings by the Ministry of Defence (the Service Departments had by now been amalgamated into a single ministry) for any purpose in National Parks and Areas of Outstanding Natural Beauty, with a view to improving access for the general public and giving greater scope for recreation and leisure activities.

The Nugent Committee (Nugent, 1973) established that the total land holdings of the Ministry of Defence were 284,000ha and that in many areas where the landscape was protected, notably in the National Parks, there was limited scope for releasing some of this land and ameliorating the impact of military use, even though it felt that the overall amount of land available for training was barely adequate. The conflicts identified by the Committee were almost identical to those highlighted in the Dower and Hobhouse Reports a generation previously, but the proposals for resolving them were generally weak and unspecific. Altogether there were 26 recommendations, of which the following bore most directly on National Parks:

(i) 'There should continue to be no major expansion of an existing Defence site, nor development of a new one . . . within a National Park . . . without consultation with the local planning authorities and . . . with the National Park Authority. There should also be consultation with the Countryside Commission (the successor to the National Parks Commission), where this is not already provided for' (paragraph 7.27).

(ii) 'The Ministry of Defence should review arrangements for access to its sites, particularly those . . . which interrupt long distance paths and those to which so far no access has ever been given; every effort should be made to improve access where possible, as soon as this can be done consistently with operational safety and security requirements and with agricultural and other interests' (paragraph 8.06).

(iii) 'Much more attention than at present should be given by both the Ministry of Defence and the Property Services Agency of the Department of the Environment to carrying out work to improve the appearance of Defence sites, particularly through the removal of derelict buildings and eyesores, and through greater attention to landscaping; this work should be carried out in consultation with the local planning authorities and should be the subject of regular reviews' (paragraph 8.23).

(iv) 'Fuller account should be taken of environmental and amenity considerations in all aspects of the construction and maintenance of Defence sites, and the best possible advice should be sought in this regard' (paragraph 8.25).

(v) 'In the implementation of all measures we propose, and especially those regarding improvements to site appearance and clearance, particular attention and priority should be given to Defence lands in special areas' (i.e. National Parks; paragraph 8.54).

In a number of ways the timing of the Nugent Committee report was unfortunate. The delay of more than 20 years in setting up the first, comprehensive, review of Defence land requirements after the Second World War, especially in view of the designation of the ten National Parks, allowed attitudes to harden and training areas to become established. Inevitably, this weakened the case for excluding military activities from National Parks. The effectiveness of the report in this regard was further undermined, because in 1971, while the Nugent Committee was in the middle of its deliberations, the government appointed the National Parks Policy Review Committee, chaired by Lord Sandford, to review the achievements of National Parks in England and Wales and to make recommendations about future policies. The coincidence of timing led the Sandford Committee to reject making any independent review of Ministry of Defence lands in National Parks, although given the widespread concern it felt bound to comment on the Nugent Committee's findings in its own final report (Sandford, 1973). All the Committee could do, however, was to reiterate the general objections to military training in National Parks, albeit in rather more specific terms than hitherto. A majority of members recommended that any extension of military training sites in or adjoining a National Park should be the subject of a public inquiry, and that there should be a quinquennial review and report to parliament of Ministry of Defence sites in National Parks (paragraph 5.35). One member of the Committee, John Cousins, went even further, recommending that, in the light of the Nugent report, all military activity in National Parks be phased out (paragraph 5.36).

The government response to both these reports was predictably cautious, rejecting the call for a quinquennial review and extolling the benefits of consultation between the Ministry of Defence and National Park Authorities (Ministry of Defence, 1974; Department of the Environment, 1976). The firmest statement to emerge was an expression of hope that it might be possible in the future to release more land from military training.

Of all the National Parks, the greatest and most sustained concern over military training has surrounded Dartmoor. The Nugent Committee received more representations about it than any other site in the whole of the United Kingdom and their report revealed a deep division as to how the conflict should be resolved (Nugent, 1973, pp. 120–3). Even in a National Park, the majority of the Committee did not feel justified in recommending the disposal of a site fulfilling a vital military function, unless they were able to offer a sure alternative in the form of land already owned, leased or held on licence by the Ministry of Defence. One member, John Cripps, the then Chairman of the Countryside Commission, felt that such a restrictive concession did not go far enough and argued that everything possible should be done to find alternatives, especially where there was such a clear conflict as land designated as a National Park.

There was some marginal reduction in the amount of land used on Dartmoor for military training in the wake of the Nugent Report (from 137 sq km to 132 sq km), but this in no way satisfied local opposition and, eventually, in 1975, Baroness Sharp was asked jointly by the Department of the Environment and the Ministry of Defence to inquire into whether the military training carried out on Dartmoor could be met elsewhere in south west England. Given such limited geographical terms of reference, it is hardly surprising that, apart from reiterating the inappropriateness of military training in a National Park, Baroness Sharp's report did little to resolve the fundamental land use dilemma as to how National Park and Defence policies were to be reconciled.

The government's response to Baroness Sharp's report was to state unequivocally that the continuance of military training on Dartmoor was unavoidable for the foreseeable future. The Dartmoor National Park Committee was thus left with very little room for manoeuvre and felt impelled to back improved consultation, rather than open opposition. A steering group was set up under an independent chairman, appointed by the Department of the Environment and the Ministry of Defence, with the membership drawn from the National Park Committee, the services, the relevant government departments, statutory agencies such as the Countryside Commission and the Nature Conservancy Council, and the more important of the affected landowners.

The initial contribution of this group can only be described as disastrous. Its meetings were private and therefore regarded with a mixture of suspicion and scepticism by all those bodies opposed to military training. The Dartmoor Preservation Association, the main pressure group fighting for the primacy of National Park values in land use policies for Dartmoor, believed the group was merely a secretive device for legitimising uninterrupted military training. Its worst fears were confirmed when the National Trust refused to renew the lease on part of Ringmoor, one of the training areas it owned in the south west of the National Park, when it ran out in 1976. The Ministry of Defence insisted that an alternative site had to be found on Dartmoor and, eventually, the Dartmoor National Park Committee reluctantly acquiesced to land being leased from the South West Water Authority at Cramber Tor in the middle of the high moorland.

Although the land substitution went ahead, the resulting outcry forced the Dartmoor National Park Committee to reassess both its policy on military training and its role in the steering group. In 1981 it resolved not only to try to reduce the level of military training on Dartmoor, but actively to resist any further investment in military facilities and any licensing of new land for training. Whereas, previously, it had participated in the steering group without a declared, clear-cut, policy, it now adopted a much more rigid and unambiguous stance.

In principle the policy conflict on Dartmoor is the same as in all the other National Parks, but it is more sharply focused than elsewhere. The scale and variety of military training are large and the location on the south west peninsula means that possible alternative training grounds are a considerable distance away and inconvenient for meeting the local service needs. However, the most important reason for the spotlight being pointed so persistently on Dartmoor is the strength of the opposition and the formidable organisation of the Dartmoor Preservation Association. This pressure group has succeeded, better than any other in the United Kingdom, in highlighting the conflict and sharpening the arguments against military training in National Parks. As a direct result of its activities the incursions by the services into Dartmoor have been the main focus of the conflict with the military throughout the 1970s and 1980s.

THE NATURE OF THE MILITARY PRESENCE

The Ministry of Defence actually only owns or leases 2.4 per cent of the total area of National Park land in England and Wales (32,644ha), though it enjoys some rights over a further 0.9 per cent (11,860ha). This is less than half the area administered by the Forestry Commission and somewhat less than the area owned by the various Regional Water Authorities. Nevertheless, the nature of the activities pursued in the course of military training are a peculiar irritant to the general public, because they restrict access, involve the movement of large numbers of people and quantities of equipment, are noisy, and frequently cause damage, especially to ancient monuments.

In fact the activities carried out under the guise of military training are extremely varied and, while some are patently incompatible with the aims and objectives of National Parks, others impinge very little, and some seem ideally suited to such areas. The greatest offence is caused by live firing, a term which includes the use of all types of gun, from heavy artillery to small arms. Artillery is only used extensively in Dartmoor, Northumberland and the Pembrokeshire Coast, though there is live firing of some description in all but three Parks (Brecon Beacons, Exmoor and the Lake District) (Council for National Parks, 1985; MacDiarmid, 1985). The worst clashes occur in Dartmoor and the Pembrokeshire Coast, where extensive live firing is in direct conflict with heavy visitor use. The Northumberland National Park, which has by far the largest military training area, has experienced relatively little difficulty in accommodating service use, visitor pressure being low in comparison with the other National Parks. In addition, most of the visitors are attracted to Hadrian's Wall, which is well away from the training area.

Overall the most extensive military use is what is known as 'dry' training, which involves manoeuvres without the use of live ammunition. From the point of view of the National Parks this sounds more innocuous than it actually is, for 'dry' training can involve the widespread digging of trenches and other minor earthworks and the use of pyrotechnics and blank rounds, as well as heavy vehicles.

Like open moorland throughout the United Kingdom, the unenclosed parts of all ten National Parks are used for adventure and survival training. For the most part this involves much the same activities as any rambler would indulge in, though frequently under more severe weather conditions. So long as the numbers taking part do not become excessive, when in any case they would largely defeat the object of the exercise, there can be little objection on aesthetic grounds to this type of use by the services, or anyone else.

Some of the most vehement complaints about military activities in National Parks are not directed against ground training at all. Fixed facilities in the form of barracks, airfields, military roads and large gun targets are permanent reminders of the military presence and are especially obtrusive in a number of Parks. There are two camps near Brecon in the Brecon Beacons; on Dartmoor the Okehampton camp has introduced a number of roads and other fixed facilities into the heart of the open moorland; at Fylingdales on the North York Moors the radar early warning station is an alien, though impressive feature; and the Llanbedr Royal Air Force camp and airfield in Snowdonia are unsightly permanent reminders of the military presence. Indeed since the Nugent Report was published in 1973, considerable efforts have been made to remove unwanted fixed facilities and to restore land to its moorland state, though these have not always been successful. The disused rifle range at Rippon Tor on Dartmoor is a veritable landmark, but cannot be bulldozed to the ground, because there is so much lead hidden inside that it would pose a health hazard to animals and humans were the interior exposed!

Finally mention must be made of the noise from low-flying aircraft, the most ubiquitous and frequently cited complaint about a military presence. To some degree all the National Parks are affected by it and, just because they are so unpredictable and inescapable, aircraft arouse a special fury. Most National Park Authorities have negotiated some reduction and rescheduling of low-flying exercises, but the sparsely populated moors of upland Britain are never likely to be free of this deafening nuisance.

It would be wrong to imply that the relationship between the services and the National Park Authorities is wholly negative. In a recent survey by the Council for National Parks (Council for National Parks, 1985), four authorities specifically recorded their appreciation of the contribution by the services to their National Parks: in the Pembrokshire Coast the Royal Air Force provided an invaluable air-sea rescue service and the army helped with conservation and heavy lifting work; in Snowdonia the Royal Air Force contributed to the mountain rescue service and to heavy lifting work; in the Yorkshire Dales and the Brecon Beacons there was appreciation for the help given with heavy construction projects.

THE SCALE OF MILITARY TRAINING

The use made by the services of National Parks in England varies both in its nature and extent, making it difficult to generalise about the military presence. In Table 9.1, however, an attempt has been made to summarise the overall situation and a number of broad trends do emerge. The most important point is the concentration of military activity, especially of areas for live firing, in three National Parks: Dartmoor, Northumberland and the Pembrokeshire Coast. In all three the conflict is considerable, being most acute in Dartmoor and the Pembrokeshire Coast where visitors are prone to clash directly with military exercises. It is also clear from Table 9.1 that there has been a slow general reduction in the size of the area primarily devoted to service training in National Parks since the Nugent Committee reported. However, against this, there have been increases in Dartmoor and in the Peak District, in both cases fuelling the tension. The situation on Dartmoor is extremely sensitive, for as Baroness Sharp's inquiry revealed, there is no foreseeable prospect of reducing the size of the training area (Sharp, 1975). In the Peak District, on the other hand, negotiations are in progress for the National Park Authority to acquire part of the Harpur Crewe Estate,

Table 9.1: Military training in National Parks, 1985

	a	b	c	d	e	f
Brecon Beacons	1,138	5	418	–	–	yes
Dartmoor	14,026	6	792	874	9,797	yes
Exmoor	–	–	–	–	–	yes
Lake District	783	2	–	–	–	yes
Northumberland	22,869	1	–	–	11,320	yes
North York Moors	1,073	1	8	–	–	yes
Peak District	1,456	2	24	121	239	yes
Pembrokeshire Coast	2,599	6	94	–	2,428	yes
Snowdonia	238	2	–	–	8	yes
Yorkshire Dales	322	1	3	–	321	yes

a = Area in ha in military use.
b = Number of separate areas.
c = Area in ha released since publication of the Nugent Report in 1973.
d = Area in ha acquired since 1973.
e = Area subject to restriction by live firing.
f = Low flying aircraft.

Sources: Council for National Parks, 1985; MacDiarmid, 1985.

currently used by the services.

As with almost every other aspect of National Park administration in England and Wales, there have been major improvements in the relationship between the ten Authorities and the Ministry of Defence since 1974. Even the cautious recommendations of the Nugent Committee enabled the reorganised and enhanced National Park Authorities to make a fresh start in the latter half of the 1970s (Blacksell, 1986). For the most part this has taken the form of better consultation and co-operation over small matters, but it has helped lift the veil of secrecy which shrouds so much of military activity and led to a modest reduction in unnecessary restrictions on public access.

CONCLUSION

In their challenging survey of the first three decades of National Parks in England and Wales, Anne and Malcolm MacEwan take a bleak view of military activity: 'Military training presents in its starkest form the contrast not merely between conflicting government policies, but between conflicting aspects of human nature and society. The supreme irony of Dartmoor is to go there in search of freedom and to find its centre dominated by a jail, or to go there in search of peace and natural beauty and to find them blasted to pieces by men being systematically trained in violence' (MacEwan and MacEwan, 1982, p. 244). They brook no compromise between the needs of the National Parks and the demands of military defence. Without doubt they are right to single out the value of the conservation achievement. The National Parks in England and Wales are a unique experiment, which has protected the landscape while at the same time safeguarding the rural economy (Blacksell, 1982). To risk jeopardising this success for anything other than a proven and specific military requirement would be irresponsible, but even so the prospects for any further reductions in the scale of military activity seem remote. The present government has significantly expanded the size of the Territorial Army and the part-time recruits need land on which to exercise and train. The services are in no mood to relinquish rights on land to which they already have access. Many of the buildings and other works also seem destined to remain: for instance, the Fylingdales radar early warning station is part of a fixed European network, currently being upgraded, so that for all practical purposes any idea of relocation is little short of fanciful. For better or worse in the foreseeable future military training and its associated activities in National Parks are going to remain and, realistically, only a pragmatic policy of seeking to *ameliorate* the conflicts seems likely to lessen them.

REFERENCES

Blacksell, M. (1982) 'The Spirit and Purpose of National Parks in Britain', *Parks*, 6, no. 4, 14–17.

Blacksell, M. (1986) 'National Parks and Rural Land Management', in D.G. Lockhart and B. Ilbery (eds) *The Future of the British Rural Landscape*, Elsevier, Ch. 10, forthcoming.

Council for National Parks (1985) *Military Use of National Parks*, mimeo, available from CNP, 45 Shelton St, London WC2H 9HJ.

Department of the Environment (1976) *Report of the National Parks Policies Review Committee*, Circular DoE 4/76.

Dower, J. (1945) *National Parks in England and Wales*, Cmd. 6628, London: HMSO.

Hobhouse, A. (1947) *Report of the National Parks Committee*, Cmd. 7121, London: HMSO.
MacDiarmid, S.M.J. (1985) 'The Use of Land by the Ministry of Defence within the National Parks of England and Wales', unpublished BSc field study, Wye College, University of London.
MacEwan, A. and MacEwan, M. (1982) *National Parks: Conservation or Cosmetics?*, London: George Allen & Unwin.
Ministry of Defence (1974) *Statement on the Report of Defence Lands Committee 1971–73*, London: HMSO.
Nugent (Lord) (1973) *Report of the Defence Lands Committee*, Cmd. 5714, London: HMSO.
Sandford (Lord) (1973) *Report of the National Parks Policies Review Committee*, London: HMSO.
Sharp (Lady) (1977) *Dartmoor*, London: HMSO.

Index